Market, Schmarket

Market, Schmarket

Building the Post-Capitalist Economy

Molly Scott Cato

with cartoons by Polyp

New Clarion Press

© Molly Scott Cato, 2006

The right of the above named to be identified as the author of this work has
been asserted in accordance with the Copyright, Designs and Patents Act 1988.

First published 2006

New Clarion Press
5 Church Row, Gretton
Cheltenham GL54 5HG
England

New Clarion Press is a workers' co-operative.

A catalogue record for this book is available from the British Library.

ISBN paperback   1 873797 50 8
     hardback   1 873797 51 6

Typeset in Times New Roman by Jean Wilson Typesetting, Coventry
Printed in Great Britain by The Cromwell Press, Trowbridge

For Jairo, who represents the millions of children who have been killed for the sake of the capitalist system

For the children and young people in my life – Rosa, Ralph, Josh, Emma, Joe and Nelly – for whose sakes I hope this book helps to build a more humane economy

Aedh wishes for the Cloths of Heaven

HAD I the heavens' embroidered cloths,
Enwrought with golden and silver light,
The blue and the dim and the dark cloths
Of night and light and the half light,
I would spread the cloths under your feet:
But I, being poor, have only my dreams;
I have spread my dreams under your feet;
Tread softly because you tread on my dreams.

W. B. Yeats, from *The Wind Among the Reeds, 1899*

Contents

Figures

Tables

Boxes

Preface

We are living in interesting times. Far from the fall of the Berlin Wall marking the end of history, it has opened up all sorts of possibilities and freed our minds from the hegemony of capitalist ideology. The debate has been released from the straitjacket of the false dichotomy between capitalism and communism. This is a timely turn of events, because we will need all our powers of creative thinking to solve the significant and urgent problems that we face as human beings sharing this beautiful planet.

Although problems such as climate change and global poverty are now figuring large in the public debate, the penny has yet to drop that these are but two consequences of a wider problem, caused by the way our economy is organized, caused by capitalism. Many concerned citizens make commendable efforts with individual problems, when their time would be more efficiently spent addressing the source of those problems. In this book I hope to convince readers that capitalism is that source, to dissect its internal workings, and to share the progress that the green movement has made in addressing these both at the level of policy and in terms of grassroots initiatives.

Like all over-ambitious projects, this book can be criticized for being thin on detail. Since I wish to attack capitalism along a broad front, this is inevitable. I hope readers will be indulgent with my apparent dilettantism and follow up the many suggestions for seeking further information on the individual subjects covered. I also hope readers will indulge the cultural prejudices that have resisted editorial scrutiny. This book is all about a new sort of economy, one which is culturally sympathetic and grounded in place. For that reason I have avoided the temptation to adopt a mid-Atlantic tone to appeal to that large old publishing market that is divided from me by a common language. It was pointed out to me at an early stage not only that there were many potential readers across the Atlantic, but that they were just the sort of people I needed to convince. So I have done my best to remove the worst excesses of anti-US chauvinism which so many intellectuals in Europe easily fall prone to, but I will not apologize for using English turns of phrase and references. I have explained these for the benefit of US and other English-speaking readers from different cultures, but I did not want to lose what is, after all, my natural idiom. And if I can survive *Friends* and *Fahrenheit 9–11* without subtitles, surely I can expect my overseas readers to extend their cultural knowledge in a similar spirit?

Finally, I am offering this book as a source of hope rather than despair. My own study of economics has been a liberating, although at times gruelling, experience. It has led me from frustration and confusion to a position of confidence about what is wrong and what we need to do about it. I also see many signs of hope. Capitalism is far from the towering giant of its imagination. If we identify the home of capitalism in the USA, as I believe we should, then we see many competing power blocs. Russia is resisting the takeover of its resources by US-backed oligarchs and US corporations. Cuba and Venezuela are developing novel solutions to economic problems in spite of being in the USA's backyard. China appears to have worked itself into a situation of financial dominance over the USA; we wait to see how it will use its new and growing power. Meanwhile India, with its vast and increasingly skilled workforce, has wisely maintained control over its currency, and its people showed in the latest election their judgement of the slavishly pro-corporate policies being followed by their leaders.

We in the English-speaking world have a unique responsibility because of our position closer to the heart of capitalism, because of our mastery of 'the language of business', and because of our privileged access to both education and freedom of expression. In spite of what we are all taught in school, history is not a battle of arms but a battle of ideas. My intention is to challenge the way you think about the economic system you are part of, and to inspire you to change it.

Acknowledgements

I would like to begin these acknowledgements with a special tribute to Mike Woodin who, as many friends and colleagues will know, died unacceptably young in 2004. His restless energy was an inspiration to many and was the spur to my putting my own thoughts about global capitalism into print when I heard that the book he had written with Caroline Lucas would shortly be coming off the presses. Both of them have contributed immeasurably to the grounding and publicizing of the green message, and their book will always serve as testimony to that.

I am fully aware of how fortunate I am to enjoy that rare thing in the late capitalist economy: a supportive and comfortable workplace. I do not underestimate the efforts of Len Arthur and Mike Newth over many years in protecting the niche which has allowed me to develop my ideas. I would also like to thank Russell Smith and Tom Keenoy for intellectual support, as well as latterly Rebecca Boden.

It has been wonderful writing this book for a publisher who I know is on my side and knowing that it would be published in the spirit in which it was written. My thanks to all working for New Clarion Press.

Amongst the many whose ideas have shaped my own, and been borrowed shamelessly throughout this book, I would identify especially Frances Hutchinson, for her championing of ideas the capitalists would rather were eliminated from history, Richard Douthwaite for his creative response to the need for a post-capitalist economy, and James Robertson, the grandfather of the new economics. The Green Party has been a lively hotbed of debate over green economics since its foundation more than 30 years ago and the innumerable contributors to these debates should be remembered here.

Spencer Fitzgibbon has been a literary, political and personal support through dark days of loss of confidence and failing conviction. David Weston's useful email postings have been invaluable and are used throughout. He has spared me the time I used to waste reading newspapers, and the rage they often provoked. Andy Pike has provided some useful ideas about the power of the shareholder. Thanks to Chris Hart for reading and engaging constructively with various bits of the manuscript.

Where would an author be without a library? I am lucky to live in a town with a copyright library as well as a beach and extend warm thanks to the staff of the National Library of Wales, whose cooperative spirit made them resist any individual naming.

This has been a difficult couple of years for me, and I have leant heavily on the support of family and friends. Thanks to mum and dad, Jane and Nick, Rich and Sue. For constructive engagement over many years I am grateful to Ev, Karen and Linda. Special thanks for Bob. And finally, thanks to Barbara: what would I do without you?

1

Warning the Frog: An Anatomy of Market Failure

> The modern economy is propelled by a frenzy of greed and indulges in an orgy of envy, and these are not accidental features but the very cause of its expansionist success.
>
> Schumacher, *Small is Beautiful*

When was the last time you felt really happy? If you think back to that time, did the feeling arise from anything you bought in a market using money? I can fairly confidently predict that in most cases the answer is no. As a species we are brought delight by the birth of our children, by a curious juxtaposition of ideas, by the misty beginnings of a glorious spring day. The tragedy of the modern economy is that, although the well-springs of our joy are found in our shared humanity and our beautiful planet, we have allowed ourselves to become enslaved to a market and its hegemonic ideology.

There is no longer any need to characterize those who question the efficiency and ubiquity of markets as communist fellow-travellers. We have the liberty to explore an infinite range of different ways of deciding how our resources should be shared, how goods and services should be manufactured and distributed. Rather than ensuring the final victory of capitalism, in fact the ending of communist domination of eastern Europe and its retreat in most other parts of the world has opened up the space for debating these different approaches to economics. This is an urgent task for, let us be frank, the system we have is not a very good one. Any system that allows deaths from over-consumption in some countries and from under-consumption in others can hardly claim that it achieves efficient distribution. An economic system whose twin objectives are profits and expansion can no more claim to meet our most fundamental human needs for security and well-being.

I have frequently been told that if I oppose capitalism I must be a communist. This sort of comment betrays a sad lack of imagination on the part of my interlocutor. My response is that I refuse to believe that a species that has produced the likes of Shakespeare and Gandhi can really not

1

achieve something more exalted in terms of an economic system than capitalism. This is the challenge for us all, if only because if we fail to rise to it, the planet on which we all depend will begin to fail to support us. It is a challenge which I make some effort to contribute towards in this book.

In this first chapter I concentrate on justifying my firm belief that capitalism is not a very good economic system and does not serve the interests of the vast majority of humanity very well. The reason we are stuck with it is twofold: those whom it does serve are canny and powerful, and the rest of us have not put enough effort into imagining, creating and justifying something better. I address four of the most obvious negative consequences of our profit-driven economic system: obesity and over-consumption; the epidemic of drug-taking; global instability and war; and climate change.

Fat profit

Food offers a perfect case study of how the domination of the profit motive distorts the system of distribution in our globalized world. Economics is defined in the *Oxford Dictionary of Economics* as 'the study of how scarce resources are, or should be, allocated'. How can capitalism possibly justify itself as an efficient system, never mind the only system in town, when it achieves this so badly that we have some people dying of starvation and others dying of obesity? No, it isn't the vending machines, or the corrupt dictators, it is the economic system that is to blame. Green politics is about limits and meeting needs, and an efficient economic system would respect these; conventional politics is about profit, and profit can be increased by the encouragement of greed. That is the central explanation for the rise in obesity.

We are encouraged to be greedy, to buy a new sofa to sit on while we over-consume and absorb advertising to persuade us to consume even more, interspersed between programmes instilling our patriotic duty to keep the economy afloat by shopping, and terrifying us that we are heading for premature death because of, yes, over-consumption. This is the sort of self-contradictory message which generates internal confusion and mental dis-ease. No wonder that rates of anti-depressant prescription increased by 125 per cent between 1993 and 2002. Profits are made by advertisers, food corporations and drug manufacturers, while the costs are borne by us, not consumers but human beings.

Is it too outrageous to see a link between the pseudo-religious commitment to growth amongst policy-makers and the accompanying growth in our waistlines? Clive Hamilton identifies the addiction to growth as a 'fetish', which he compares to the cargo cults that grew up in Papua New Guinea in the 1930s. 'Cargo cults and the growth fetish both invest magical powers in the properties of material goods, possession of which is believed to provide for a paradise on earth.' The fact that ever-increasing consumption does not bring happiness is not an exciting new thought for most environmental campaigners, but the fact that a book called *Growth Fetish* received such wide publicity may be.

The Worldwatch Institute makes the same point with a more statistical bent in its 2004 *State of the World* report, in which it chose to focus on consumption under the headline 'Richer, Fatter, and not much Happier'. It quotes the Centre for the New American Dream slogan 'More fun, less stuff' as guidance for better living. And if you ever meet anybody who still believes that ingenuity can find a way around planetary limits, just try whispering the single word: China. Famous as a nation of cyclists Chinese rates of car ownership went from virtually none in 1980 to 5 million in 2000. More than a billion consumers still wait unsatisfied, but not for long if General Motors has anything to do with it.

Another internal tension results from our dependence on the car, which is causing problems from wars to secure oil to a whole range of health problems, in addition to the 3,000 people who die and the 30,000 who are seriously injured on the world's roads every day:

> Car use and the corresponding decline in physical activity is an important cause of the obesity epidemic in the United States and the United Kingdom, and physical inactivity increases the risks of heart disease, diabetes, osteoporosis, and hypertension. Car based shopping has turned many small towns into ghost towns and has severed the supportive social networks of community interaction.

The relationship between over-eating and health has been found to be related to the structure of society under capitalism, rather than a class-related propensity for eating too many chips. In *Britain on the Couch*, Oliver James argued that the competitiveness inherent in a capitalist economy and the hierarchy it generates leads to low serotonin amongst the 'losers' in society. Later research has shown that the levels of serotonin in the brain are, indeed, lower in middle-aged men and women in lower social classes. A relationship has also been identified between lower serotonin and over-eating, as well as smoking and drinking alcohol to excess. In other words, it is the unequal distribution of power, and the chemically based depression this creates, that is a central cause of the increase in obesity.

Food is the most basic of all human needs. Capitalism is failing to meet our need for food adequately. The food that is available is often so adulterated and so lacking in basic nutrition that it creates ill-health and cravings for other, more satisfying foods. The connection between food and the locality, the identity that is built through seasonal foods or local cuisines, is being destroyed by a global fast-food culture. More fundamentally still, the distribution of food between the West and the South is so poor that we sit unhealthily on our sofas, obediently over-eating, while

---

Box 1.1 Evidence of an epidemic of psychological distress

Last year at the Institute of Optimum Nutrition we surveyed 22,000 UK citizens. Most were urban dwellers aged between 20 and 30. We found that:

76 per cent of people are often tired
58 per cent suffer from mood swings
52 per cent feel apathetic and unmotivated
50 per cent suffer from anxiety
47 per cent have difficulty sleeping
43 per cent have poor memories or struggle to concentrate
42 per cent suffer from depression.

Welcome to the 21st century. Despite immense improvements in standards of living, modern man is not so much a naked ape, but a knackered ape.

Source: Patrick Holford in *The Ecologist*, 22 March 2003.

---

watching our brothers and sisters starve in Africa or North Korea. This is my first indictment of capitalism as an *economic* system: it is failing in the central role of an economy, the efficient distribution of our most basic commodity, food.

Numbing out

I have often wondered about the moral panic over drink-driving when so many of us are actually under the influence of drugs for most of our lives. The drug epidemic I am concerned about is not centred on the coca fields of Colombia or the vice dens of south London. It is a society where people are so confused and in so much pain that they display a range of psychological and physiological symptoms typical of experimental rats under stress. The other side of this coin is a pharmaceutical industry ever ready to treat these symptoms for a profit, and in addition to create a whole range of imaginary diseases for which they have already invented drugs that might have an impact.

The first of these invented 'syndromes' is attention deficit hyperactivity disorder, or ADHD, whose symptoms appear to be a list of characteristics typical of childhood, such as noisiness and inability to sit still. This disorder only exists because one of the major drug companies has a treatment for it. They have a drug, therefore they invent a disease for

which it is a cure. Ritalin 'works' because it increases the amount of do-pamine in the brain – this is the chemical which is produced in inadequate quantities in depressed people. Cocaine has a similar effect. In other words the children displaying these symptoms are depressed, but instead of dealing with their problems we are drugging them.

The medicalization of everyday life is one way that our health, which used to be a personal matter or a matter for the public sector – that is, areas outside the profit-realm of the market – has been sucked into capitalism:

The latest chapter in the relentless 'medicalisation' of human behaviour was announced last year by Stanford University, where scientists announced a cure for compulsive shopping disorder. A study of 24 people, published in the *Journal of Clinical Psychiatry*, showed that the powerful anti-depressant citalopram – known in Britain as Cipramil – could help the eight per cent of Americans obsessed with shopping.

Like obesity itself, 'shopaholia' is now defined as a disease, for which there is a profitable treatment. No mention is made of the sources of that disease: the absence of satisfaction in life which shopping is intended to fill, and the advertising industry that self-consciously confuses needs and wants, and sells empty, valueless products on the basis of their apparent ability to bring us love, success or attractiveness. Normal human characteristics such as shyness and difficulty with public speaking have also been converted into medical 'conditions' which can be treated. An economic system that pressurizes people into unhealthy and stressful situations can then cure the symptoms those unwanted and unpleasant situations cause in the normal human beings who are forced into them.

The two other most common expressions of a low level of mental ill-health are expanding steadily. In the case of anxiety:

This has been proven by a study which measured increases in anxiety levels among American young adults and children between 1952 and 1993. Anxiety levels rose steadily during that time, to such an extent that the average level of a normal child today is the same as that which was found in children who had been sent for psychiatric treatment in the 1950s.

James locates the source of this increase firmly in the US form of capitalism, as he does the tenfold increase in depression in the USA since 1950. The World Health Organization estimates that by 2020 depression will be the biggest global health concern after chronic heart disease. Globally, 532 million tranquillizers and 463 million sleeping pills are consumed every year; an estimated 1.5 million people in Britain are addicted to such drugs. One might also suggest that 'heart dis-ease' is also related to a failure of life to live up to our expectations rather than a propensity to eat too many chips.

The most frightening aspect of the chemical alteration of our personalities is what is happening to children, whose normal behaviour is being pathologized and then drugged out of existence. Figure 1.1 plots the rise in Ritalin prescriptions from 92,000 in 1997 to 254,000 in 2002, a 326 per cent increase in just six years. In the USA, 10 million children are on the drug. The idea that ADHD was invented by drug company Novartis to sell a drug which it had developed but could not manage to sell is now being tested in a class action in the USA.

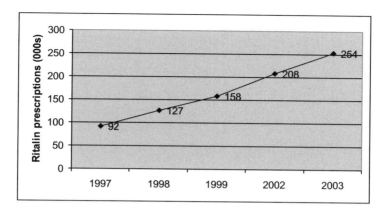

Figure 1.1 Department of Health figures for Ritalin prescriptions, 1997–2003

Figures from the UK government's drugs watchdog indicate how older children are seeking chemical escape from the pressure that the competitive educational system puts them under. In 2003, 140,000 children between the ages of 16 and 18 in full-time education had been prescribed an anti-depressant. Since 1996 the number of young people under 16 being given Prozac and the related SSRIs has risen from 76,000 to 110,000.

A record 587 million drug prescriptions were written for UK citizens in 2001, an increase of one-fifth since 1997. The total cost of prescriptions was £6.1 billion, a figure which has increased by more than 10 per cent since 2001. This rise in the level of prescriptions in the UK is also an indication of dis-ease, a vague sense that something is wrong in life. For those of us without religion we find nobody to turn to for help except our GP.

Drug companies are encouraging this trend, for obvious reasons, including making available online questionnaires so that anxious net-surfers can find out what ails them online. While researching this section I have discovered I have a very serious case of adult deficit disorder and will need substantial doses of amphetamines to live my life effectively. A similar offline survey that asked women about seven sexual 'problems', including anxiety about sexual performance and lack of desire, unsurprisingly found that 43 per cent of women suffered from 'sexual dysfunction'. Two of the survey's authors had close links to Pfizer, manufacturer of Viagra.

Prozac is the classic 'numbing out' drug; it takes the edge off the suffering caused by living in this competitive, unsatisfying society, but does not prevent you from playing your part as an economic unit. Levels of prescribing have mushroomed during the past 20 years in the UK: in the decade up to 2001, prescriptions increased from 9 million to 24 million a year. In 2002 doctors wrote out 26 million prescriptions for it and related SSRIs.

This represents easily half the adult population of the UK who cannot face the reality of life without a chemical crutch. The levels of Prozac being prescribed are now so high that the quantities of it passing through the body and into groundwater are building up to levels where the Environment Agency considers them 'a potential concern' and some environmentalists are talking about 'mass medication'. Are we, intentionally or unintentionally, moving towards the science-fiction scenario where opposition to unpleasant political and economic realities is lulled by chemical means?

Most of the discussion of drug use in the media is part of the moral panic about the 'underworld' of illegal drugs portrayed in films like *Trainspotting*. This discourse focuses entirely on the poor moral health of both the users and the suppliers of drugs. It ignores the euphoria that must be associated with, say, injecting heroin (why else would people do it?) and the widespread use of drugs amongst 'respectable' members of society. When media figures are exposed as drug-users they are immediately shunned and removed from their positions. This is a hypocritical response by managers who may themselves have a containable, and affordable, drug habit. It also fails to question why it is that so many people feel the need to remove themselves from this world into a drug-induced virtual reality, and why the drugs of choice have seen a progression from the reality-enhancing drugs popular in the 1960s and 1970s, to the numbing-out drugs of the 1990s and later.

Whatever your take on the morality of drug use, the scale of the issue cannot be ignored in a consideration of the consequences of a life spent under capitalism. Data from the 2001/2 British Crime Survey show that 34 per cent of 16–59-year-olds had used an illicit drug, while 12 per cent of these adults had used such drugs in the last 12 months. For most people the illegal drug they had used was cannabis. However, the UK also features at the top of the European league for a range of heavier drugs: number one for amphetamines, second only to Ireland for ecstasy and second only to Spain for cocaine. The situation may well be more serious than these official figures suggest, since in an illegal area the real situation is hard to measure. Research from three British cities (Brighton, Liverpool and London) indicates that rates of regular drug injection of heroin and crack cocaine could be as high as 1 in 50; amongst 30–44-year-old men the rate rises to 4 per cent.

In this section I am trying to avoid the distinction between legal and illegal drug use, since it is my view that much of the routinely prescribed 'medication' is a comfort against the pain we feel in the inhumane society that capitalism has created. The website of the drug pressure and education group Drugscope has a section for 'analgesics', which it defines as 'a drug which is a pain-killer such as heroin, opium, morphine, codeine and paracetamol'. In this context, the rise in the misuse of 'legal' drugs is entirely predictable. The US pharmaceutical industry is having to deliberately introduce chemicals to cause unpleasant side-effects into its painkillers because of an 'epidemic' of addiction to opiate-based painkillers. According to Dr Clifford Woolf, professor of anaesthesia research at Harvard Medical School, 'The problem of prescription painkiller abuse is much bigger than people realize ... No other drug type in the last 20 years had been so abused in such a short period of time.' According to the Substance Abuse and Mental Health Services Administration, more Americans abuse prescription opiates than cocaine and the abusers far outnumber those who misuse tranquillizers, stimulants, hallucinogens, heroin, inhalants or sedatives. After marijuana, pain pills are the drug of choice for America's teenagers and young adults. In recent decades between 5 and 10 per cent of people prescribed opiates for pain relief became addicted to them.

The official distinction is that there are mad people, who suffer mental illness and are prescribed psychiatric drugs; there are bad people, who obtain drugs illegally for 'recreation'; and there are sick people, the cause of whose pain is physiological and who are to be pitied, and given expensive drugs. These distinctions are quite artificial. In other cultures and other ages the categories would have been differently defined, with roles for supernatural forces in all three removing individual responsibility and hence the need for punishment of some groups. I take the USA as the paradigmatic example of the late form of capitalism, and therefore it is not surprising to find a plethora of irrational and inhumane cultures predominating there, of which the born-again Christian (now accounting for one-third of US citizens) is the most influential and disturbing. To waylay suspicion that this is mere chauvinism I should point out that half of all Americans express their belief that 'the Bible is the actual word of God and is to be taken literally, word for word'. It is also unsurprising that the USA, as well as generating a whole range of previously unknown forms of sickness, also has more people in the bad and mad categories.

I take this level of childish or insane belief as evidence of the need to escape the painful reality that capitalism creates. For those without such belief, there is a solution to the pain of an unfulfilling life to be found in the multitude of legal and illegal drugs. In a capitalist culture, drugs that work to remove pain or alienation are profitable, whether the wealth accrues to Afghan poppy farmers, Mafia mobsters or the shareholders of GlaxoSmithKline. There are also important questions still unanswered about the distinctions between psychological pain and illegal behaviour, and between organically rooted and environmentally engendered illness.

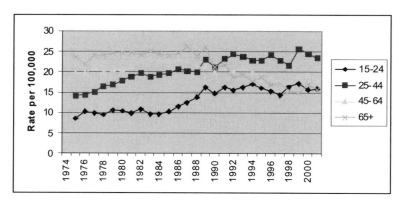

Source: Office for National Statistics, Series DH2.

Figure 1.2 Rates of suicide and open verdicts in England and Wales, males, 1974–2000

This section is called 'Numbing out' because some strategy is necessary to deal with the psychologically negative consequences of capitalism. We are programmed to be cooperative and to have meaningful and trustful social interactions. Capitalism has created a dog-eat-dog world of competition and spitefulness. This has a psychological cost which we deal with in whatever way we can: whatever gets you through the night.

The final part of this section addresses the situation of those who cannot face having to get through another night and decide that death is preferable to the sort of life on offer in our never-had-it-so-good society. Suicide is one of the many side-effects of living in an alienating and disconnected modern society. Amongst young people, 19,000 make an attempt to commit suicide every year in the UK and about 700 of those are successful, in their own terms. Suicide accounts for 20 per cent of all deaths amongst younger people aged 15–24 and is the second most common cause of death amongst young people, after accidental death.

In the matter of suicide amongst young people there is a distinct tendency in favour of young men, with young women being more likely to make a gesture of desperation by attempting suicide, rather than being successful. Amongst young men, the suicide rate has doubled since 1985, meaning that they are catching up with the rate of suicide amongst men in the 25–44-year-old age range, who are the most likely age and gender group to kill themselves. Between 1971 and 1998, the suicide rate for women in England and Wales almost halved, while in the same period the rate for men almost doubled; the rates are illustrated in Figure 1.2. Interestingly, this pattern is only found in the UK and the USA, the two countries where the competitive, capitalist ideology is most forceful. As the same report continues:

> At the beginning of the twenty-first century, men appear to be more vulnerable to death by suicide than ever before: suicides by men make up 75 per cent of all suicides in the UK. Suicide rates for men are higher than for women across all age groups. In the 25–44 age range, men are almost four times more likely than women to kill themselves, while men aged 45 and over are more than twice as likely to commit suicide as women in the same age range.

Suicide can be interpreted as a failure to accommodate the self-contradictory pressures of capitalist society. It is little surprise, therefore, that those who are most expected to succeed within this type of economic system, young to middle-aged men, are most likely to find the conflict intolerable and decide life is not worth living.

Turning up the heat

We live in a world scarred by a continuing cycle of wars. I describe in Chapter 3 how war serves the interests of corporations, but it plays a more fundamental role in supporting the capitalist system, according to Ramón Fernández Durán, a radical Spanish economist and member of the environmental action group Ecologistas en Acción. His thesis traces the origin of our present economic system to the Spanish and Portuguese invasion and domination of the Americas. The Iberian peninsula became the first global hegemon, a single power which is able to dominate all others because of its superior wealth and military might. Its power was based on the gold discovered in South America, which paid for the men and materiel. By the middle of the seventeenth century the power had moved to Holland, which had invented an innovative method of banking that enabled it to expand its trade without access to gold. Its domination was in turn broken by that of France and Britain, which struggled for the right to dominate the economic and political world in the early nineteenth century. Britain won, and created a global empire in which military and economic interests were inextricable. This role was finally ceded to the USA following the Second World War.

This short paragraph is a summary of a centuries-long struggle for economic power. It conceals beneath its bland surface bloody tales of the warfare that is the most distinctive feature of the history of the western world, because the hegemonic power does not give up that role willingly. Each transition is marked first by widespread civilian unrest, a reaction to the unfair settlement that the capitalist system requires and that the military might of the dominating power keeps in place. This unrest is followed by full-scale war, as the hegemon struggles to maintain its status. The transition from Spanish to Dutch rule was marked by the Thirty Years War; that from Holland to Britain by the Napoleonic Wars, as Britain and France fought to be the superpower; and the world wars of the twentieth century can be interpreted as the death throes of the British Empire, which fell apart as the USA became dominant at the end of the Second World War.

At the beginning of the twenty-first century there can be little doubt about which country is the hegemon: the USA is widely considered the world's only superpower. Its central role is to defend the interests of capital, especially finance capital, in return for which it is allowed to operate above international law and its people enjoy a higher standard of living than those of other countries. In an era of 24-hour media, the role of defending capital is especially demanding, since market traders respond to every hint that its position is weakened.

The attacks of September 2001 challenged the power of the hegemon and the wars we have seen since were necessary to prove the hegemon's power. As the hegemon proved its military strength by attacking first Afghanistan and then Iraq, the jitters on the financial markets ended – until the next time. Most critics of globalization recognize the importance of confidence to a financial system that is massively over-indebted; few appreciate that what impresses the markets the most is the flexing of superpower muscles. It is this, not weapons of mass destruction, that guarantees that the war in Iraq is only one on a list of global show-wars.

Liberals the world over shrink from the vision of US imperialism bestriding the world from Venezuela to Equatorial Guinea. Moral arguments aside, one is forced to ask how on earth they can pay for it. In terms of its debt-to-GDP ratio the USA is in a worse position than countries generally perceived as basket-cases and regularly breaks the equivalent of the strict Eurozone rules. The USA owes a total of $2,500 billion and runs a massive trade deficit with the rest of the world. So how can it afford to prosecute foreign wars and spend more on military equipment than the next 14 biggest-spending countries combined?

The explanation lies in the world trading system established at Bretton Woods in the wake of the Second World War. It is not an accident that this system was designed at a conference in the USA and that its three controlling bodies – the International Monetary Fund, the World Bank and the World Trade Organization (formerly GATT) – are all based there, because the system guarantees the USA a dominant role in the global economy. There were two controls in the system that prevented the USA from excessive economic domination. The first was its obligation to maintain a link between its currency and gold, which was abandoned in 1971, when the costs of the Vietnam War made it impossible for Nixon to continue to prosecute the war and maintain national solvency. The second was the controls over currency that countries abandoned when financial markets were deregulated during the 1980s. Since these controls were abandoned, the USA has literally had a licence to print money: the dollar that all the world's economies use for trade. It makes the dollars, it controls them and it spends them, largely on arms.

This currency domination is well understood amongst Washington policy-makers. Professor Thomas Barnett of the US Naval War College wrote in January of 2003: 'We trade little pieces of paper (our currency, in the form of a trade deficit) for Asia's amazing array of products and services. We are smart enough to know this is a patently unfair deal unless we offer something of great value along with those little pieces of paper. That product is a strong US Pacific Fleet, which squares the transaction nicely.' Barnett's argument is that an implicit exchange is being made: the rest of the world allows the USA all the consumer goods and military materiel it wishes to have, in exchange for which it guarantees global security.

According to green economist Richard Douthwaite:

> The US plans to spend $379bn on its armed forces next year. This is almost exactly equal to its trade deficit in 2001, so the transaction would indeed be 'squared nicely' if the rest of the world was happy to have the US play the role of global policeman and also to pay that policeman by allowing him to fill in a blank cheque for pretty well whatever sum he likes. But, given the policeman's record of destabilising or overthrowing governments with which he has had ideological differences and the fact that he would continue to put his 'particularistic national interests' ahead of those of the rest of the world, I doubt if many countries would be entirely happy with the arrangement.

As I write this, the USA is on a high state of alert. Armed guards surround the key institutions of US capitalism: the New York Stock Market, the World Bank and IMF, the headquarters of several large banking corporations. The USA feels itself under threat precisely because it is the key player in an unjust and iniquitous economic system. It feels itself under attack and in need of defence. As Table 1.1 shows, this expense is a very costly business. Who is the USA defending itself against? Its military budget is already eight times larger than that of China and 29 times as large as the combined spending of the seven 'rogue' states (Cuba, Iran, Iraq, Libya, North Korea, Sudan and Syria). This budget is larger than the combined spending of the next 23 nations. The USA is suffering from a very expensive case of paranoia. This paranoid delusion is no accident. As Michael Moore points out in his latest diatribe against corporate USA, this state of terror is created deliberately, both to expand the profits of the arms corporations, and to allow an erosion of civil liberties.

Table 1.1 US 'defence' spending, 2000–5

Year	Budget ($bn)	% increase
2000	288.8	
2001	305.0	5.6
2002	343.2	12.5
2003	396.1	15.4
2004	399.1	0.7
2005	420.7*	5.4
2000–5		45.7

*Budget request.
Source: www.armscontrolcenter.org.

Skating on thin ice

Climate change is not a single problem, but rather an interrelated system of climatic changes linked by unpredictable feedbacks. Part of the reason that the sceptics were able to hold sway for so long – and put off the necessary changes, making the policies ultimately required to preserve our planetary support systems that much more painful – is that the scientific evidence was conflicting and did not seem to fit any existing patterns. This is exactly the sort of area that policy-makers like least. Their activities are based on known patterns, measurable outcomes and reliable projections. With climate change none of these is possible, but what we can say is that the evidence is now very clear that climate change is with us. We have effectively turned our planet into a meteorological laboratory and we, along with all other species, will have to live with the consequences.

No lesser authority than the government's Chief Scientific Adviser, Sir David King, has said that there is more CO_2 in the atmosphere than at any time in the last 55 million years and that the warming it will precipitate is enough to cause melting that will submerge cities including London, New York and New Orleans. His prediction for New Orleans came true quicker than he might have expected; how long will it be before he is proved right about London as well? At a speech given to launch the scientific expedition to the aptly named Cape Farewell in the Arctic in July 2004, Dr King stated that when the Greenland ice cap melts, the sea level will rise by 6–7 metres and when the Antarctic ice melts it will be another 110 metres. Clearly this is a scientist with the wind up:

> Records of the 3 km deep Antarctic ice core showed that during ice ages the carbon dioxide in the atmosphere was around 200 parts per million (ppm), and during warm periods reached around 270 ppm, before

sinking back down again for another ice age. That pattern had been repeated many times in that period but had now been broken because of the
intervention of man. Carbon dioxide in the atmosphere had reached 360
ppm in the 1990s and now was up to 379 ppm and increasing at the rate of
3 ppm a year – reaching a level not seen for 55m years when there was no
ice on the planet because the atmosphere was too warm.

In spite of the failure of the US administration to take any action, if
anything the noises coming from its advisers are even more millenarian.
In February 2004 a secret report from the Pentagon was leaked to the *Observer*. It predicted the catastrophe that will result from climate change
and stated that it is more of a threat to global stability than terrorism. The
report concluded that 'disruption and conflict will be endemic features of
life . . . Once again, warfare would define human life.' They warn of
chronic shortages of energy and water by 2020, little more than a decade
away.

Work by the Geological Survey of Greenland and Denmark has found
an alarming acceleration in the rate of ice-sheet melting in Greenland,
which is now shrinking at a rate of 10 metres a year, rather than the 1
metre a year previously observed. No scientist is prepared to put a date on
the final melting of the Greenland ice, but this recent survey provides evidence that the timescale has been reduced. With all the Greenland ice
gone, sea levels will have risen by 6 or 7 metres, leading to the engulf-
ment of sea-level cities including London. Melting of ice on this level
also affects the salinity of the sea around the UK's coast, greatly reducing
or perhaps eventually ending altogether the Gulf Stream.

As long ago as 1999 scientists were already predicting that the main
support system for the UK's balmy climate, the Gulf Stream, might be beginning to fail. This warm water is transported to the UK coasts by the
North Atlantic Drift, an ocean current that operates like a pump, relying
on differences in seawater temperature and salinity. The melting of the
Greenland ice is causing a fall in salinity and a rise in temperature of
water flowing back into the Atlantic, switching off the pump. The loss of
the Gulf Stream could cause cooling of 5 °C or more.

In 2004 these worst fears were confirmed by Bill McGuire, Benfield
Professor of Geophysical Hazards at University College London. Again
the news appears to be that predictions made with the timescale of a century or more may come true much more rapidly. The outflow of cold,
dense water that balances the Gulf Stream has been reduced by 20 per
cent since 1950. The implications may go wider than the predicted chill-
ing of northern Europe, with some suggestion that a disruption of the
Atlantic currents might bring about a dramatic global climatic change.

The first significant and obvious impact of changing climate on European populations was the extraordinary heatwave during the summer of
2003. During the speech by Sir David King quoted above, he pointed out
that the heatwave had killed 25,000 people, far more than terrorism, and

---

Box 1.2 Some consequences of climate change before 2020 *pace* **the Pentagon**

- Future wars will be fought over the issue of survival rather than religion, ideology or national honour.
- By 2007 violent storms smash coastal barriers rendering large parts of the Netherlands uninhabitable. Cities like The Hague are abandoned. In California the delta island levées in the Sacramento river area are breached, disrupting the aqueduct system transporting water from north to south.
- Between 2010 and 2020 Europe is hardest hit by climatic change with an average annual temperature drop of 6°F. Climate in Britain becomes colder and drier as weather patterns begin to resemble Siberia.
- By 2010 the USA and Europe will experience a third more days with peak temperatures above 90°F. Climate becomes an 'economic nuisance' as storms, droughts and hot spells create havoc for farmers.
- Access to water becomes a major battleground. The Nile, Danube and Amazon are all mentioned as being high risk.
- A 'significant drop' in the planet's ability to sustain its present population will become apparent over the next 20 years.
- More than 400 million people in subtropical regions will be at grave risk.

Source: Secret Pentagon report summarized by Townsend and Harris.

---

yet had not been given anything like the same level of attention. It was the 2003 heatwave that made a lot of Europeans sit up and take notice of climate change. Beyond our personal, selfish arena of concern, the changing global climate has been causing crises to other human populations and other species. Island countries like the Maldives and Kiribati are beginning to disappear beneath the waves, while low-lying countries such as Bangladesh are suffering more devastating floods.

Evidence is emerging all the time that the effects of climate change are beginning to be felt. The failure to breed of hundreds of thousands of Scottish seabirds is just one example from summer 2004, which was identified as 'the first major impact of climate change on Britain . . . a rise in sea temperature is believed to have led to the mysterious disappearance of a key part of the marine food chain – the sandeel, the small fish whose great teeming shoals have hitherto sustained larger fish, marine mammals and seabirds in their millions'. The last census of seabirds in the islands in 2000 identified 172,000 breeding pairs of guillemots, but last summer the birds produced almost no young. The same census found 6,800 pairs of great skuas, while as few as 10 were found in summer 2004. McCarthy reaches a depressing conclusion:

> This is being seen in the North Sea in particular, where the water temperature has risen by 2°C in the past 20 years, and where the whole ecosystem is thought to be undergoing a 'regime shift', or a fundamental alteration in the interaction of its component species. 'Think of the North Sea as an engine, and plankton as the fuel driving it', said Euan Dunn of the RSPB, one of the world's leading experts on the interaction of fish and seabirds. Research last year clearly showed that the higher the temperature, the less sandeels could maintain their population level, said Dr Dunn. 'The young sandeels are simply not surviving.'

This is just a small selection of the evidence that climate change is real and is already with us. In spite of this forming a part of my personal reality for at least the past couple of decades, I have frightened myself in reporting this incontrovertible evidence of the big climate experiment. It is easy to respond to this fear by defence mechanisms designed to maintain mental equilibrium. Mayer Hillman suggests that these include repression, suppression, denial, projection and dissociation. We tell ourselves things like 'it isn't true', 'there's nothing I can do anyway so I might as well enjoy what's left', 'technology will find a solution', 'it's the government/rich people/the Americans' fault' and so on. I am here to tell you that none of these is true, but that also there is no need to panic. Whatever you made of the other sections of this chapter, I would have to grant that the evidence used to support them is debatable. In the case of climate change it is not. Climate change is happening because of our increasing impact on the planet, which is a direct consequence of the economic system called capitalism and its addiction to growth. The good news is that, together, we really can change this and, better still, the alternative way of organizing the economy that we will build as a replacement will leave almost all of us – excluding the super-rich and super-powerful capitalists – leading happier and more fulfilled lives.

Warning the frog

Something is wrong. I have presented evidence here under just four headings, but I could have produced a whole book of evidence that capitalism is destroying lives and destroying our planet. That is not the point of this book, but I need to start by convincing you that there is a problem and that we need to work together to solve it urgently.

A recent article in *The Economist* used the metaphor of the frog in the experimental vat in a discussion of the problem of debt. The point about the metaphor is that, because the heat is turned up so slowly, the frog does not realize it is being slowly boiled alive. This sounds to me like the folk myth of the dog in the microwave, since I cannot believe anybody would be allowed to conduct the experiment required to test the idea, but as a metaphor for how our economic system is cooking us all without our really noticing, it cannot be bettered. So the message of the first chapter of this book is: 'Wake up! Jump out of the vat!' The chapters that follow offer a series of areas where our economy is going badly astray, with suggestions for improvements.

2

How Perfect is the Neoclassical Market?

I think, therefore I think about buying things.

Marbles advert

Chapter 1 has presented a pretty devastating critique of the practical consequences of the market system. It leads us to an irresistible question: how have we allowed things to get so bad? How have we permitted such an inefficient and destructive system into so many areas of our life? How dare the proponents of capitalism smugly tout its superiority like so many latter-day priests? The answer lies in the discipline of economics, which has been used as an intellectual forcefield, warding off all but the most dauntless of the academic critics of capitalism. With its unattractive jargon and its insistence on a qualification in advanced mathematics, economics has defended its territory ferociously. For more than 100 years, and with increased force since the Second World War, the particular form of academic economics developed in the USA and spread worldwide has deterred any serious criticism of an economic system which, as the previous chapter shows, is clearly doing more harm than good.

There have been many attempts to undermine this exalted position that academic economics has achieved for itself. Here I will limit myself to dissecting just one of its many misguided notions: that of the perfect competition that is yielded by the market. I am sure I am not the only teaching economist who has experienced moral qualms when passing this stuff on to students. The flaws are so obvious that most students who are actually concentrating in a lecture can spot them instantly. This is what reveals the real purpose of the theory, which was never intended to provide a true picture of how markets function, as most economists would admit, but rather (which they would not) to provide intellectual refuge for those defending an indefensible economic system. First we need to explore briefly the concept of the market and the powerful role it plays in supporting the hegemonic economic system we all endure in our daily lives.

How the market is central to capitalism

It has become a cliché of the political debate that if something fails it should be 'marketized' and this will solve the problems. This is now a general solution to political problems that is proposed for areas as diverse as depressed local economies and overcrowded hospitals. In spite of the images of beast-infested jungles that abound in the marketeers' discourse, this solution is not seen as throwing a group of vulnerable people to the lions; rather it is offered as a panacea for all the ills of a late capitalist society and economy.

If, as is often the case, this solution fails, it is not reversed. We are told not that the market as a system has failed but rather that this particular market has failed, and it is generally concluded that the failure results from the fact that the market was not 'free' enough. Although Joanna Bloggs can clearly see that a train system does not work well within a culture of competition, she is silenced by the ideologues who will offer the free marketeers an infinite number of opportunities to kill consumers, whether from BSE or the string of rail crashes. So convinced are they of the supremacy of their market mechanism that they will accept these sacrifices to the market fetish in their own societies, and numerous more overseas.

So the dissection of the market as a concept is essential before we begin to rebuild our economy. The first step is to question what we really mean by the market. For managers and politicians it is simply shorthand for an economic structure that advances their ideological position; but economists actually mean something by it. They are the keepers of the Holy Grail of the market mechanism, whose beautiful qualities are passed on to all students of economics within a year of reaching university. The purpose of this chapter is to demonstrate that the central assumptions on which the claimed supremacy of the market system is based are universally flawed and anachronistic.

This task is not intellectually demanding. Testing the market against reality invariably results in its demonstration as a hollow icon. However, if you try publishing a swingeing attack on this ideal view of the market as the best system for the distribution of goods, not to mention money and people, you will find your arguments dismissed on the basis of naivety. The attack is unfair, the economists will claim, because nobody really believes the world works that way. But if not, where is the justification that the market is the best system? And, perhaps more importantly, why is this non-existent ideal system taught to all first-year students of economics? Here is the answer given by one standard introductory economics text:

> These assumptions are very strict. Few, if any industries in the real world meet these conditions. Certain agricultural markets are perhaps closest to perfect competition. The market for fresh vegetables is an example. Nevertheless, despite the lack of real-world cases, the model of perfect

competition plays a very important role in economic analysis and policy. Its major relevance is as an 'ideal type'. Many on the political right argue that perfect competition brings a number of important advantages. The model can thus be used as a standard against which to judge the shortcomings of real-world industries. It can help governments formulate policies towards industry.

This paragraph constitutes a fascinating admission of intellectual manipulation. It explicitly states the theory of perfect competition as an ideological tool rather than a scientific theory. Without it governments would not be able to justify their policies so, although it is a completely inaccurate portrayal of the world we live in, it is of vital political importance. Perhaps most telling is the claim that this 'model', meaning something that is not real, which does not exist in the real world, can now be used as an ideal against which we can compare other systems of allocation which do exist in the real world. In other words, we can assess how efficiently tea-bags are being distributed and if this does not match up to our model we can legitimately criticize it, even though we are aware that our model is an impossibility. It is at least admitted in black and white that, like the Camelot of the Monty Python film (the Holy Grail one), the market is 'only a model', it is a chimera against which a real system can be compared, against whose perfection we who exist in the grubby world of monetary exchange can match our imperfections. This is a far cry from the laws of physics claimed by those who use market theory to justify strict competition laws.

The imperfect theory of perfect competition

At the heart of the justification of the supremacy of the market system within academic economics lies the theory of perfect competition, so it is high time to carry out a reality check on this theory, which is itself based on a series of assumptions. Others have produced similar critiques, so we may conclude, as do Gaffney and Harrison, that the theory remains for ideological rather than rational reasons. In order for the market to be effectively challenged, we need to provide a superior distribution system. This chapter merely clears the ground for us to begin that more important and more challenging task in the chapters that follow. It is an old joke in the economics profession that if there is some fact about the real world that makes modelling difficult, you deal with this by assuming it away. This technique is used with gay abandon in the case of the theory of perfect competition, which is based on a series of fundamental assumptions without which it is assumed not to be valid.

The list of assumptions of perfect competition is taken from the 2003 edition of a standard economics text (I refer to it from here on simply as

'Sloman'); similar ones could be found in any introductory economics text. In fact, a rapid search of the internet will find plenty of examples of university courses teaching approximately the same theory as is critiqued below. The paucity of change over the past 30 years or so, during which economic conditions have changed beyond all recognition, is evidence of the theory as catechism rather than science. The last time I taught this theory to undergraduates I was issued with a US text. It explained the theory of perfect competition by reference to suppliers of two competitive products: ice-cream and frozen yoghurt. This seems to epitomize some of the problems with the theory and with economics in general. First, it clearly originates in a foreign, US culture: how many UK kids have ever tried frozen yoghurt? Secondly, the example is trivializing. I felt embarrassed explaining these issues which influence so many lives (and deaths, in the developing world) in terms of an irrelevant, self-indulgent good such as ice-cream. For many of those who are the victims of the market ideology, ice-cream is a luxury which, although far better suited to their climate than ours, they will never have the pleasure of enjoying.

Assumption 1: there are so many firms in the industry that each one has no power whatsoever to affect the price of the product

The first assumption is intended to guarantee that neither individual buyers nor individual sellers can have undue power within any market. This is because, with so many sellers, it would be impossible to operate an effective cartel, since the cost of finding information from so many sources would preclude such an arrangement. Again, because there are so many sellers, none can individually influence the price of the good s/he is selling. Large buyers might also come to have too much power in a market, so the assumption applies also to the demand side of the market.

Is this a realistic view of how modern markets operate? In reality, it flies in the face of the consolidation that has typified capitalism at least since it was critiqued by Marx. Perhaps in this Information Age we should be most concerned about the heavy consolidation in the world of media, as demonstrated by the merger of AOL and Time-Warner, two of the largest global media corporations, in 2001. Since the merger, the group has gone from strength to strength, now out-competing other providers of high-speed internet connections and seeing profits increase by 76 per cent in the last quarter of 2004.

Let us carry out that manoeuvre so detested by economists and test out this assumption against the reality of the market for food in the UK at the beginning of the twenty-first century. The reality is that the market is dominated by a small number of very powerful players – the supermarkets. As middlemen, standing between producers and consumers, they both buy and sell food, and ensure that what economic theory might consider the 'sellers' have to meet their needs in terms not only of price, but also of quality. According to Corporate Watch research, in 2000 the major supermarket chains controlled 88 per cent of the UK food market, a concentration of retail power far greater than in continental EU countries or the USA. Later that year, analysts predicted that the number of major players would be down from the existing five – Tesco, Sainsbury's, Safeway, ASDA, and Somerfield – to just two. So much for competition: without a large number of potential entrants to the market, what mechanism does the market offer to constrain their behaviour?

Competition only works when there are large numbers of suppliers who cannot unduly influence our purchasing decisions or prevent other producers from entering the market and improving on their offer to us as consumers. This view may have made sense why you consider the eighteenth-century market that Adam Smith visited, where he might have bought meat, potatoes and shoes, but it has little relevance in a complex, modern economy where purchasing decisions are based on advertising and goods do not reach the market without many years of development and massive R&D investment. Sloman deals with advertising as follows: 'There is no point in advertising under perfect competition, since all firms produce a homogeneous product (unless, of course, the firm believes that by advertising it can differentiate its product from its rivals') and thereby establish some market power; but then, by definition, the firm would cease to be perfectly competitive' (p. 156). As I tried to imagine what kind of advertising might conform to the world of the perfectly competitive theory, Mr Cholmondley-Warner sprung into my head, kindly pointing out in his received pronunciation that Mr McVitie is now producing his digestive biscuits with chocolate on top. If this were all advertising is about, why would companies spend millions on it every year? Why would there be whole journals dedicated to informing company executives of the most effective ways to manipulate the minds of potential buyers?

If advertising were not effective, why would companies focus almost exclusively on building their brands, to the exclusion of considerations of quality and at extreme expense? Interestingly, the textbooks make no connection between advertising and brands and the assumption about the homogeneity of products, to which they are clearly linked (see Assumption 3). In reality, a corporation in the global economy focuses on holding its market share and defending it against all-comers. The business of corporate capitalism is not about perfect competition but about obstructing competition. This is done not only through creating and defending the corporation's unique identity through its brand, but also through investing in advertising and PR to support its brand and litigation to attack those who transgress it, and through concealing virtually everything about its operations, from the details of how its products are made (remember the Coca-Cola secret recipe?) to how it spends its profits. Given the savagery with which corporations defend their right to control the markets they operate in, the next assumption seems fairly extraordinary.

Assumption 2: there is complete freedom of entry into the industry for new firms

This assumption follows directly from the first and is necessary to ensure that there continues to be a large number of buyers and sellers so that competition between them occurs. In order for entry and exit to the marketplace to be free, there must be no 'barriers to entry'. As just explored, it is obvious that in the market for complex products, the need to invest in R&D, to prepare a product for the market, and then to advertise it all create barriers too huge for all but the largest corporate investor. James Dyson has described in detail his experience of trying to break into the market for vacuum cleaners with a new product which he wanted to sell himself, rather than selling the idea to one of the corporations controlling that market. On the company website he describes 'The patent nightmare':

> The Dual Cyclone™ was nearly never made due to patent and legal costs. Unlike a songwriter who owns the song he writes, an inventor has to pay substantial fees to renew his patents each year. During the development years when James Dyson had no income, this nearly bankrupted him. He risked everything, and fortunately the risk paid off. Then in 1999, Hoover tried to imitate a Dyson and James Dyson was forced back to court to protect his invention. After 18 months Dyson finally won a victory against Hoover for patent infringement.

The whole concept of 'intellectual property', enshrined as TRIPs (Trade-Related Intellectual Property) in the WTO agreement, makes a mockery of free entry into the market, since patent or licensing laws will operate to restrict this assumption. So one of the central assumptions used to argue that markets are the ideal way to distribute goods relies on the fact that producers can have free access to information about products they might wish to produce, that the inventor of the process cannot use the law to protect his right to extract profits from that invention while preventing others from producing it more cheaply; that, in fact, the 564 pages of *Blackstone's Statutes on Intellectual Property* do not exist. In reality, of course, this is the kind of law corporations use to protect their profits. How surprising that an organization like the WTO, which claims to be the foremost global promoter of 'free' markets, in fact defends the right of corporations to extract profits in this way that wholly invalidates the free operation of markets.

We may take the example of the pharmaceutical industry, since it is a clear case where every moral pressure, never mind the strictures of a genuinely free market, suggests that knowledge about how to cure disease should not be restricted. Patents have long been used in the pharmaceutical industry to protect the fruits of research. The justification used is that, if companies could not be guaranteed the right to be the sole profiteer from their discoveries, they would not invest the money in the initial research. However, when faced with dire humanitarian need, few think that the global protection of what is referred to as 'intellectual property' under the TRIPs agreement can be maintained. This is why, with 25 per cent of its people of working age being HIV-positive, the South African government decided to ignore international law and import generic AIDS drugs from India. The price difference is staggering – $350 for a year's supply compared with $10,000 for the branded medicines – so a poor country like South Africa had little choice. Under the TRIPs agreement, South Africa was clearly able to justify its actions under clauses exempting countries facing public-health disasters, but its actions were legally challenged by the US trade representative and action was taken against the government of South Africa by the Pharmaceutical Manufacturers' Association. The courage of the government was rewarded and the PMA eventually withdrew its case in 2001, coming to a deal with the government over reasonable pricing and availability of AIDS drugs.

In a world where corporations are prepared to take legal action to protect a patent for a life-saving drug needed by a significant proportion of the inhabitants of an impoverished country, how can the free movement of information have any meaning? Corporations live and die by their sole right to sell their products, whether these involve scientific intellectual property, as in the case of a drug, or merely a trade mark. The true free marketers are the Asian manufacturers of imitation Rolex watches, who are likely to find that, rather than being awarded the Hero of the Global Market, they are prosecuted and put in gaol and their goods destroyed. Many of these goods find their way into the only true markets many of us still have access to, on the stall of our own local market heroes, who flourish in spite of the scourge of the local trading standards officers, who fail to respect their right to market freedom.

The reality in the pharmaceutical market, as in many markets, is that businesses will produce what they can make a profit from, not what is in the public interest. This is why there are no high-tech cures for sleeping sickness and malaria, which poor people die from, while there are a superfluity of treatments for the concerns of the affluent, from skin products to slimming pills. It is a recognition of the fact that research for profit is not directed in the public interest that leads to the awarding of research grants for the development of a range of important recent drug successes. A report from the US Congressional Joint Economic Committee in May 2000 established that 7 of the 21 most important drugs introduced in the USA between 1965 and 1992 (including tamoxifen, AZT/zidovudine, Taxol, Prozac and Capoten) were developed with the help of federal funds. AZT, the leading anti-AIDS drug, was originally synthesized in

1964 as a result of a National Cancer Institute grant. However, GlaxoSmithKline determined the drug's anti-AIDS properties and were granted a patent for this use, and hence profited from its worldwide sale. Many of these drugs that are so jealously guarded have been developed partially, often to the extent of half the funding, by public money. And yet the 'intellectual property' reverts to the corporations and we, the public who funded the research, have to pay them for the benefits of the knowledge they developed at our expense.

The other side of the free-entry-and-exit coin is the need for 'factors of production', i.e. labour and capital, to be perfectly mobile. Just in personal terms it is clear that labour is far from mobile: restrictions range from family or neighbourhood ties to the loss of pension rights. But the most glaring 'restriction' is found in the strict immigration rules that govern the freedom of movement of labour. What is the value of basing a claim to the superiority of the market on the fact that workers can move freely to better-paid jobs in a world where they are not actually allowed to enter Britain, are condemned as economic migrants and, if they succeed in entering, are put in gaol as illegal immigrants or deported? Even in a labour market with apparent free movement of labour, as the EU has been since 1992, there is actually very little movement of workers from one country to another, since they are dissuaded by language and cultural barriers. The devastating consequences of genuine free movement of labour can be assessed by comparing the minimum wage in the UK with the sorts of wages paid to workers in the Chinese SEZ (special economic zone, or specially exploitative zone) in Guangdong, exposed by Corporate Watch. A shoemaker there earns only £40 per month of 14-hour, 7-week days, out of which s/he has to pay for food and bedding. It is the working conditions faced by people like this that turn them into economic migrants, and their desperation and willingness to be exploited that frightens European governments into undermining the free market they officially support by preventing their freedom of movement into our labour market.

Assumption 3: all firms produce an identical product

This assumption is necessary to achieve the required situation where we make our purchases solely on the basis of price; it is often referred to as the homogeneity of the product, while consumers are defined as being indifferent between the different products on offer. We are indifferent between the products of different suppliers, since we 'regard all units of the industry's product as identical'. For this to be true, we would have to be sure that our teenage children would be equally happy with a Primark tracksuit for Christmas and one emblazoned with the latest trendy sports brand. Or that a pair of trainers with Michael Owen's face appliquéd to the side would offer no more delight than another pair without this childish repository of England's hopes. One textbook deals with consumers' lack of indifference by explaining that this assumption is unlikely to be met in practice, citing the example of the car industry where, even if there were many firms, perfect competition would not be possible because the Ford Mondeo and the Vauxhall Vectra cannot be considered homogeneous goods; consumers have individual preferences for one or the other. The assumption can then be slightly qualified so that, if a producer decides to produce a slightly different product then this does not invalidate the assumption, but rather a new market is created. This may hold water if we think of the market for shoes being divided into the market for shoes and the market for trainers. But we can hardly make sense of a theory that would require a different market for trainers with each different sportstar's face, or for each different team's football shirt. Yet it is clear that young people are far from indifferent between these goods.

Again the proof of the irrelevance of this assumption is found in the actions of the global corporations. If indifference between similar items were part of their understanding of the market, why would they expend so much energy shoring up the uniqueness of their brand, as shown by Naomi Klein? The purpose of the brand is directly to undermine the homogeneity of products, to achieve a situation where indistinguishable brown liquids become of hugely different value because they are marked with the label 'Somerfield Cola' or 'Virgin Cola'. The advertising industry is explicitly dedicated to undermining this assumption by establishing consumer preference for one brand or another.

Assumption 4: producers and consumers have perfect knowledge of the market

Of all the assumptions of perfect competition, the assumption about knowledge of opportunities to buy and sell has failed the test of time perhaps worst of all. In Adam Smith's eighteenth-century market it was a reasonable suggestion that you might be able to have 'perfect information' about all the goods between which you were making your choice. There were, let's say, three shoemakers and you could stroll from one stall to the next, and on to the third. In markets and fairs of this time, producers of similar goods helpfully located themselves alongside one another, which is why we are left with street names such as Butcher's Row or Shoe Lane. Pretty nearly perfect information was possible then, because there was such a limited range of goods.

Proponents of market capitalism frequently list the expanded range of goods as one of the achievements of their favoured economic system, yet they have failed to consider how this impacts on the assumption about perfect knowledge. With millions of goods currently available, how could we possibly know about all of them? Evidence that we do not comes in the form of advertising campaigns like the one by Superdrug claiming 'If you find it cheaper elsewhere, we'll refund twice the difference.' Clearly, if you had perfect information, you would know it was cheaper somewhere else to start with and, if you wished to 'maximize your utility', buy it there. Such advertising campaigns manipulate us on the basis of our well-founded fear that our knowledge of the market and its goods is far from perfect.

This assumption comes in two parts, and far from reality though the side relating to consumers is, that relating to producers takes us once again into the realms of fantasy or farce. For the assumption to be true, sellers of goods must have perfect information about all the opportunities to sell. As Sloman puts it: 'Producers are fully aware of prices, costs and market opportunities.' But in the global marketplace this would have to include selling opportunities right across the globe. In reality the only players who have this sort of reach are well-established, well-capitalized corporations. What chance do you or I have of finding out about market opportunities in Montevideo or Novosibirsk?

The focus of this point about the perfect knowledge of sellers is that they must have knowledge of market opportunities. This will fulfil the need for a constant entry of new sellers, which is the way that prices are kept low and racketeering is prevented – the basis of why the market system is a good system for distributing goods in the first place. Potential entrepreneurs are expected to scan the economy for market opportunities for them to exploit, where existing suppliers are making the largest profits – 'abnormal profits', as economic theory calls them. But how are we to know the size of these profits, normal or abnormal, when such knowledge is constrained by commercial confidentiality? Modern corporations pay accountants to distort the financial figures they are required to declare, while most others are kept secret to protect their commercial position.

As a final point it is important to note that the whole theory of perfect competition specifically excludes certain categories of goods, which are defined as being mutually inconsistent with a competitive system of supply and distribution, namely public goods and goods which enjoy a natural monopoly. Examples of public goods are public services such as the police and flood defences, i.e. services which can be considered 'non-rival' (nobody else is providing them) and 'non-excludable' (if somebody pays for them, we all benefit). Education and health are frequently excluded from this view of services and defined as 'merit goods', although my own view is that these are also public goods and have been redefined elsewhere for ideological reasons – to make them available for the rapacious market. Examples of natural monopoly goods are the water supply and telecommunications, where the nature of the good makes it senseless to have more than one supplier because of the large and inevitable economies of scale involved in establishing its provision.

So we have arrived at a situation where, in spite of the theoretical necessity that markets can only be justified as offering economic superiority in the case of pure private goods, the global 'free market' is at this very moment seeking to extend its tentacles into every public good and service imaginable. If the supremacy of the market can only be demonstrated in the case of pure private goods, why were we forced to suffer the disaster of Railtrack and the chaos of the General Agreement on Trade in Services? Why is it that markets are being forced into areas, such as health care and education, where they are neither appropriate nor efficient, and on the basis of a market justification that they cannot even theoretically live up to? Of course, in terms of economic theory we know this is a rhetorical question because the answer lies in the realm of politics.

It is because of political pressure that the World Bank, which is a leading ideologue in the cause of markets when it comes to Structural Adjustment Programmes, promotes the drive for the privatization of the supply of water in the developing world, water being almost the classic case of a natural monopoly. This is why water dominated the agenda at the Johannesburg Summit in 2002 and why 2003 was declared by the UN as the International Year of Fresh Water. Once the market was opened to profiteering, suddenly there were plenty of companies prepared to provide water to the world's poor. When the ideology has achieved its purpose, it is the citizens of the world who have to live with the consequences. It was inevitable that market economics would not be in the interests of consumers of water: even the theory said so. So did a report from the World Bank's own research unit, which questioned the efficiency of markets in the distribution of water and underlined the importance of firm state intervention. In the UK, consumers have suffered from the monopolization of the natural monopoly of the water supply. The reality of privatized water in the UK is that none of the companies has really had to compete for its regional monopolies; rather they were given 25-year concessions when they were established in 1989.

Adam Smith, who is often touted as the originator of the theory of market competition, wrote about the invisible hand of the market. According to Smith, each participant in a competitive market is 'led by an invisible hand to promote an end which was no part of his intention'. However true this may have been in Smith's day, it has never been demonstrated in the complex, global economy of the twenty-first century, when the invisible hand has made itself visible, and for many it is making a gesture that Smith would never have expected.

Privatization and corporatization

I have spent some time exploring the central myth of market superiority, and exposing it as hollow. This is important because this myth supports the extension of capitalist, corporate power into more and more areas of our lives, areas where the theory, even if it were internally coherent and its assumptions correct, has been proved not to be valid. It is almost a cliché amongst critics to identify capitalism with the shark because of its need for constant forward motion. This is the explanation for its advance into areas where it is entirely unsuited; there the profit motive will reduce quality and invalidate the purpose of the economic activity, as in the case of high-tech medicine, which requires a huge level of energy input, the production of which itself creates further disease, either cancer through nuclear power or asthma through fossil-fuel combustion.

Economic theory itself states that anything which is defined as a public good cannot be efficiently provided by the market. This is because the benefits it brings are shared by society as a whole, so individuals are not prepared to pay enough for companies to consider it worth their while to provide the good or service in sufficient quantity or quality. The recent history of our railways and universities proves this principle. As a society we would rather people travelled by train than car, for practical and environmental reasons; as a society we benefit from a higher level of knowledge and culture amongst our people. However, individuals will choose to travel by car when that is cheaper than the train, and will cause a devaluation in the quality of university of education when there are twice as many of them per academic as there were 20 years ago. However, in this case the privateers are happy to fly in the face of the theories they usually hide behind and propose full-scale marketization of not only public goods but the whole public sector.

This policy is unpopular, which is why it is being introduced by sleight of hand rather than openly. The first move down the road were the Private Finance Initiative (PFI) and Public–Private Partnerships (PPP): bringing private money into the public sector. An organization that has no particular bias against private money has concluded that these deals offer extremely bad value for money to taxpayers. The report, from the Association of Chartered Certified Accountants, assesses the cost of 21 roads and hospital projects financed by PFI as compared with the standard public-sector borrowing approach and shows a 30 per cent differential. The costs of PFI projects routinely rise significantly once the deals are signed, resulting in vast profits for the contractors at the public expense. The report is also critical in terms of accountability, concluding that 'financial information about PFI is opaque, partly because of government-imposed confidentiality'. This is Enron-style off-balance-sheet accounting, and the government does not want us to know about it.

The ongoing process of hospital privatizations results in similarly bad deals for the people who have to use these hospitals. One example is Walsgrave Hospital in Coventry, which Alan Milburn, the Health Secretary, announced would be built under PFI in July 1997. A copy of a confidential report into the PFI proposal, written by two public health scientists and an economist, was leaked to George Monbiot. The bidding consortium would only make sufficient profit to entice it to enter the deal if the new hospital had 25 per cent fewer beds and 20 per cent fewer staff. Far from the private sector's profits being achieved by market-generated efficiency gains that proponents of PFI have promised, in reality they will be achieved, in Coventry and elsewhere, by offering a much poorer level of service.

The truth about PFI is that it is another one of Gordon Brown's cunning plans. This latter-day Baldrick of the Treasury is smart enough to work out how the financial system prevents public investment to improve the lives of citizens, which is his primary political objective – we should give him that much credit. So from Third World debt to the NHS he has come up with a whole range of financial fiddles, most of which have three-letter abbreviations such as PFI, PPP and IFF (international finance facility). He has been twisting the rules of the financial game for our benefit – but only our short-term benefit, because in the long run this accounting scam will cost us all. In the case of PFI, the £105 billion commitment it represents should really be added to government borrowing, showing the truly horrendous size of the national debt. But by keeping some of the responsibility for the debt in the private sector, Brown can keep it off the books. Unless we assume that Gordon Brown is gambling on the collapse of capitalism as a result of its own internal contradictions – which is not impossible given his orthodox Marxist past – his generosity in the short term will cost all of us dear in the future.

Unison has identified the shortcomings of this privatization-by-the-backdoor approach in its Positively Public campaign. It assessed the £35.5 billion of PFI deals that have already been signed in terms of value for money and risk allocation. The union concluded that the audit trail for such projects was obscure, they offered bad value for money, and the risk still stayed with the public while the profits went to the private sector. From a commonsense perspective, private borrowing to fund public services is bound to be more expensive, between 2.5 and 4 per cent more expensive, since local authorities can achieve the lowest borrowing rates and the government even lower ones. The National Audit Office offers figures showing that the interest-rate differential increased repayment costs by 1 per cent per year, costing an additional £140,000 for every tenth of a percentage point difference on each £14 million borrowed. So value for money is clearly not the point; privatization is the point.

At the global level, the encroachment of the market is validated and underpinned by the General Agreement on Trade in Services. Some sectors, such as tourism and computer services, are already required to be open to competition as 'basic obligations'. Other more sensitive areas, such as health, education and postal services, are specifically excluded at the initial stage, although poorer countries are being pressurized to open up these markets and the same will follow in Europe. The definition of public services used is specifically limited to those with no private element, and so is being invalidated by the PFI/PPP initiatives, which are being used deliberately as a wedge to open up our health service to GATS.

The next proposed advance of the market is by way of the proposed EU directive on 'services in the internal market', aiming to 'remove barriers' to the market in the services sector. This means that public bodies can no longer choose domestic suppliers of basic social requirements, such as postal or health services. Providers of services will only have to meet legislative standards in the country where they are based, leading to the inevitable situation where corporations will base themselves in countries with low wages and health-and-safety standards, probably in eastern Europe, and then compete for contracts to provide services in countries which would never accept these conditions of employment for their own citizens. The opportunity for profiteering is clear, but again there is nothing to uphold the standards of service or the ethos of public service in these vital areas.

In early 2005 the pressure was on again with a spokeswoman for the European Union executive stating that liberalization of the services sector was a 'crucial element' in the relaunch of the so-called Lisbon Agenda, the EU's flagging plans to 'boost competitiveness'. This is the watchword to look out for: business is using the Lisbon Agenda to drive forward its invasion of our cherished public sector. France is opposing the move, with President Chirac saying that he wants the services directive go 'back to the drawing-board' – particularly the 'country of origin' clause, which allows countries to apply their own legislation rather than that of the country where the company is based.

In the UK, the onward march of the market in the public sector is taking place under the rubric of the Wider Markets Initiative. This comes at the problem (from a market perspective) of the public sector from the other end: rather than encouraging private sector companies to bid for public contracts, it encourages public-sector bodies to engage in private market business. The incentive or bribe, depending on how you look at it, is that public sector bodies that start to behave more like businesses will be less constrained by Treasury borrowing rules. The official line is that 'it is government policy to encourage wider markets activities in order to achieve best value for money from assets, to foster entrepreneurism [*sic*] and because of the extra economic activity it generates for the UK'. In reality it is another blurring of the distinction between public and private to allow privatization to take place without our knowing about it. A similar tactic is to move public services into the third sector, such as by selling council housing stock to housing cooperatives. This has an intrinsic appeal to those who favour local, mutual solutions, but it leaves these small coops vulnerable to being picked off by larger players once their public protection is lost.

The rhetorical justification for selling off our public sector to market sharks is that it does not really matter who provides the service so long as it is quick and cheap. This is entirely spurious reasoning for areas that have emotional impact, such as our health or the education of our children. We would not apply this economistic calculus to the way we choose our life partners, or when we are burying our loved ones. The truth is that the health and education sectors represent around 20 per cent of our national economy that is currently unexploited by corporations. No profits are being made there, which makes it a likely area for corporate targeting. This is the source of the widespread propaganda about inefficiency and poor service. However, this is apparently failing to convince the public, who hold their health service close to their hearts. Perhaps this is unsurprising, given the disasters we have endured at the hands of the privatized transport sector, particularly the railways. With propagandizing at home and GATS abroad, it is a stiff challenge to prevent the movement of the market into these final areas of our lives.

Conclusion: market myths and market realities

At the level of intellectual debate, the assassination of the case for the supremacy of the market is embarrassingly easy. But we must credit economists with more intelligence than a robust defence of such transparent nonsense would allow them. No economist would defend the bald assumptions of perfect competition, which are always portrayed as textbook simplifications, good enough to be passed on to students, but not providing a true reflection of a far more complex world. In reality, however, the critique is so wide ranging and the assumptions so wide of the mark that highbrow, maths-infested sophistications cannot be enough to save the theory. It is deeply and fundamentally flawed and needs to be replaced with a new theoretical model of the market which makes an attempt to approach reality. There are some promising candidates in the theories of globalization and in post-Marxist works such as the theory of the international division of labour.

Perfect competition is the central myth of the market system – Maria Mies called it capitalism's 'creation myth' – which is why I have spent space dissecting it here. But there are many others. Perhaps the most personally alienating for me is that of 'rational economic man'. The perspective of economic theory is so phallocentric that even personal relationships are reduced to bargaining games, so that children are produced to care for us when we are too old to work, and wives and husbands trade off good looks against power or earning potential. Apart from making a firm mental decision never to marry an economist, there is little to learn from this thin, mean and grossly unrealistic theorizing. Another prominent myth, of the eternal goodness of growth, has been admirably dissected by Richard Douthwaite, and is shown to have only ever had any power as the result of a faulty accounting system.

A more recent critique of the reliance on the concept of growth has described it as a 'growth fetish' and it is not the only example of a situation where anthropologists are more useful in describing our economic behaviour than economists. Marx wrote of the fetishism of commodities, where material goods, which are central to the functioning of capitalism, are endowed with pseudo-religious power to give us satisfaction. The fact that they are all shown to be false gods is all to the good, encouraging us back on to the treadmill of work to earn money for further consumption. In terms of our psychological and spiritual well-being, this commodification is disastrous, draining real value and compassion out of our lives, which are then filled up with things of no intrinsic worth: 'The essence of the capitalist market system is commodication: the turning of human activities and natural resources into commodities to be bought and sold in the marketplace.'

If capitalism is a religion then economists are its high priests. Economists are privileged within our political system as though they were invested with a superior knowledge of right and wrong, and this superiority is apparently based on a theory which we have seen is tragically flawed. None the less, using their qualifications as 'economists' as justification, they find fault with the views of the electorate, who are too foolish to see the value of neoclassical policies.

Polls before the German *Länder* elections in autumn 2004 indicated that Chancellor Schroeder's policies to cut payments to the unemployed by around €2.5 billion, reduce working protection and cut healthcare benefits, were sufficiently unpopular to cause him to lose elections in several of the *Länder*, including falling behind the former communists in what was East Germany. Rather than seeing this as a democratic mandate for keeping the German social welfare model intact, economists drew attention to voters getting it wrong: 'Schroeder has rightly discovered economic reform as his main theme but voters are too afraid to follow,' said Holger Schmieding, co-chief economist at London-based Bank of America Corp., in an interview. 'It's tough for the government.' Schroeder's policies, including forcing the increasing number of unemployed into low-paid jobs, are particularly unpopular in former East Germany, where unemployment rates are highest. But voters are not given freedom to express their political right to choose strong welfare policies. In fact, they are only so foolish as to choose these because of poor communication on the part of Schroeder: 'This is indeed a major departure from the welfare policies followed by governments for far too long,' Schmieding said. 'But Schroeder has done a bad job explaining why he's doing what he's doing – public anger would be much less if there was greater awareness.' These quotations make clear the way economists are used as apologists for an economic system that favours the interests of capital over those of the citizen, and how they are accorded an undemocratic and unwarranted power in making judgements that fly in the face of the democratic will of the people.

Theory aside, we can gain the best idea of how markets function by studying what happens in the real world that we all live in. We can take the example of the global market for bananas. Under the Lomé Convention, the EU had gained the right, for political, post-colonial reasons, to favour bananas from the Caribbean over bananas from Central America, imported by Chiquita, which were subject to limits and tariffs. Acting under lobbying pressure (for which read bribery in the form of a $415,000 donation to the Democrats from Chiquita chairman Carl Linder Jr), the USA complained of 'discrimination', and the WTO dispute panel found in favour of the USA. The interesting point to emerge from the story is not which side won – in the case of the recent US tariffs on steel the boot was on the other foot – but rather that the decision was made on the basis of political power and corporate lobbying, not the democratic will of the world's people, or even benign, yet inanimate 'market forces'.

And what of the ability of perfect competition to ensure that companies behave efficiently and cannot make abnormal profits? The lie to this is provided by the record-breaking corporate profits reported by Shell in January 2005. The company made £9.2 billion after tax, up 55 per cent on the previous year. These profits were made in 2004, which even friends of the company would have to agree was a disastrous year. During the year Shell saw its share value plummet as it cut its estimate of reserves four times during 2003, and by a full 20 per cent in January. If you are an oil company, this effectively is your value, and it seems that Shell had been deceiving its shareholders about the value of the company for years.

In September 2004, Shell paid £82.7 million in fines to stock-market regulators for misreporting offences. Following the emergence of the deception, its chairman, Sir Phil Watts, and production chief, Walter van der Vijver, both resigned. At the end of 2004 finance chief Judy Boynton also left after it was revealed that she had taken no action following receipt of an email from van der Vijver which said the firm had 'fooled' the market about its reserves. She received a half-million-pound golden handshake. The reason Shell was able to make these profits was that the oil market had been manipulated by policies such as the war in Iraq to inflate oil prices, so that we paid more for oil, which went directly to corporate profits. It clearly had nothing to do with efficiency.

A more tragic illustration of the pernicious nature of competition is the destruction of the British social firm Remploy. It has long provided employment to those with physical or learning disabilities, thus allowing them independence and self-respect. But competitors believed that it was being allowed to compete unfairly and had not won contracts on the basis of price alone. They took Remploy to the European Commission, which ruled in their favour. The outcome clearly did not serve the public interest, and shows how competition rules are now preventing us from improving the lives of citizens. Disabled workers were sacrificed on the altar of the competition fetish.

So what would be left of the market in a system of green economics? In theoretical terms, the market would be removed from its place on the altar and situated instead amongst our other social institutions. Green political economy views markets as socially constituted rather than a natural creation: 'Markets are simply exchange mechanisms set up by the polity and government through the legislature. To view the market as "free" or "natural" is reification.' But there is no parallel fetishization of planning or state provision. Green political economy is opposed to: capital accumulation and the resultant growth imperative; the reduction of values to prices; and the anti-social anti-environmental effects of powerful corporations. Green economists are similarly aware that 'the capitalist market cannot resolve the problems of the environment. It is geared to short-term profit-making, not to long-term conservation.' But bearing these significant constraints in mind, in the area of private goods and services markets, when adequately constrained by environmentally and socially oriented taxes and regulations, such as global basic health and safety standards and resource taxes, markets would be allowed to function as distribution mechanisms. The markets we might end up with would be smaller and more tightly regulated but paradoxically also considerably freer than the globalized corporate-dominated market at the heart of the late capitalist economy.

By the end of this chapter you should have reached the point of peeping behind the curtain and noticing that the Wizard of Oz is in fact a small bald man sitting on a high stool. For younger and cooler readers the reference is the point in the film *The Matrix* where Neo has to choose between the red and blue pills. It is time you shook off the illusions about the reality of the economic system you have grown up within, as well as its magnificence and omnipotence. Capitalism is just one way of running the economics show, and in reality a rather immoral and shabby one. The rest of the chapters in the book focus on different important aspects of capitalism, attempting to anatomize them and suggest alternatives.

3

We Have to Learn to Share: Mutual Approaches to the Economy

El pan para mí es un problema material, pero el pan de mi prójimo es un problema espiritual.

My own bread is a material problem; my neighbour's bread is a spiritual problem.

José María Arizmendiarrieta

I have a story in mind that I would like to share as I begin writing, very unfashionably, about how it is the essence of humanity to help one another. Around the time I began writing this book in earnest, there was an explosion in a plastics factory in Glasgow. This was during the heat of the Iraq War, with new pictures emerging daily of degradation of prisoners by soldiers, at a time when it would have been easy to become disillusioned about the way human beings can treat each other. The other side of our human selves was revealed in the aftermath of the accident, during an interview with a large Glaswegian factory worker, his face covered with debris and blood. He explained how, from the darkness and fear following the explosion, he and his mate, who was unfeasibly called Jimmy, held hands as they felt their way through the rubble to safety. That is an image I hold in mind whenever the market ideology threatens to overwhelm me with its attempts to pit us against each other for the gain of the few.

The purpose of this chapter is to identify a central flaw with capitalism: it relies on inequality. Policy fig-leaves have abounded over the years in an attempt to conceal this embarrassing reality. But within this economic system, inequality is not a temporary aberration that we must live with while waiting for wealth to trickle down or for some of the boats further inside the harbour to rise. These are rhetorical lies as insincere as the policies and institutions apparently dedicated to resolving the problem of poverty. Because capitalism needs inequality; it is the engine that keeps it moving forward. It is our attempts to catch up with the material standards of others that keep us moving our feet forward and turning the capitalist treadmill.

In this chapter I begin by identifying inequality as a problem. To those with a more philosophical or ethical bent this may seem superfluous, but even for entirely self-centred reasons it is simply not a good idea to leave a vast segment of the human family outside the party while gaily advertising its delights. Blatant inequality generates resentment and anger, and when channelled by the unscrupulous, those understandable emotions can easily be turned to violent conflict. As well as concentrating wealth in few hands, globalized capitalism does the same with power, and the next section of this chapter explores the privatization and corporatization of our economic and social life.

There is evidence that the New Labour government in the UK has abandoned any attempt to achieve equality, favouring instead a strategy of increasing the size of the pie so that even those with the smallest and most unfair share still have enough that it does not raise too many complaints from them or others. Given the evidence presented below that an unequal society is an unhealthy society, this would appear to be a bad idea for all of the UK citizens. While policies have successfully drawn those at the bottom of the distribution out of the direst poverty, they have done nothing to address social inequity. The situation is particularly serious in terms of the proportion of children growing up in poverty, where, despite the economic boom, the UK has only risen from bottom of the European league to eleventh out of the EU 15, only surpassing Italy, Portugal, Spain and Greece. Unsurprisingly for a New *Labour* government, the tie between unemployment and poverty is unchallenged, meaning that the workless suffer particularly badly in Labour Britain. Figures for assets indicate that this is where the real inequalities lie in our society, with the very rich controlling a far larger proportion of the wealth than they did before the years of neoliberal economics and the Thatcher revolution: the richest 1 per cent of the population controlled 6.5 per cent of the wealth in 1985; this had risen to 13 per cent by 1999.

So capitalism is found to be an economic system where political and financial power are shared unequally and increasingly unequally as the system develops. This is, in a sense, a self-limiting process, since those without power become increasingly desperate and take matters into their own hands using the weapon of their own bodies. Others, however, take a more positive course and work together to organize their own economic system. This is what we call 'mutualism' or 'cooperation', and the remainder of this chapter gives examples from history of mutual economies, which have developed in times when capitalism has been at its most rapacious. The origins of the cooperative movement can be traced to the overweening power of capital towards the end of the nineteenth century. This unequal power distribution generated violent resistance and revolution, as well as intellectual opposition and practical alternatives. We see all three of these responses again today.

I favour the mutual model because it is something we can just decide to do together without legislation or permission or very much capital, and especially because it is a constructive non-violent response to oppression. The message of this book is that, if we find the economic system we have inherited unappealing or distasteful, we should use our imagination and our ingenuity to come up with something better. The cooperative movement represents evidence that a better alternative is not only possible but actually exists.

The dangers of inequality

The US power structure responded to the attacks on the World Trade Center by declaring a 'war on terror' that was misplaced as well as definitionally challenged. There were many reasons why being in a state of war and keeping the domestic population in a state of fear might serve those who wish to exercise an unreasonable amount of power over others. However, the declaration of war was perhaps not so misguided. The attacks of 11 September 2001 were a well-directed message that certain forces in the world were launching their own war, against a hegemonic economic system whose aims they detested and whose inequality they found inherently immoral. The response from the USA's corporate bosses has been violently repressive. This has gained the support of the testosteroned, gun-slinging voters of the Midwest, and also lined the coffers of several teetering US corporations, as I outline later. But it has not dealt with the cause of the attacks, which certainly in part is the gross inequality of economic power and financial resources in today's world. The message from the hijackers was fairly clear from their choice of target: it would be hard to find a more appropriate apotheosis of US capitalism than the vaunting twin towers.

Following the World Trade Center attacks, a group of 100 Nobel Laureates made a public statement at the Nobel Centennial Symposium in Oslo, where the annual peace prize was awarded. In December 2001 they stated that:

> The most profound danger to world peace in the coming years will stem not from the irrational acts of states or individuals but from the legitimate demands of the world's dispossessed. Of these poor and disenfranchised, the majority live a marginal existence in equatorial climates. Global warming, not of their making but originating with the wealthy few, will affect their fragile ecologies most. Their situation will be desperate and manifestly unjust. It cannot be expected, therefore, that in all cases they will be content to await the beneficence of the rich. If then we permit the devastating power of modern weaponry to spread through this combustible human landscape, we invite a conflagration that can engulf both rich

and poor. The only hope for the future lies in co-operative international action, legitimized by democracy.

In 2004 two prominent members of the UK Green Party provided a useful account of how globalization, rather than ending global inequality as its supporters claim, is in fact creating it. They quote the following statistics:

> Measures of absolute poverty also reveal a grim picture. Of the world's 6 billion people, 2.8 billion – almost half – live on less than $2 a day, and more than 1.2 billion – a fifth – live on less than $1 a day, with numbers having increased during the 1990s in most regions of the world apart from India and China.

Robert Hunter Wade considers that even the apparently impressive economic growth in India and China results from 'statistical sleights of hand', and within the latter country he identifies that 'surging inequality is now greater than before the Communists won the civil war in 1949'. Wade concludes his analysis as follows:

> On income distribution, the strong conclusion is that world inequality has risen since the early 1980s when income is expressed in terms of market exchange rates; and the same is true for PPP incomes [purchasing power parities: an attempt to make a realistic assessment of the value of an income based on its ability to buy goods to eliminate value differences caused by relative currency values] when a top-to-bottom ratio is used (rather than an average). A rising share of the world's income is going to those at the top. Moreover the absolute size of the income gap between countries is widening rapidly.

In the face of statistics like these, it becomes clear that the economists at the World Bank and academic economists the world over are acting as apologists for a system that is responsible for the deaths of thousands of children every year. The only other possibility is that they really are too ignorant to draw the inevitable conclusions from their own research papers. A more compassionate interpretation is that they have begun to believe their own fantasy and that the numerous redefinitions of purchasing power parities and poverty indicators are their best attempts to convince themselves, as well as us, that the economic system they are managing is not causing the devastation and death we see in the poorer countries of the world.

The good guys in this global debate are, unfortunately, not doing much better. It is sad to see that some of the best-intentioned development charities have missed the point on this one and, instead of tackling capitalism head on as a system that is inherently unfair, are wasting energy lobbying for fairer trade rules. The Make Trade Fair campaign is a classic example of a well-meaning mistake. It is like arguing for a change of game in a bent casino. It is missing the point that, even if we change this set of rules,

the global corporations will invent another game to enrich themselves at the expense of others, until we wake up to the fact that we need to control their power.

Debating the exact percentage of this tariff or that quota is the equivalent of petitioning an absolute monarch for the right to keep slightly more of the corn you spent your energy growing. In that case you might have been wise to tug your forelock since he had an army and you had only a pitchfork. But we live in a democratic system: the USA itself lays claim to the invention of the system where the power resides with the people. So we should be working together to use that power to remove our representatives, who have taken a wrong turning, and require them or others to represent our interests rather better than they are doing. If they happen to be unreasonable about it and turn nasty then perhaps we will be justified in claiming, along with Monty Python's medieval peasant, that we have identified 'the violence inherent in the system'. While we continue to acquiesce in solutions that reinforce global inequality, and timidly argue for a slight shift in nuance here or there, we really have only ourselves to blame.

Inequality and war

Amongst those who opposed the Iraq War there are a wide range of explanations for why it happened, some taking the form of bizarre conspiracy theories. The most obvious explanation that 'it was all about oil' has some merit, although it is also too simplistic. The reasons why those behind the Bush administration decided to provoke and then fight this war are complex, but the salvaging of some of the giants of US corporate capitalism has to be high on the list of reasons.

Halliburton is the most obvious example of a corporation that has benefited hugely from the war and it also, appropriately, has the Vice-President of the USA as a former chairman. Like most global players today, Halliburton is a 'group' of associated companies, which styles itself as offering 'a broad range of energy services', which may be some explanation for why it became notorious by being offered the first post-war Iraqi contract: to extinguish the pipeline fires. Like most of the corporate front organizations, it has bought up a range of smaller players including some who control operations you may be more familiar with. One of its subsidiaries, Kellogg, Brown & Root, has the contracts for Aldermaston and the Royal Devonport Dockyard.

In spite of its lucrative, politically connected contracts, Halliburton was far from secure, and as corporate capitalism rocked in the wake of the Enron collapse, its position was increasingly precarious. Halliburton had used the same technique of counting 'unbilled receivables' to inflate the profits it reported to shareholders and the stock market. Enron and Halliburton shared many similarities: their place in the energy sector, vast borrowing, and close political ties with the White House. Like Enron, Halliburton had postponed losses and counted money it had not even invoiced for as revenue: according to the pressure group Judicial Watch, it overstated profits to the value of $445 million during 1999 to 2001. Living on the accounting edge like this might have worked during the boom of the 1990s, but it was becoming impossible in the insecure new century, especially once the foundations of the corporate world were cracked by the World Trade Center attack and the fall of Enron.

George Bush's election to the White House, with his running mate Dick Cheney, chief executive of Halliburton from 1995 to 2000, was crucial in saving the company. When things got sticky after the collapse of

Enron, the attack on the World Trade Center was used as an excuse to increase US defence spending hugely. Halliburton almost immediately received billion-dollar contracts from the Pentagon to build operational bases for the so-called war on terror. It was also saved from lawsuits it was facing from former employees who had been poisoned by asbestos: a legal reform capped the value of such suits, causing Halliburton shares to rise by 43 per cent. Cheney is not entirely in the clear – he is still facing a fraud case filed by Halliburton investors in the Dallas court.

Halliburton has not been the only carrion crow corporation to feed on the corpse of Iraq. When the *Guardian* writer Julian Borger recently called his article 'Bush Cronies Advise on Buying Up Iraq', again he was not talking figuratively. Here is how his colleague Rory McCarthy, in Baghdad, explained what is going on:

> Under the new rules, announced by the finance minister, Kamil Mubdir al-Gailani, in Dubai, foreign firms will have the right to wholly own Iraqi companies, except those in the oil, gas and mineral industries. There will be no restrictions on the amount of profits that can be repatriated or on using local products. Corporate tax will be set at 15%.

And here again we see Halliburton, this time in the guise of its subsidiary Kellogg, Brown & Root, where Dick Cheney cut his corporate teeth, winning a big contract, this time worth $7 billion and again to repair Iraq's oil infrastructure. A company that was on the verge of a spectacular crash is now making good business again. This may be one reason why the intelligence warnings about terrorist attacks were not heeded.

The corporatization of Iraq and the extraction of the country's national oil wealth to inflate the profits of US corporations continue apace. Before retiring to safety and leaving the administration in the hands of a puppet regime, Paul Bremer (head of the Coalition Provisional Authority) instituted a system of orders bearing his name. Bremer Order no. 39 covers foreign investment:

> Bremer Order #39, enacted on September 19, 2003, has five key elements: (1) privatization of state-owned enterprises; (2) 100% foreign ownership of businesses in all sectors except oil and mineral extraction, banks and insurance companies (the latter two are addressed in a separate order); (3) 'national treatment' of foreign firms; (4) unrestricted, tax-free remittance of all funds associated with the investment, including, but not limited to, profits; and (5) 40 year ownership licenses which have the option of being renewed.

The changing of the fundamental economic laws of a country is illegal under international law. An occupying power is only permitted to reinstate a functioning state; that state's citizens should have the right to make choices about the nature of their political and economic systems. Other Bremer orders deal with such issues as the obligation of Iraq to comply with WTO rules and the organization of its taxation and banking systems.

Naomi Klein describes how the corporate 'feeding frenzy' in Iraq is fuelling the resistance to US control. She claims that the State Department has transferred $184 million earmarked for drinking-water projects to the refurbishment of the new US embassy, and that the reconstruction is deliberately being slowed down to give Ambassador Negroponte leverage to ensure US military bases are allowed to remain in perpetuity and desired economic 'reforms' are introduced. She is scathing about the performance of the US corporations:

> Rather than models of speed and efficiency, the contractors look more like overcharging, underperforming, lumbering beasts, barely able to move for fear of the hatred they have helped generate. The problem goes well beyond the latest reports of Halliburton drivers abandoning $85,000 trucks on the road because they don't carry spare tyres. Private contractors are also accused of playing leadership roles in the torture of prisoners at Abu Ghraib. A landmark class-action lawsuit filed by the Centre for Constitutional Rights alleges that Titan Corporation and CACI International conspired to 'humiliate, torture and abuse persons' in order to increase demand for their 'interrogation services'.

For those with a normal, ethical take on life, war is an evil to be avoided, but for those corporate executives whose financial mismanagement and corporate debts are making their futures feel increasingly uncertain it may begin to look like a lucrative and profitable opportunity, an attractive market niche with growth potential as long as the 'war on terror' lasts.

In the face of such arrant immorality, sometimes humour is the only psychologically tolerable response. Hence the conclusion of an article published under my name in the *Morning Star:*

> The big silver lining in this particular war cloud is that when you bomb a country back to the stone age – especially if you've already bombed it back to the stone age a dozen years previously – that country will simply beg you to rebuild it back to at least the feudal period, if not all the way to the Dickensian era. Benevolent capitalism would come into its own. Doubtless there will be socialists and Greens who will, in their ever-such-a-wet-blanket manner, borrow the words of Homer Simpson and say, 'This is starting to look like some kind of scam, or possibly scamola.' But don't be misled. The world will be a better place after this war, just as it was after all those other little English wars and honorary English wars, like Vietnam and Grenada and Suez and the First, Second and Third Anglo-Afghan Wars and the Crusades, and the Opium Wars and the Anglo-American War of 1812 and that little one I can't remember the name of when the British gassed the Kurds; and so on. So you can sit back, read your copy of the *Sun*, enjoy the tales of derring-do in Iraq, and think oh, what a lovely war.

Warning: inequality is bad for your health

As I mentioned in the introduction, the capitalist system requires inequality for its operation, so that any theorist who suggests that once there is enough money it can be shared with the poor is either a deceiver or has not understood the system. Capitalism operates like a pump, where the energy of those who have least pushes them upwards to become those who have most. Inequality is the motor that drives this pump; it causes the capitalist machine to function to its maximum, but caught up in that machine are human lives and the costs of inequality on those lives is very great.

First, the inequality has damaging psychological consequences. There is understandable anxiety in the medical community surrounding the statistical evidence that those in professional occupations live considerably longer than those in manual occupations. Data from the Office for National Statistics indicate that men in social class I live 7.4 years longer than men in social class V; for women the difference is 5.7 years. More surprisingly, US researchers have found that inequality is bad for the life expectancy of all in a society, since the relationship they found between a measure of inequality across society as a whole (the Gini coefficient, calculated at the level of individual US states) and the life expectancy of that society remained after they had controlled for poverty. They called this finding the Robin Hood Index, suggesting that Robin Hood's redistribution deserves the warmth it has always received. The authors conclude:

> The paper suggests that that there is a relation between income distribution and life expectancy. It concluded that variations between states in the inequality of income were associated with increased mortality from several causes. Relative poverty, i.e. the size of the gap between the wealthy and less well off, seems to matter in its own right: the greater the gap between the rich and poor, the lower the average life expectancy. This association is independent of that between absolute income and life expectancy. Therefore it matters, not only how affluent a country is, but also how economic gains are distributed among its members.

Jeremy Seabrook argues that what is so damaging about inequality under capitalism is that it is used to spur us to greater economic effort and to do this we must feel ashamed of our relative lack of affluence. Our desire to remove the shame of poverty is what generates our energy to engage in capitalism, to increase our monetary holdings, to ensure that we are on the winning side of the unequal distribution:

> If at the earlier moment of industrialization the persistence of poverty could be explained by a productive capacity only rudimentarily established, such an excuse is no longer possible. It becomes clear, therefore, that the survival of poverty is essential for ideological and not material

reasons. Indeed, the maintenance of a felt experience of insufficiency is essential to any capitalist version of development.

The feeling of insufficiency, what has elsewhere been called 'the ethic of scarcity', becomes part of our drive to accumulate more, in a rat-race that we can never win. The advertising industry plays its own part in increasing our feeling of 'deprivation' and our felt need for a range of wholly worthless gadgets that we are sure the person behind the Leylandia hedge must already own.

Related findings on 'status anxiety' draw similar conclusions about the negative effects of our feelings of inferiority and the importance of our quest to be found admirable in the eyes of those around us. Marmot, who is famous for his pioneering Whitehall Studies into this subject, found that control over our lives and opportunities for social participation were the key factors in determining our health, based on more than 25 years of research from a multitude of societies around the world. Commenting on his work, a colleague wrote that 'Despite the widespread belief that molecular biology will soon vanquish disease, there remains the discomfiting fact that health can be predicted to an astonishing extent by being poor, *feeling* poor, and being *made* to feel poor.'

James identifies the psychologically damaging effects of late capitalism, of which he takes the USA to be the paradigmatic example. His exploration of the impact of child-rearing practices on the mental health of citizens identifies the high rates of daycare for children during their first year, combined with the inculcation of a punitive conscience and a powerful drive to succeed through dominating discipline, to be the cause of the psychological problems of US young people. His conclusion is that 'in comparisons between developed nations the degree to which a social group has an American style of advanced capitalism would predict the extent to which those who have been made vulnerable to Disorder by their childhoods would fulfil that potential'. He also relates this to the right-wing move in US politics and in other countries dominated by pro-capitalist ideology: 'I have come to the conclusion that a disproportionate number of leaders and chief communicators in our society suffer from Personality Disorders, or symptoms of them; they are often unable to acknowledge the dependence of children on parents or increasingly, of citizens on states.' His conclusion that a psychologically disturbing and disturbed economic system favours the advancement of psychologically disturbed citizens is an unsettling one.

By contrast, a rare piece of psychological research into cooperation found that it is good for your health. Rilling and colleagues from Emory University, Atlanta, conducted an experiment on women based on the prisoners' dilemma game while carrying out an MRI scan of their brains. They found that the pleasure centres received stimulation if they chose a cooperative strategy, suggesting that there may be fundamental psychological rewards available within a cooperative workplace. It seems to me fairly obvious that we have needed to rely on cooperation to survive as a species, and that there should be a selection advantage to cooperation, which is the pleasure derived from it. However, it is also of interest that the research was conducted only on women.

You have to learn to share

In the days before NHS dentists became an endangered species, I was lucky enough to have a very good one. When she gave me an injection, she would always do it in two goes: the first one to numb the gum, so the second, deeper one would not hurt. She told me that this was standard practice with children and she did not see why adults should suffer unnecessary pain either. This also reminds me of a poster I once saw extending the laws of the nursery classroom to life in general. It gave such recommendations as: if you see somebody is upset, hold their hand.

'You have to learn to share' is one of the key messages we teach our children when they first start interacting with others. It goes along with 'You shouldn't tell lies' and 'Don't hurt other people'. Strangely, however, all these messages are qualified or abandoned altogether once we enter the complex world of adults. We justify our dishonesty and selfishness by explaining to ourselves and others that we must put away childish things because the world is fall of dangers and confusions that we could not imagine as children. I would beg to differ. It seems to me that what we teach our children is a fairly good system of rules for how we should live together as adults. For the time being I am going to focus on sharing, because I think as a society and as a human species we are not doing very well with this rule. I will discuss the gross failure to share the planet's resources on a global scale in the following section, but for the moment we could benefit from spending some time putting our own society under the microscope.

The endless rhetoric opposing taxation is a prime example of the self-reinforcing resistance to sharing encouraged by capitalism. The understandable reluctance to give up an advantageous position is encouraged by Thatcher's anti-society politics. Greed is good; taxation is bad, ran the message communicated directly and subliminally over nearly 20 years while inequality between households spiralled. Remarkably, this discussion has still failed to entirely dent the commitment to a commonwealth on which our welfare state was built. Polly Toynbee finds that the rhetoric outstrips the reality when people are actually polled about their attitude to tax. The media over-represent the revulsion from paying higher taxes for better public services, which is a form of sharing. She reports a Reform poll which found that 50% of those asked agreed with the statement 'I would be willing to pay more tax to increase spending on public services.'

Box 3.1 The moral of Air Florida Flight 737

On 13 January 1982 a passenger aircraft crashed into the freezing Potomac river after crashing into the 14th Street Bridge shortly after take-off from Washington Airport. The Bridge was later renamed the Arland D. Williams Jr Memorial Bridge after a passenger on the flight who saved his fellow passengers but at the cost of his own life. He passed life-vests and the life-line to rescue other survivors. The story was a crumb of comfort to come out of the disastrous tragedy and its commemoration shows how much we value a selfless non-monetary motivation in others.

Source: From 'A hero – passenger aids others, then dies', *Washington Post*, 14 January 1982.

An equally disturbing trend is that towards gross intergenerational inequity, which has reached epidemic proportions. A whole range of macroeconomic and demographic factors, ranging from the 1970s inflation to the baby boom, mean that the generation currently in retirement is controlling a grossly unfair proportion of available capital. This trend has been exacerbated by rapidly increasing house prices, meaning that members of older generations can not only live in houses larger than they need while their offspring remain inadequately housed, but also engage in 'equity release' to fund a SAGA-sponsored life of luxurious consumption. This decision to re-engage in debt transfers the value that might have been passed down the generations back to the banks which create the money that is loaned against the mortgage. There is evidence that it is related to the increasing incidence of age discrimination.

There is no sense of immorality amongst those who enjoy an unfair level of consumption, which they justify on the basis that 'they worked hard for it'. There are so many unspoken assumptions in this phrase that I devoted a whole chapter to it in another book. For now I will limit myself to suggesting three. The first is that it is impossible to suggest that hard work is fairly remunerated, when a simple observation of the workplace from Bangkok to Bangor indicates quite clearly that, as Ewan McColl put it, 'them as works the hardest are the least provided'. Secondly, in the case of retirement, there is the assumption that working during a period of your life entitles you to an unfair share in perpetuity, even when you are no longer working. The financial investment world may facilitate this, but there is no way that it is morally justifiable. Thirdly, the ability to acquire a high-paying job has very little to do with dedication and effort, and everything to do with contacts and various types of inherited capital, whether cultural, social or financial. The stalling of class mobility makes this abundantly clear.

Box 3.2 Rational economic man?

A Comins Coch man who risked his life to rescue a toddler and his mother from a burning car has been hailed a hero. Alan Munro Forrester, 57, was on his way home on Friday night, on the A44 near Sweet Lamb, when he saw a Renault Megane leave the road, plough into a tree and burst into flames. He managed to rescue the pair, who are not being named, by cutting them free from their seatbelts with a knife.

Police, who say Mr Forrester's quick thinking saved lives, have also commended his bravery. A spokesperson said: 'There is no question that this gentleman saved the lives of this mother and her baby. What he has done is extremely heroic. He took a great personal risk, not knowing if the car was going to explode and we commend him for his actions.'

But Mr Forrester, who was later treated for smoke inhalation, said he just did what he had to do. 'People warned me not to go near the car because it might explode but I had to help the people inside', he said. 'Fear just goes out of the window and something else takes over. You hope that someone would do the same thing for you or your family.'

The thought of Mr Forrester's grandson spurred him on. 'When I saw the baby I saw my grandson's face. Jamie is about the same age and I just thought, it could have been him trapped in the car. The little boy was screaming, he was hysterical and he was screaming at me to get him out.'

Source: *Cambrian News*, 21 October 2004, p. 1.

Just do it (together)

Having spent our adult lives in a competitive, individualist, selfish world, how can we hope to imagine an economy based on sharing? Fortunately, we have no need because the model has been not only developed in theory but operating in practice for more than 150 years: the cooperative model, also known as mutualism.

Mutualism developed historically as a response to the first rampant emergence of capitalism, which brought with it the movement to the cities and the breakdown of traditional agrarian societies and their parish-based social support systems. Mutualism was the response of people working together to solve the problems that capitalism had created. Writing in 1902, Kropotkin reports the following account from a friend who was involved with a workers' club in Whitechapel:

Nursing neighbours, in cases of illness, without any shade of remuneration, is quite general among the workers. Also, when a woman has little children, and goes out for work, another mother always takes care of them. If, in the working classes, they would not help each other, they could not exist. I know families which continually help each other – with money, with food, with fuel, for bringing up little children, in cases of illness, in cases of death. The 'mine' and 'thine' is much less sharply observed among the poor than among the rich. Shoes, dress, hats, and so on, – what may be wanted on the spot – are continually borrowed from each other, also all sorts of household things.

These informal support networks were extended into formal structures where very small contributions were collected to support social services such as libraries and welfare institutions, or put by in mutual savings societies against calamities such as illness (and hence unemployment and poverty in days before the dole) and death.

The formal cooperative movement was begun by a group who became known as the Rochdale Pioneers, as a result of the need for fresh, wholesome food in the industrial cities, and the inadequacy of the adulterated and over-priced supplies offered by commercial shopkeepers. This was not the first cooperative activity in the economic sphere; there were other widespread examples before the middle of the nineteenth century, including cooperative cornmills built in Woolwich by dockworkers reacting against monopolistic mill-owners as early as 1760 and a cooperative shop owned by weavers in Fenwick, Ayrshire, in 1769. What was different about the Rochdale example was a formalized structure and system of rules which has since developed into the cooperative principles still operating today.

The Rochdale pioneers operated according to principles of open membership, democratic control, dividend on purchases, limited interest on capital, political and religious neutrality, cash trading and the promotion of education. These principles were established in 1844 and form the basis of the values still followed by the international cooperative movement. It is important to note that Rochdale was not only about food but has influenced the development of the whole cooperative sector with its commitment to equity and democracy. From food the cooperative pioneers moved to consider work and why it was that the value generated from that work was so unfairly shared. Having taken control of the consumption side of the equation, they devised a means to control the production side, by owning their own businesses and sharing the surpluses generated.

Many have attributed the surplus-value hypothesis to Marx, but in fact he was merely reporting the conclusions of disgruntled workers who noticed the profits that were being made from their labour while they remained in direst poverty. An example is an anonymous pamphlet sent to Lord John Russell (a reformist Whig member of parliament and later twice Prime Minister) in 1821. The author of the pamphlet makes the central point that 'It is admitted that the interest paid to the capitalists, whether in the nature of rents, interests of money, or profits of trade, is paid out of the *labour of others*.' Her/his central thesis is that workers are paid the minimum that allows them to physically survive and continue to work, allowing the employer to accumulate capital. Marx elaborated on this account at great length, but I cannot see that he has actually improved on it.

The theory of cooperatives owes its origin to Robert Owen, who dedicated much of his life to developing an economy based on fairness and sharing. Owen wrote that the capitalist system 'has made man ignorantly individually selfish; placed him in opposition to his fellows; engendered fraud and deceit; blindly urged him forward to create but deprived him of the wisdom to enjoy'. As a self-made owner-manager in the Lancashire cotton mills, Owen was in a privileged position to make this sort of judgement. He established labour exchanges and developed time-money, where employees could be paid an hour of their time rather than various quantities of money. He derived this idea from his early recognition of the importance of the labour theory of value and its extension to conclude that the value of a product should equate to the amount of labour time invested in it, not the amount of money exchanged when it is bought or sold. Such a time-money system would also make each person's time equal, of course. Although Owen's practical experiments with cooperation met with mixed degrees of success, 'Owen's aim of opposing the competitive individualism and exploitation of capitalism remains central to co-operative thought'.

The central theme in cooperative thought is the importance of sharing the benefits of labour between all those involved in its production, and balancing their competing interests within the business. Green economics would add the planet into consideration of stakeholders, so that the concept of productivity must be balanced by the need to respect the limits of our ecosystem.

In the UK the cooperative ideal built a huge movement which represented around a third of the retail market and covered people's needs in areas of their lives ranging from financial services to funeral services. Many of these companies still exist. In France the ideas took a different turn amongst artisans in the 1830s and received a boost in the revolutions of 1848, developing into syndicalism. 'Syndicalism differed from socialism on two counts. Syndicalists did not seek alliances with socialist political parties, regarding the ballot box as an irrelevance. Further, French syndicalism was based upon direct worker ownership and control of the factory and the workplace.' Unlike the UK movement, the French version, which also spread to Spain until the civil war there, was devoted to violent, revolutionary activity.

Unfortunately these early developments were swamped by political movements to encourage reformism and state socialism. In the UK this position was typified by Beatrice Potter (later Webb), who along with Sidney Webb established the London School of Economics and many other bastions of socialist life in Britain, which have hampered the development of genuinely mutual and local solutions to economic problems. Potter supported consumer cooperatives but argued against worker cooperatives on the basis that 'Restricted to the dwarfish forms into which individual wage slaves can elaborate it by their private efforts, the cooperative system will never transform capitalistic societies.' The concern was that the workers' revolutionary potential could be deflected from political agitation into self-help. The rest is the history of the twentieth century, disfigured as it was by features such as Stalin's death camps and the destruction of socialism in the UK by Thatcherism and New Labour. How much easier it was for supporters of capitalism to win control of a single, unified political party than a thousand locally based and worker-owned businesses.

The cooperative movement had a rough time in the second half of the twentieth century, struggling with, on the one hand, the monopolization of mutual activity by the state that took place in the post-war years and, on the other, the carpet-bagging of its profitable, financial institutions spurred by the loadsamoney culture of the 1980s. Having formerly been the leading innovator, introducing the self-service shop in 1948, the Coop shop suffered as a result of the ending of retail price maintenance in 1964, which led to competition based on price rather than quality. The following decades were a difficult time for cooperative retail in the UK, and by the last decade of the twentieth century it was a shadow of its former self, retaining only some rather drab shops indistinguishable from the more attractive private competitors. But it is now undergoing an ideological and commercial renaissance affecting the main Cooperative Group itself, but also seen in the flourishing of smaller food coops, often based around wholefoods, Suma being the best-known example in the UK.

There is a corner of southern Europe, however, where a large proportion of economic activity is organized along cooperative lines. In the Basque country of northern Spain, the Mondragon cooperatives are providing a model for how other regional economies could be organized to maximize the benefits of mutual organization and to share the proceeds of economic activity fairly. The movement began when the local priest, José María Arizmendiarrieta, founded a technical school in the 1940s because of his conviction that knowledge was the key to economic success. In 1956 several of his students started the first producer cooperative, Fagor, which has grown to become a European leader in the production of domestic electrical goods. The Mondragon Group now consists of 67 industrial enterprises, 8 involved in distribution, and 15 which serve the group as a whole, primarily in the educational field. It also has Eroski, the leading chain of hypermarkets in northern Spain and with outlets throughout the country, and Caja Laboral, the workers' bank.

Wales also has its own unique workers' cooperative which is a source of great pride to its local community: Tower Colliery, in the Cynon Valley near Hirwaun. It is the only worker-owned deep mine in the world and a rare sign of hope to come out of the destructive political battle over coal-mining in the UK. Following closure of this modern and well-endowed pit as a result of politically motivated government policy, the miners organized to buy it themselves, 239 of them investing their £8,000 redundancy money to fund the buyout. Since 1995 they have managed the pit themselves with enthusiastic support from the local community. They have now operated with surpluses in each of the past 10 years. Tower is the largest deep mine operating in the South Wales coalfield, employing 300 men, 90 per cent of whom are shareholders. In 2002 it was one of Wales' top 300 companies, with a £28 million turnover, a surplus of £2.7 million and a 26.8 per cent return on capital. It also provides its employees with high-quality employment in which they feel pride and for which they do not need to sacrifice autonomy or self-respect.

Internationally, the cooperative movement is flourishing. The International Cooperative Alliance (ICA), the international coordinating body of the cooperative sector based in Geneva, has organizations for agriculture, fisheries, banking, consumers, health, housing, insurance, tourism and workers. It is a truly global movement, which provides a positive slant on globalization. The ICA is the largest non-governmental organization recognized by the United Nations. It represents nearly three-quarters of a million cooperatives worldwide, providing employment for over 100 million people – more than are employed by all the multinational corporations in the world. International Cooperative Day 2004 focused on 'fair globalization' and identified the important role that cooperatives can play in improving the lives of those who live in the world's poorer countries. Iain MacDonald, Director-general of ICA, made a strong statement in favour of fair trade:

> We are by nature inclusive and international. It is galling, therefore, to see 'globalisation' and 'anti-globalisation' so misrepresented. Global trade, especially of a co-operative nature, has to be encouraged. What we are against is the way in which non-co-operative trade, with its emphasis on minimal service and maximum profit, is distorting world trade and causing untold damage and misery – the opposite of our values . . . There is a huge void which we should be filling – one which advocates fair and ethical trade through co-operation . . . The everyday activities of co-ops are helping to build fairer globalisation. Their Fairtrade initiatives, community focus and development activities, plus their advocacy and lobbying efforts are all helping.

I outline in Chapter 4 my concerns about using trade, fair or not, as a response to global inequality, but although the volume of international trade will certainly be reduced in a sustainable economy, what is traded should be traded for a fair price. Much of the fair trade produce sold in the

UK comes from cooperatively organized farms: it is the cooperative structure that puts the 'fair' into 'fair trade'.

New growth opportunities

The rampant greed demonstrated by the late form of capitalism is offering significant advantages to those seeking to organize their business along co-operative lines. The emphasis on vast and rapidly growing profits means that parts of conglomerates that are viable and have a good level of sales none the less drag down corporate performance and can be made available for sale. This offers employees an opportunity to bring about a buyout.

Non-viability is often determined by accountants who are operating with an agenda, rather than providing honest figures, resulting in a pro-cess known as 'destructive accounting'. Tower Colliery was a beneficiary of this process, since the National Coal Board estimates of the value of its coal reserves were extremely pessimistic to justify closing the pit. Figures were massaged to indicate unduly grim forecasts, a process that miners referred to as 'fiddling' and that included the purchase of unused equipment and unnecessary and expensive refurbishments to in-flate the cost side of the balance sheet. According to miners:

> In the 12-month after 1984, they decided to install a new railway system to make the transportation of coal more easy – new rails, new roads, new

weighbridge. They installed a new control with an estimated cost of £2 million. They decided to open up a new face with new advanced machinery – all to no avail. I don't think that they close a pit overnight as a result of a whim; it must have been on the cards. So why go to the expense of spending all this money? Building up people's hopes, then having them dashed like that. Most of the money was spent since the end of the strike. God knows how many millions it cost.

In other cases, dishonest accounting can impede buyout attempts. This happened in the case of the Vaux Brewery on Teesside, where a management buyout was attempted but because of an over-estimate of the value of the company, sufficient funds could not be found. In the end the disparity between the amount the buyout team could offer and the value of the asset was far less than the City bankers' estimate.

> The out-turn was over £15m less . . . than BTAB [City-based Bankers Trust Alex Brown] estimated. Given that the gap between the value of the MBO bid and the closure/asset disposal was claimed to be £30.5m, this was based on an over-estimate of proceeds worth £15m. The real difference between the MBO and closure/asset disposal may have been only £15m – just £5m more than that £10m difference the Swallow Board publicly claimed would have been acceptable.

As capitalists turn their attention away from extracting surplus labour value to speculation, it offers opportunities to those prepared to work to take advantage of the idle assets. The Movimento dos Trabalhadores Rurais sem Terra (MST: Movement of Landless Rural Workers) in Brazil has led the occupation of unused land which has been worked by cooperatives of farmers. Less than 3 per cent of the population owns two-thirds of Brazil's arable land; many of them are absentee landlords who leave the land abandoned. MST members have been seizing this land since 1985, and 250,000 families now work more than 15 million acres. This is dangerous work: more than 1,000 people have been killed in the past 10 years, but MST is supported by UNICEF and radical Catholic priests. It has now moved beyond agricultural cooperatives and created 60 food cooperatives. This has allowed perhaps a million of Brazil's poorest people to become subsistence farmers, avoiding the exploitation of the labour market.

The ability of cooperatives to survive in corners where corporations have less interest in engaging in their particular form of rapacious economic activity is also demonstrated in Argentina, where following the financial crash of 2001, factories were left empty in spite of workers wanting to work there and raw materials being available. The workers responded by expropriating their own workplaces and transforming them into democratically organized factories. There are now over 200 such 'liberated' workplaces in a diverse range of sectors including ceramics, textiles, footwear and printing. A film by Naomi Klein and Avi Lewis tells the story of these workers who took up residence in their own abandoned factories and, by refusing to leave, turned them into cooperatives. For a real economy to function it is necessary to have raw materials, people wanting to buy the products, and workers prepared to work for wages that ensure the price of the product is within the price range of the purchaser. These three conditions were satisfied in Argentina, which was destroyed by the activities of financial speculators on the international currency markets rather than any intrinsic weakness in its real economy. As the focus of attention for capitalists shifts from production and sale to speculation, the field is wide open to those wishing to regain control of the real, bread-and-butter economy.

The related tendency of corporations to cast aside viable and profitable businesses because they are not making profits fast enough to satisfy shareholders offers opportunities for spreading mutual ownership models. An example is Datrys Consulting, which was a successful branch of a Dutch-owned firm of consulting engineers that learned of its demise as part of a company restructuring plan. With the support of Wales Cooperative Centre the employees bought the company, based in Caernarfon, north Wales, as a going concern from the Dutch parent and they began trading as a cooperative in October 2002. The workforce continue to provide bilingual civil engineering services, maintaining the five well-paid and highly skilled jobs in a depressed rural economy, and increasing them now to eight.

The need for the economy of the future to be ecologically respectful is a basic tenet of green economics, but it seems clear to me that for this to be possible the economy must also be organized along cooperative lines. In the case of wind power, the government appears to have reached the same conclusion. A recent Department of Trade and Industry seminar focused on sharing the experience of Denmark, where much of the wind-energy capacity is organized by the community which uses the energy or benefits from its sale. The Global Watch mission visited Denmark in October 2004 under the auspices of Cooperatives-UK. The support of the UK government suggests that it recognizes the need to offer local communities the value of wind power if the large-scale expansion it plans is to succeed. Communities are only prepared to accept the upheaval a wind farm will cause if they benefit directly from it. Wales is leading the way in community wind farm development in the UK, with the country's first community wind farm, Bro Dyfi, being opened in April 2003. The company has 59 shareholders, with holdings ranging from £100 to the maximum £1,000. The single turbine, known as *Pwer Pobl* or People Power, has a maximum output of 75 kW, enough for nearly 50 households. The Renewable Energy Investment Club is following this up by offering another share issue in a similar venture.

What is the nature of the link between sustainability and cooperative organization of the economy? I would suggest that the key is responsibility. I recently interviewed some members of environmentally focused worker cooperatives to explore their views on this issue. Jan Cliff, the prime mover behind the renewable energy consultants Sundance Renewables in Ammanford, south-west Wales, made the point: 'The trouble with the corporate model, as I see it, is that it is based on a very hierarchical structure and that does disempower people working within it even with the better run or managed corporations, that have managers with a degree of corporate social responsibility.' The nature of the employment relationship in the era of downsizing and outsourcing is a tenuous and distrustful one. You take your pay but think little about the strategy of the firm or the moral consequences of its activities. This is the direct opposite of a mutual economy, where your prime motivation is solving a problem and being embedded in the community you are providing a good or service for. As Jan put it, 'Workers [in a conventional business] can think it is the bosses' problem; it's not my problem.' Mutualism, by contrast, is about taking responsibility for solving one's own problems, and in the environmental niche this appears in the form of taking responsibility for the need to live in harmony with the planet.

Conclusion: if you don't like the heat . . .

We need to develop and design a system for the production and distribution of goods that balances the needs of producers, consumers and the planet. Since we all rely on the planet for our survival, and play the other two roles at some points in our lives, this is only sensible. Otherwise we would be robbing Peter to pay Paul, or rather robbing ourselves to pay ourselves in our other incarnations. The robbing that we want to see an end to is the robbing of value by those who do nothing but use their money to make more money. That was the original purpose of the cooperative movement and it remains valid today.

The cooperative model has long been marginalized within conventional economic theory. More recently it has attracted increasing amounts of positive comment from theorists of regeneration:

> [The social economy] is becoming seen as a holistic solution for social exclusion in a number of ways. First, by encouraging collective self-help, confidence and capacity building, and nurturing the collective values of the economy via socially useful production. Second, by humanising the economy via an emphasis upon autonomy, associational values, and organising the economy at a 'human' scale. Third, by enhancing democracy and participation via a decentralisation of policy to local communities and place. Fourth, by bringing about a greater degree of systemic coherence to the local economy via the local production and consumption of goods and services (a fortiori if this is linked to the

creation of a local currency). Fifth, by acknowledging the relationships between economy, environment, politics and society.

Other commentators are aware of the radical potential of cooperation as an alternative form of economic organization to capitalism. That explains why, at the same time that it is being explored and streamlined into more business-friendly forms, it is also being ideologically marginalized:

> This article is about the tensions between efforts at gradualist reform within existing circumstances, and the possibility of fundamental social change and liberation through the creation of radical alternatives to the mainstream. For this is the duality which has always existed in the social economy: on the one hand, its pragmatic, incremental, cooperative attempts to ameliorate conditions, in the face of need and adversity, versus, on the other, its utopian vision of a bright and self-sufficient commonwealth, based on principles of mutual cooperation, in which social needs and usefulness would be key to the production of goods and services, and everyone would be able to realize their fullest potentials.

If this alternative were not viable, why would the capitalists work so hard to marginalize it? A more worrying sign is the recent degree of political attention attracted by the sector, including the setting up of the Cooperative Commission by Blair and his New Labour hordes. Mutualism is a valuable tool bequeathed to us by those who worked to protect themselves against capitalism in its early years. It is worth protecting and developing rather than reinventing the wheel. Why should we engage in exploitative employment relationships when a fairer model is available? Rather we should share the mutual model, which is not only fairer but, by sharing rewards equally, increases incentives to improve both efficiency and productivity:

> The key to unlocking interest in the co-operative form of enterprise lies in demonstrating that co-operatives can serve the mutual interests of all stakeholders. Employee-owned businesses are more productive when the entrepreneurs and employees have a financial stake in the growth of the enterprise. Customers are more loyal to businesses they have a financial interest in.

So cooperation makes sense within a conventional economic mindset, but more importantly it enables us to feel good about what we do as both producers and consumers, knowing that we are operating fairly and with justice. And, if the link between sustainability and cooperation is an essential one, as I believe, then it also guarantees our ability to treat the planet with respect while engaging in economic activity.

4

From Free Trade to Trade Subsidiarity

The law doth lock up both man and woman,
Who steals the goose from off the commons,
But lets the greater felon loose,
Who steals the commons from the goose.

Anon., sixteenth century

Trade at any price

I wish I had space in this chapter to undertake a dissection of theories of
trade to match the one focused on markets in Chapter 2. But space, and
your patience, are limited, so we will have to concentrate instead on the
sort of trade system that would form part of a green economy. The initial
ground clearing will have to be limited to raising a few questions about
what trade is, and challenging the Mandelsohnian mantra that trade is
necessarily a good thing.

If we think our way back to the earliest historical example of trade that
we can recall, the Vikings or the Hanseatic League, perhaps, the first
thing we notice is that the trade was an exchange of exotic items that were
not available in the locality. The Vikings brought Baltic amber to the
Dark Age Britons, who sent back tin or gold in return. If the traders had
had nothing we could not find at home, we would not have involved ourselves with them. How simple life was in the happy days before capitalist
exchange!

The early economists also theorized trade as an exchange of goods that
could not be produced locally. In Ricardo's theory, British woollen goods
are exchanged for Portuguese wine. The sleight of hand that underpins
the 'trade is good' mantra is his theory of comparative advantage. It is
clear that if you have a British climate, you cannot have an absolute advantage in the production of wine. There are inevitably going to be
countries where the sun shines for more of the year, whose citizens can
produce better wine more cheaply. But what of the situation facing a
country that is less efficient in the production of all goods than its

neighbours? According to the theory of comparative advantage, it will still gain from trade if it focuses on producing the goods it can produce most efficiently with its own resources.

The reason this is a sleight of hand is that there are assumptions built into the concept of 'efficiency' that are not politically neutral. For one, the trade that takes place is denominated in a currency, and that currency is owned and controlled by a nation-state which can therefore use it to gain advantage in the trade. This explains why the east Asian tigers and now China are benefiting far less from their trade with the USA than are that country's citizens. It also explains why the USA is so keen to open up trade with the poor countries and persuade them that this, rather than self-sufficiency, is their best route out of poverty.

The gains from trade, whatever one's degree of productive efficiency, are determined by the terms of trade, which are always dependent on the relative levels of political or military power. The Vikings were traders, but they were also thieves. Some of their trading was always carried out in terms of offers people found it very difficult to refuse. The sorts of negotiation conducted today at the WTO are little different. The USA and EU use their political and military influence to achieve trade settlements that suit their interests, limiting the prices paid for the sorts of goods – raw materials and textiles – which the poorer countries have to offer.

The British Empire was built on trade, always described as 'free trade', but in fact trade backed up by the threat of violence. Simon Schama's analysis of the British Empire focused on its foundation on the iron law of free trade: that the market should have its way. Enormous sacrifices were demanded to maintain the sacred status of the market. The first shock came from Ireland, where oats were being shipped out to the UK market by landlords while potatoes lay rotting in the fields. The logic of capitalism dictated that prices should not be cut, that tenants should not be allowed to eat the food they were growing in their fields, which was rather sold to an overseas markets to be consumed by horses. If the landlords could not make a profit from tenants, they would turn them out of their homes and make a profit from sheep and cattle instead. The iron law of the market resulted in a million deaths in Ireland, less than 200 years ago, with another 2 million people emigrating to the USA and elsewhere. The population of Ireland declined from 8 million to 2 million in just one century. The iron law of the market is having very similar effects in Africa today, where farmers are producing green beans for our winter tables while their children starve.

The Indian famine of 1877 was similarly caused by a religious but immoral attachment to the law of the market. While thousands starved in Mysore and Madras, the British imperial authorities refused to intervene in markets and exported grain to other parts of India, out of the famine region. The resistance was to artificially lowering prices, because the market must be free to set its price. Schama concludes, 'common sense, not to mention common humanity, was sacrificed to the fetish of the market and millions were abandoned to perish'.

Gandhi learned the historical lesson. He knew about the cotton trade, which ensured markets in India for imported English goods in which India had been self-sufficient for thousands of years. Inferior cotton goods from the Lancashire mills were forced on to Indian markets, while local production was banned and punished. This is the explanation for the spinning wheel on the Indian national flag. It represents a symbol of the resistance to capitalist imperialism in the production of cotton. The early anti-imperialist fighters in India wore homespun *khadi* as a mark of their independence and resistance, as many leading politicians still do today. The tactic of resistance that was Gandhi's favourite was in fact invented in Ireland and named after an Irish land agent: Boycott. Although the elites of the poorer countries are being inveigled into the global trade system, the people of those countries will be its victims. A strategy of boycotting the global market and embracing self-sufficiency would serve their interests far better.

But why this obsession with trade? Why allow millions to die for the sake of what seems an empty fetish? The importance of trade is that it justifies the extraction of value from production. And the wider the area of trade, the more distant the sites of production and consumption, the larger the value that can be extracted. Hence globalization. And hence also the sucking of more and more areas of our lives into the market, where profit can be legitimately extracted. Our response should be to create economic systems which have three characteristics:

- localization, so that the distance between producer and consumer is minimized;
- self-provisioning, where the first criterion is perfected and the good or service does not enter the marketplace at all;
- cooperatives, so that the additional value accrues to those who produce the good rather than those who trade it.

It is important to remember the human consequences of the era of 'free trade' because the wolves in sheep's clothing are so eager to paint themselves as friends of the poor, kindly offering them the opportunity to better themselves by trading with us – and to paint alternative economists as hard-hearted and selfish by contrast. The following sections attempt to unpick further this piece of capitalist doublethink by exploring in more detail the problems of the increasing volume of world trade for the planet and the world's poor. I then offer a conceptual framework for reorganizing world trade within a carbon-limited global economy, which I call *trade subsidiarity*.

Who benefits from trade?

One of the most powerful political messages of our time is that trade is the solution to global poverty. As I identified in Chapter 1, capitalism is a system which inevitably generates inequality, but because humans find this morally repugnant, excuses have to be found to cover up this unavoidable truth. We have gone from the trickle-down theorem, through the rising of all boats on the tide, to the more visceral and hence appropriate quotation from Galbraith, 'If you feed enough oats to the horse, some will pass through to feed the sparrows.' The latest in the long string of such excuses is that the reason the poor countries remain poor is that they do not involve themselves enough with capitalism. They are losing out not because the market is a mechanism for generating inequality, but because too much of their activity takes places outside the market. They need more capitalism not less and this will lead to less poverty not more. Needless to say, this is the opposite of my view; the evidence from the 50-odd years since we ceased to exploit these countries through colonialism and began to exploit them through trade is clearly in my favour.

It has been established by a researcher working for the World Bank that 'Globalization generally widens the income gap between the world's poorest people and the richest.' His study was based on a review of national surveys of household income in 88 developing countries between 1985–91 and 1992–7, and concludes that trade and investment liberalization only promote income equality among middle-income and rich countries. The study was conducted during the boom-time for globalization, with both goods markets and financial markets being extensively liberalized. The countries studied saw an increase in the proportion of imports and exports relative to their economic activities of between 62 and 77 per cent. But during the same time, the average income of the poorest 10 per cent of people in the countries studied fell from 30.7 per cent of the average income to 24.8 per cent. By contrast, the income of the richest 10 per cent increased from 273.5 to 293.4 per cent of the average.

The World Bank's many papers showing improvements in absolute standards of living in developing countries are subject to question. There is a strong suspicion that the only way they can be shown to have grown richer is by a classic tactic of corrupt science: averaging. Based in the utilitarian paradigm which assesses the overall rather than the individual good, this tactic is clearly part of a capitalist worldview which privileges the needs and benefits of the elite over those of the mass. It is from this perspective that a national income measure that has increased and can then be divided equally between all the heads in the country – even when the wealth itself is clearly not – can indicate an improvement in the poverty situation facing that country.

This represents a tactical change for capitalist apologists on the issue of poverty, foremost among them the economists of the World Bank. It has proved necessary in the face of the striking evidence of starvation, destitution and death. The use of average income measures also has the benefit of being conducted at the level of macroeconomic indicators, which are far easier to manipulate and obfuscate than starving children. The evidence that the gap between rich and poor is widening is irrefutable, although in some, but not all, of the countries following the IMF model the poor may be becoming better off in absolute, and usually monetary, terms.

Direct evidence of the impact of trade indicates that this small and distorting increase in national income is bought at a high price. An UNCTAD report in 1997 showed that in a sample of ten Latin American countries, nine recorded an increased differential between skilled and unskilled workers as a result of opening up markets to international trade, and that in most of the countries the real purchasing power of the least skilled workers actually declined, in several cases by more than 20 per cent. International Labour Office data show that among 30 countries studied in Africa, Asia and Latin America, wages in two-thirds of them had fallen between the late 1970s and late 1980s, and the wages of the least skilled had fallen fastest.

In 1999 a paper from the World Bank reported on data for a sample of 38 countries between 1965 and 1992 to show that opening markets up to trade had reduced the incomes of the poorest 40 per cent of the population, while increasing those of the richer groups. The World Bank's commentary was that 'The costs of adjusting to greater openness are borne exclusively by the poor.' Mies and Shiva argue that the liberalization of markets is a deliberate policy to reduce subsistence and force the poor of the world into the capitalist labour market: 'The displacement of small farmers is a deliberate policy of GATT.' The policy has had a serious and negative impact on levels of hunger: 'A conservative estimate of the impact of so-called liberalization on food consumption indicates that in India, by the year 2000, there will be 5.6 per cent more hungry people than would have been the case if free trade in agriculture was not introduced. Free trade will lead to a 26.2 per cent reduction in human consumption of agricultural products.'

Developing countries have spent these 30 years on the economic rollercoaster of international trade because of the dogma from international bodies suggesting that this will end poverty. The richest people in these societies have used this international game to increase their own wealth, while the poor in the same societies have grown poorer. The overall gains from trade are minimal to the countries producing agricultural products: between 1986 and 1996 Ghana increased its exports of cocoa by nearly 80 per cent but earned only 2 per cent more in return.

According to Richard Douthwaite, this is exactly what economists would have predicted, in spite of their claims that trade is the solution to world poverty:

> This widening of the gap between the least well paid and all other income earners in their societies is, in fact, exactly what standard economic theory predicts. In the 1930s Eli Heckscher and Bertil Ohlin developed the theorem which is now named after them and which states that each country tends to export goods that use the highest proportion of its most abundant, and hence relatively cheapest resource. For most 'developing' countries this resource is its unskilled labour and, as competition in international markets between such countries will tend to force the prices of their exports down, the earnings of the unskilled will be reduced by more than those of more highly skilled workers less exposed to foreign competition. All workers in sectors exposed to international competition may therefore see their wages fall as markets open up, but those most exposed will fare the worst.

So, for once there is a fairly clear answer to our question. Those who benefit from trade are the rich elites in the poorer countries and those in powerful positions within the global corporations. The losers are far more numerous, including most of those who work within the globalized economy in the West, whose gains of a paltry range of consumer items have to be balanced against their loss of power and identity in their work (see Chapter 7). The losers in the South, as usual, lose far more: the ability to be self-reliant, their traditional ways of life as they are sucked into the production centres in the cities, and often their lives, as the globalized economy leaves them prey to famine and illness.

Why the planet cannot afford profit-driven trade

Some countries have certainly achieved considerable 'progress' towards a western industrialized and consumerist lifestyle through involvement with the global economy. However, it is interesting to note that most of these countries have faced disastrous economic crises as a result of their open involvement with the global marketplace. The most prominent example is Japan, the *Wunderkind* of global capitalism during the 1970s and 1980s. It was followed by the 'Asian tigers' of Thailand, Malaysia and the Philippines, which enjoyed their short time as favourite mistress of the financial sovereign before being cast aside.

When considering this history of boom-and-bust amongst the new Asian economies, you can't help being reminded of a comedy sketch where a succession of small and puny boxers try their luck with the prizefighter in the ring, who also has odd pieces of heavy metal in his gloves. How long is it going to take the smarter members of these societies to work out that they are not doing very well out of the global competition? Since stupidity is rarely an explanation for seemingly irrational behaviour, I would suggest an alternative explanation: while the majority of people in these poorer countries do not benefit, the elites who control policy benefit very nicely. The reasons for the bruising nature of the encounter lie primarily in the rigged structure of the global financial system rather than the trade system. To suggest, as Oxfam does, that sorting out the trade rules will be sufficient to make trade work for the poor is to miss the crucial role that money, its creation and control, plays in the global system called capitalism.

We have witnessed the degree of popular energy that can be aroused by appeals to Make Poverty History. Yet from a critical perspective the focus on *poverty* is part of the problem, since it concentrates on what is only a symptom of an unequal power structure. Way back in 1920 G. D. H. Cole pointed out the flaw in addressing only poverty rather than its root causes in political and social structures:

What, I want to ask, is the fundamental evil in our modern society which we should set out to abolish? There are two possible answers to that question, and I am sure that very many well-meaning people would make the wrong one. They would answer poverty, when they ought to answer slavery. Face to face every day with the shameful contrasts of riches and destitution, high dividends and low wages, and painfully conscious of the futility of trying to adjust the balance by means of charity, private or public, they would answer unhesitatingly that they stand for the abolition of poverty.

The force of this argument has not faded with the years because the system of exploitation at the heart of capitalism has not changed. Unless we establish an economic system that does not rely on expropriation and exploitation, no amount of aid or trade is going to end world poverty. It is worse than naïve; it is a deception to argue that it might.

One of the foremost proponents of localization has also been one of the most trenchant critics of the move amongst development charities and organizations to portray trade as a positive response to world poverty. Colin Hines's Jekyll-and-Hyde image is a good one, not only for Oxfam but for many of those whose hearts appear to be in the right place but who have been, frankly, scammed by the globalizers. Supporting market 'solutions' to the problem of global poverty is really like suggesting that a person suffering from poisoning should just be given a large dose of the same poison! The poison in question is the utterly bogus and increasingly discredited trade theory, and its increasingly shaky foundation in the hypothesis of 'comparative advantage'.

Hines's critique of the trade justice position focuses on what he calls the three Cs: control, competition and climate change. Control is the key point, since opening up a small, vulnerable economy to the globalized marketplace leaves a country vulnerable to the power of the corporations which dominate that marketplace. These corporations control trade through their influence on the World Trade Organization and on individual governments. This is simply an extension of the way western governments have used international institutions to gain cheap resources and markets for their goods. More important still is the way the trade is mediated through the reserve currencies, so that nations controlling them can obtain their imports for virtually no cost (this system is discussed in more detail in Chapter 6). It would be far better for the economies of poor countries to be run by the citizens of those economies and for their benefit. This is what Hines refers to as 'self-reliance' and it is the only way that we can avoid the disgrace of finding African fruit and vegetables on our supermarket shelves while there is famine in the countries that produced them. The inefficiency of growing cash crops for western markets, the cash from which is then used to buy food that has been grown in the West is obvious to everybody except the middlemen who organize the trade and profit from it.

Hines's second C – competition – is illustrated in the markets for such commodities as coffee, sugar and tea, as well as in manufactures such as textiles. The south-east Asian tsunami brought this issue into relief, since the over-development of the coasts of countries like Sri Lanka is a direct result of competition for foreign cash via the development of the global tourist industry. Tourism is the world's biggest industry: it accounts for 10.4 per cent of global GDP and provides 8.1 per cent of jobs worldwide, employing an estimated 200 million people. The tourism industry allows countries to trade their climates if they have nothing else of value to rich westerners. Sri Lanka has turned to tourism because it is losing the fierce competition in the global textile industry, which still represents 65 per cent of its industrial production. Western consumers, and those who organize and profit from their markets, have demanded 'free' trade and ever lower prices, so that textile manufacture moves down the downward spiral to Vietnam and China, countries with even lower wages and worse conditions of exploitation. Sri Lanka's protected quotas came to an end at the beginning of 2005; this was the big national concern before the tsunami struck. In spite of a unilateral decision by China to reduce its textile exports, the effect on the Sri Lankan economy will be devastating. It had turned to an expansion of tourism precisely to insulate itself against this. Of course, this sort of competition serves western consumers, and those who supply them, since poor workers across the South will be competing against each other, driving each other's wages and conditions of employment down in what has become known as the 'race to the bottom'. It does not, however, serve the people of these countries, who face greater vulnerability in an ever-widening pool of reserve labour.

Finally, the big one: climate change. This is the issue that is going to put the brake on global trade: the limits set by our planet make trade on the scale that we presently have it impossible. Reports such as *Collision Course* by Andrew Simms have painted a disturbing picture of the environmental cost of the expansion in global trade. The report made clear the costs of trade to both the poor world and the planet. OECD data show that, during the period of their international adoration as Asian tigers, Indonesia, Malaysia, the Republic of Korea and Thailand increased their carbon dioxide emissions by between 100 and 278 per cent. Figure 4.1 shows how the increase in total global trade is matched by the increase in carbon dioxide emissions. Perhaps the most disturbing fact is that the corporate lobbyists managed to have trade-related CO_2 emissions excluded from the Kyoto limits, thus driving a coach and horses through the whole agreement and explaining why this is the fastest-growing source of CO_2 emissions, particularly air freight.

Now that the phoney and corporate-sponsored debate about climate change is over, we must respond to the fact that we live in a carbon-limited world. Economic policy must be decided within this framework. Once that is understood, it becomes clear that every gram of

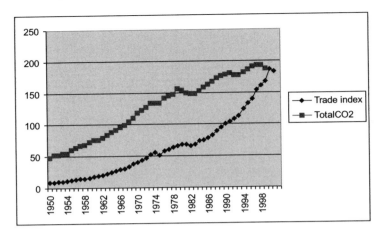

Note: The trade figures are calculated as an index based on 1990 = 100 and include agricultural and mining products and manufactures. The CO_2 emissions are for solid, liquid and gas fossil fuels divided by 33 to achieve appropriate scaling.
Sources: Carbon dioxide data are from Oakridge Research Laboratory, California; trade data are from the WTO.

Figure 4.1 Relationship between increase in world trade and global carbon dioxide emissions

CO_2 produced must be used to generate the maximum amount of human well-being, rather than the maximum profit, as at present. In such a world, the present trade system, transporting steel from one corner of the earth to the other and encouraging UK farmers to grub up their orchards so that we can import apples and pears from New Zealand or China, is plainly insane. Any CO_2 emitted for the transportation of goods that can be produced close to home has been entirely wasted.

A slightly more subtle point involves the problem of burden shifting. This is when the carbon dioxide emitted when goods are produced in, for example, China but consumed in the USA or the UK is counted as part of China's output rather than ours. Researchers at Best Foot Forward have estimated that, alongside our net per capita CO_2 emissions of 9,029 kg, we should add CO_2 embodied in net imports of 2,132 kg – a 23.6 per cent increase. This artificial reduction in our CO_2 emissions should be ended, with CO_2 being allocated where the goods are consumed rather than produced.

In a paradoxical twist, the solution to the environmental devastation wrought by the global trade system is – more trade! It is likely that any proposals made at the EU or G8 will involve carbon trading, and, in spite of our scepticism about markets, we should be prepared to work with this idea, so long as the market operates within a framework involving an absolute limit on CO_2 and measures are taken to prevent the countries controlling reserve currencies gaining an unfair advantage. The best way of ensuring this is to create a new global currency for trade in goods and in carbon dioxide. Richard Douthwaite has developed proposals for such a currency, called the EBCU (environment-backed currency unit), which are discussed in Chapter 6.

If it seems unlikely that the USA will come on board for any such scheme, we should remember how, in spite of its apparent power, the instability of the world trading system also makes the USA vulnerable. The USA's trading partners have a source of power they can use: countries from the poorer world may begin to refuse to recycle US foreign debt, in response to both US foreign policy and the risk the USA poses to sustainability by its refusal to reduce CO_2 emissions. Foreigners now own 38 per cent of US Treasury securities, which is more than twice the amount a decade ago, and this gives them considerable leverage over the US economy. The inherent weakness of the USA's position is made clear in the following quotation:

> One of the curious features of US hegemony is that it depends on the apparently limitless willingness of US allies – and even of some future competitors, such as China – to finance the apparently limitless budget and trade deficits of the US. Over the past 20 years the US has become the world's leading debtor, its net foreign debt rising from $250 billion in 1982 to $2.2 trillion in 2001, 23% of GDP – almost equal to the $2.5 trillion owed by five billion people in the whole of the developing world.

The USA relies on the purchase of Treasury bonds to remain solvent and is thus dependent on the Asian economies. So in spite of the apparent omnipotence of the USA and its currency, it is possible for the Asian economies to exercise leverage. Indeed, it seems that the two largest economies of the continent – India and China – are no longer happy to fund US consumption rather than their own. India considers its record foreign exchange reserves to be a large 'opportunity cost', and plans to spend some of this $120 billion to fund the building of roads. China is also considering whether its underpinning of the US deficit is working to its advantage, and is considering using this as leverage over US foreign policy.

Challenging the power of the dollar in world trade was always a motive for the creation of a European currency, the euro. At the EU our political representatives should focus on increasing the amount of binational trade that is conducted in euros, pounds and other non-dollar currencies, and should encourage Asian economies to do the same. But rather than using the value generated through this use of their reserve currencies to fund spending on arms, as the USA has done, EU nations should use it to purchase carbon permits from countries that are currently emitting less than their per capita allowance under the Contraction and Convergence framework (see Chapter 6), thus effectively using it for the benefit of poorer countries.

And finally, we need to find ways of responding to poverty in the South without increasing CO_2, so that standards of living can be raised without the environmental costs we in the West have always imposed in return for our dubious 'progress'. The trade in carbon emissions, if organized according to the Contraction and Convergence framework, could achieve massive cash transfers. Technology transfer is also important. The UK government plays an important role in influencing the structure of foreign trade via the payment of export credit guarantees. These export-supporting grants could be used to encourage the transfer of technologies to developing countries that would enable them to gain a headstart in creating sustainable economies. The support grants currently paid to arms industries, around 30 per cent of the total, which are a destructive influence on poorer countries' economies, should be switched towards industries which would help these countries build sustainable economies.

The solution: trade subsidiarity

Political subsidiarity is defined as exercising power at the lowest feasible level. It resonates with green politicians, whose inclination is to always work from the bottom up. The localization agenda being developed by green economists begins at the locality for sound environmental rather than political reasons (as discussed in the following chapter). A straightforward response to the issue of world trade suggests the extension of the concept of 'subsidiarity' into the realm of production and consumption, so that we naturally tend to look to purchase goods produced as close to where we live as possible.

We must be clear about what we are proposing and what this will entail in terms of the different items which enable the everyday lives we lead in a sophisticated twenty-first-century world. As well as clarifying our ideological position, I hope this concept will assist us all as individuals to make better, more informed and less guilt-ridden purchasing decisions. Once we know where we are going, the market will begin to follow and, as the decision to buy organic has shown, the difficult shopping decisions we make today will soon become commonplace.

In determining where goods should be produced, there are two important variables to consider: the physical inputs that are required to make the goods; and the amount and type of work required. Both of these really represent continua, but to simplify we can divide them into their extremes and create the grid shown in Figure 4.2.

		RAW MATERIALS	
		Local	**Global**
LABOUR	**Non-intensive**	Seasonal food	Coffee, cotton
	Intensive	Furniture, clothes	Computers, cars

Figure 4.2 People and planetary production grid: production defined by availability of raw materials and labour intensity

The grid indicates that we have generated four different types of good:

- local, non-intensive goods such as seasonal fruit and vegetables and other primary products which can be grown without much complex labour input;
- global, non-intensive goods, which do not need much labour but require a different climate from our own;
- local, complex goods that require skill and time to produce but not the import of raw materials;
- global, complex goods that need technical expertise and considerable time to produce and for which raw materials or the size of market suggests a problem with local production.

As we move up this hierarchy, the environmental problems generated by the consumption of the goods increase. The hierarchy also represents a movement away from control over the goods by local people, so that those in the final category are completely dominated by corporate, globalized trade. The grid is also helpful in identifying precisely what our concerns are about the globalized trade system. On the one hand, some commentators are concerned about the climate-change impact of the unnecessary transport of goods. Their particular concern would be the horizontal axis. For those whose concern is the migration of most productive jobs in the UK to markets in low-wage economies, the vertical axis is of more interest.

From the trade subsidiarity perspective, before we buy goods in any of the last three categories, we need to ask: could I buy the product itself or a reasonable substitute from a local source? For example, in the case of coffee, you could decide to buy Barley Cup produced in Poland and drink that; or perhaps just drink it half the time. Or you could decide to go the whole ecofeminist route and grow lemon verbena in your kitchen garden to make your tea. Similarly with the fourth category, you could decide to buy a reconditioned computer rather than engage in the global trade system even in these high-tech products. For the purposes of taking a fresh approach to trade, we need to consider each type of good in more detail.

Local, non-intensive goods

In this category what we are mainly concerned with is seasonal food. Because food travels badly and has a strong cultural resonance, this is the area where arguments for relocalizing supply have been the most developed. Evidence that this bandwagon is rolling is provided by the huge success of farmers' markets, whose numbers grew from the first in Bath in 1997 to more than 270 by the turn of the century. A more structured way to source your vegetables is via a box scheme organized by a local supplier. In the UK there are now nearly 200 produce box schemes providing vegetables and fruit to more than 45,000 households with sales to the value of £22 million. An even closer relationship is offered by a system of community-supported agriculture (CSA), which is 'the next best thing to growing your own food'.

> Farmers benefit from CSAs by having an assured and stable market for their produce and by receiving payment in advance rather than when the harvest is in. Benefits to CSA members include a lower overall price for a season's worth of food and the important knowledge of where and how their food was grown. CSAs not only enable consumers to establish a personal relationship with the farmer who grows their food, they often provide an opportunity for urban consumers to reconnect with the land.

A scheme connecting consumers and producers of milk is working well in Worcestershire, where David Kaye sells his milk direct to local people, avoiding supermarkets creaming off value.

The dominance of supermarkets in the food sector has been linked to the collapse of local rural economies and the erosion of rural communities. The ever longer food chains also create food insecurity, as the rapid emptying of supermarket shelves during the fuel protests demonstrated:

> Specialization within the contemporary global market offers an extreme example of the dangers of over-dependence on trade. An economy which has placed a large part of its domestic capital into some specialized area of production is vulnerable to the vagaries of the global market to secure the goods and services its needs . . . This example works all the way down from national economies operating within the global market, to local economies operating within national markets.

An additional concern is the loss of our innate knowledge of the culture of food production in a world where most people think that food comes from Tesco. Jules Pretty discusses these deeper, more spiritual issues surrounding food in his book *Agri-Culture*. He argues that, in resolving the problems facing agriculture in the era of globalization, it is not enough to understand economic concepts; we also need to learn what Pretty refers to as 'ecological literacy'. This is a way of learning about the land to which he gives the word *metis*, meaning 'forms of knowledge embedded in local experience'. The loss of this 'traditional' knowledge – whether it be native Americans losing their ability to name their indigenous plants and animals, or Indian healers their knowledge of traditional plants – is, for Pretty, as serious as the loss of species or languages. Pretty identifies the importance of preserving such *metis* as survives and developing more such practical knowledge about the land if we are to build a sustainable future.

As noted at the outset, the high-intensity versus low-intensity distinction is really a blurred one and it is at this margin where the local food campaigners should now be putting their energy. The types of product I am thinking about here are things like building materials and textiles. To imagine the trade subsidiarity world requires you to see the economy as one of your ancestors might have done, or how somebody in a poor village in the Third World might, or how you might if the transportation of goods carried its true environmental price. In other words, things that come from far away are either unknown, or unattainable, or impossibly expensive. When writing about regeneration of the Welsh economy I have called this kind of mind-shift 'Robinson Crusoe economics'. Instead of your consumption being determined by a desire created by the advertising industry, to which you respond by finding a means to acquire the desired item, generally through working enough hours to ensure a monetary exchange, you have to imagine yourself on a desert island. In such a situation, just like Crusoe you would begin by assessing which resources were to hand, and if you were smart you would begin with the closest resources. Following on from food, we can begin to take this approach to our other basic needs: for shelter and clothing.

The Robinson Crusoe approach to housing is demonstrated by Skara Brae, the neolithic village on Orkney dating from around 5,000 years ago. The priority was protection from the Arctic winds, hence the homes were built partly below ground level. In a landscape where trees could not survive, the obvious building material was the readily available local stone. The design for homes included covered walkways between the different houses to encourage community building in the long winter nights, and a central fireplace in each family home, a design feature which lasted until the 1960s in Orkneys houses. The houses also had in-built conveniences, such as shelves above the beds for storing personal possessions. In other parts of the country the local building materials were biodegradable, which is why little trace remains today. It was only when the Romans arrived on these shores that wealthier citizens began building to show off, aspiring after imported marble to ape the colonizers, and creating palaces as status symbols.

The appropriate building materials for homes depend on the conditions and local availability. In Wales, Ty-Mawr Farm near Llangorse Lake in the Brecon Beacons National Park runs courses in using a range of natural building materials such as earth, timber and lime. It also offers information on natural insulation using sheep wool. The Centre for Alternative Technology has been developing sustainable building ideas for 30 years, assessing the total impact of building on the environment and encouraging self-build. Empowering local communities to build their own houses in this way will enable the creation of local building cultures to replace the one-size-fits-all model of the global economy.

A Robinson Crusoe approach to clothing would suggest identifying and developing our domestic textiles: linen and hemp. Hemp has suffered from its association with marijuana, although the textile crop *Cannabis sativa* does not contain enough of the active ingredient TLC to threaten anybody's mental state. In my own local economy of Wales there is evidence of the importance of hemp and flax in various placenames such as the village of Cwm Cywarch (hemp valley) in Gwynedd and Cwm-Liniau (flax valley) in Powys.

Its proponents argue that hemp has played an important role in UK history: the earliest trace is from Scotland in the Bronze Age. Hemp was widely grown across Britain in the Middle Ages, from at least AD 800 to 1800. It was used to make textiles, paper and rope, and for oil. The fibres are believed to have anti-mildew and anti-microbial properties. It was frequently used to make sailcloth and sacking, as well as for clothing, sometimes blended with wool. A hemp resin can be used to produce a substitute for plastic. It is suggested that during the reign of George III the growing of hemp was compulsory and that the county of Hampshire is named after the crop. Hemp provided the sails for the naval and merchant ships that built the British Empire, and then ironically lost out as those sails powered the ships that brought cotton back to Lancashire to oust hemp as a textile crop.

Box 4.1 A tale of two shoemakers

Scene: a huge cluster of small-scale shoemakers (somewhere in the region of 30,000 small workshops) in the Igbo city of Aba. Numbers have swelled greatly over the last couple of decades as oil (petroleum and palm) interests have displaced a large number of previously small-scale farmers from the agricultural hinterland. The Nigerian state has little interest in supporting small-scale clusters like that in Aba and the very poor infrastructure that supports them (limited and interrupted power supplies, roads of mud, no support organizations) is an important reason why the predominant mode of production remains artisanal, with nothing that could be described as even a small factory. Almost all tasks are undertaken by hand.

On the positive side (if there is one to this story), oil riches have allowed Nigeria to resist the neo-liberal pressures for deregulation longer than most. So, Aba's shoemakers have been largely protected from international competition. Until 1999 that is, and the accession by the new Abasanjo government to the World Trade Organization.

Today, higher-quality leather is now being exported for processing overseas, driving up prices and reducing quality for local producers, while the domestic market is flooded by cheap Chinese factory-made shoes. The only producers in Aba holding their market share are those who have succeeded in reducing their costs and prices to below even the bottom of the Chinese price and quality range. This is the 'race to the bottom', with producers in over-crowded markets competing against each other purely on the basis of cost.

This is a human disaster unfolding – what are formerly displaced villagers, now displaced shoemakers, to do? Now it is undoubtedly true that this story is far more than simply a powerful illustration of the evils of globalization. A lack of support from the state, for example, was an important constraint on the evolution of Aba into a more efficient and competitive cluster. However, it does contain the key elements that I have seen in a host of small enterprise situations across Africa in the last 15 years or so.

And, in the context of this discussion, it confirms the importance of the distinction made by Richard Douthwaite between China and India on the one hand and sub-Saharan Africa on the other in terms of their response to globalization. The former have large populations, working infrastructures and (to a significant if not absolute degree) state structures that support domestic industrial concerns. Africa, with its weak, impoverished and fractured states and its small populations, is simply unable to provide the kind of political-economic context required for its producers to be able to compete.

Source: Many thanks to the anonymous development worker who sent me this story.

Flax is one of the oldest European crops, dating back at least to the Stone Age. As well as making fine cloth, the seed provides linseed oil, used in paints and varnishes, and beneficial to human health because of its high omega-3 content. Hemp and flax lost popularity as local fibre crops in competition with cheaper imported fibres and oil-based man-made fibres such as polyester.

Current concerns about the environmental impact of cotton (which needs heavy use of pesticides and is water-hungry) have now brought the debate full circle. The Bioregional Group has been running a project called Hemp for Textiles since 1994. They claim that 'Hemp merits consideration as a new linen-like, environmentally friendly, textile fabric. Hemp can be grown easily under organic cultivation as it grows so fast that it smothers weeds.' Hemp is now being seen as a solution to the reduction in rural incomes: a project to explore the feasibility of growing it on a commercial scale (called Flax and Hemp) is now being undertaken at Bangor University, funded by the European Objective 1 scheme.

Global, non-intensive goods

So far we have undertaken a desert-island-style assessment of what is available locally, but nobody is suggesting that in order to live in harmony with the planet you need to become a monk. The goods news is that life's luxuries will still be available; the bad news is that, once the producers have received a fair price and the environmental costs of moving them halfway across the planet have been reflected in a carbon tax, they will be considerably more expensive than they are now. But in a sense this is also goods news, or at least mixed news, because there is little point in having a luxury you can have every day. Before long you will be joining Jamie Oliver fans in hunting the supermarket shelves for the last lime or the last telapia because you must have exactly that (pukka) recipe tonight. This is the insane fetishism of modern consumption and actually brings far less delight than the silver-wrapped Christmas tangerines of the 1950s.

While the argument over local food has been won, the argument over low-intensity, global products is in full swing. The debate has traditionally been between proponents of so-called free trade and those who support fair trade, now transmuted into trade justice. Free trade is the dominant mode of trade, allowing corporations to exploit their transnational position and their lobbying power to gain a pre-eminent position of power which they use to extract maximum profits at the expense of people and planet. Fair trade, by contrast, is a response by well-meaning, guilt-ridden liberals in the West, who offer to pay a larger share of their income – which they can easily afford – so that the producers of these goods can have a closer to decent standard of living. In this debate about how global trade should be managed, there is now a new kid on the block: localization. This is a series of policies to control production and trade to ensure that it is more locally based, in order to guarantee social standards, employment and security of supply for local communities, as well as protecting the environment. It is discussed further in the following chapter.

Once we have developed our local economies as far as climate and resources reasonably allow, we have to find some way of dealing with the products that we need to trade. Fair trade is the obvious starting-point: the fair trade movement proves that, contrary to popular lore, price is not the key factor in determining consumption decisions. In the case of fair trade, shoppers choose a product that is more expensive not because they will enjoy it more, but because they consider it morally right that the producer of the product should receive a higher price. Within an economistic mindset this is the behaviour of a lunatic, but the figures suggest that there are a great many of us around.

Between 2002 and 2003 Fairtrade-labelled sales across the world grew by 42.3 per cent. Along with Switzerland and the Netherlands, the UK is one of the largest fair-trade markets. Retail sales of fairly traded products grew from £16.7 million in 1998 to £63 million in 2002 and fair trade coffee now accounts for more than 14 per cent of the whole UK ground coffee market. The extra benefit for coffee producers was US$30 million in 2002. A large and growing range of goods now have fair trade standards: coffee, tea, cocoa, sugar, honey, bananas, dried fruit, fruit juices, rice, wine, nuts and seeds, cut flowers, and cotton. The number of fair trade products rose from 150 in 2003 to 834 in 2005. Table 4.1 shows the rapid growth in this market.

Table 4.1 Sales of fair trade goods in the UK, 1997–2003

Year	Million tonnes	Annual % increase
1997	25,972	11.3
1998	28,913	15.8
2000	33,495	18.7
2001	39,750	22.0
2002	48,506	21.2
2003	58,813	42.3
2004	140,000	51.0

Source: Fairtrade Labelling Organizations International: www.fairtrade.net.

There is some scope for international political action to regulate trade, not through the entirely discredited World Trade Organization, but through the establishment of a new body to regulate trade in the interests of the planet and her people: the General Agreement on Sustainable Trade (GAST). The most important change would be to introduce fair trade rules like those currently operating within the fair trade movement, ensuring fair prices, decent working conditions and environmental protection. This would update the provisions of the GATT Treaty, which was subsumed and marketized when the WTO was created. GATT Article I, the most-favoured nation clause, and Article III on national treatment, should be limited to allow the protection of local economies. Article XI on the elimination of quantitative restrictions (i.e. quotas) should be removed to allow nation states to protect their domestic industries, for the purposes of

---

Box 4.2 Perfume: the real story (not by Patrick Suskind)

Natural perfume derived from flowers such as lavender or rose
following development of distillation in Arabia in seventh or
eighth century
↓
Manufactured perfumes use global ingredients: civitone, from
Alpine civit cats; muskone, from east Asian musk deer; ambergris,
from whales
↓
Chemical synthesis removes the need for natural products and increases centralization of production; Pfizer now responsible for the
perfumerie Coty as well as pharmaceuticals
↓
Branding leads to concentration on the image of the product rather
than the reality: 'Obsession' by Calvin Klein, 'Activist' from The
Body Shop (could this be the perfume for you?)
↓
Recreation of the home-grown lavender industry in London

---

employment or environmental protection. The ancillary WTO agreement
on TRIPS (trade-related intellectual property rights, i.e. the copyright of
ideas) should be replaced with an empowering attitude towards knowledge that privileges the rights of humanity rather than the corporate profit
drive. It goes without saying that the current ability to patent life-forms
would be abolished.

However, this is not enough in itself. My view is that anybody who
argues merely for a renegotiation of the rules of the WTO either grossly
underestimates the power of the corporations and the governments they
control, or else is deliberately deflecting our energy. The arguments for
localization, and policies to support it, are discussed in the following
chapter. From the trade perspective, localization also entails the re-
creation of bioregions within each country and the stimulation of their
traditional domestic crops. Inspiring work in this direction has been carried out by the Bioregional Development Group. In 1994 they began a
project to recreate the lavender fields of south London, famous for the
Yardley factory and the Lavender Hill Mob. They began planting local
lavender on a disused allotment site with the help of inmates from
Downview prison. The project generated many benefits in terms of
reinforcing the local community:

> We harvested our first crop of lavender in 1998. The event generated a
> lot of media coverage. Older residents sent us their reminiscences. The

new Christmas lights in Wallington have been designed on a lavender theme. When a local pub was refurbished, it chose the lavender story, naming the pub 'The John Jakson' after a family of lavender growers.

Reviving local crops thus also replenishes the sense of community identity that has been so battered by the globalization of markets and the homogenization of work.

Local, complex goods

Next we come to the category of goods that require large inputs of work but for which we can find the raw materials locally. An example would be the furniture we have in our homes, all of which could have been made with locally available timber. In Ceredigion, mid-Wales, the timber sector is being encouraged by the organization Coedbren Ceredigion, which produces a directory of Ceredigion's manufacturers, craftworkers and timber suppliers using timber produced from Welsh woods and forests. In one of the highest unemployment areas of Europe, it is clearly absurd for us to be importing furniture made in the Philippines and bought on an industrial estate, and yet within a globalized trade system this is what we do. In a system of trade subsidiarity we should begin by asking whether furniture produced locally from local raw materials is available.

I want to take this discussion further by considering the impact on our personal identities and human communities of a local system of production of these products, rather than one based on manufacturing them in the cheapest sweat-shop in a special enterprise zone halfway across the world. The first and most obvious point is that buying local would create productive and useful jobs in this country. The cliché that we live in a 'post-industrial age' is an untruth: there is still industrial work done; it is just that it has been exported to other countries where people can be paid less and treated in ways so inhumane that we no longer accept them for ourselves. I am not a supporter of work for its own sake, but it is important to remember the role it plays in building our lives, our family relationships and our communities.

Craftsmen and -women in my part of the world are beginning to recreate systems for distributing hand-made products, such as pottery, wooden furniture and glassware. They are organizing themselves into secondary cooperatives, to collaborate over the marketing and selling of products. The most obvious example of such an outlet in my backyard is the Craft in the Bay gallery in Cardiff's trendy reclaimed dockland. The gallery is situated in a restored maritime warehouse in the thriving bay regeneration centre and displays crafts made by guild members including ceramics, textiles, wood, leatherwork, jewellery, glass, basketware, bookbinding and ironwork. The cooperative has around 70 members and employs another three people in administrative roles. All members of Craft in the Bay are required to give an agreed number of hours per year to work in the gallery, helping to keep costs down.

The life of the craftsman should not be an isolated one. Before production became atomized in the industrial revolution, trades were organized into guilds which provided a whole range of social and economic services to their members and the community (I discuss this point further in Chapter 7). Their central role was to guarantee the quality of the product; craftsmen and women who failed to keep that standard were expelled from the guild and could not sell their output. They also fixed the price of goods, making competition between producers on price impossible. In the modern global marketplace, the ideology suggests that we the consumers should concern ourselves exclusively with price. This ignores quality, which declines as lower and lower wages are paid. The balance between price and quality in production needs to be reasserted, as does the relationship between price and the wider quality of life.

Global, complex goods

This is the most problematic category because the goods it includes require a large market in order to justify the expense of transporting the raw materials and training the workforce. This makes a strong planetary impact inevitable, so the first step should be to minimize demand for goods in this category. According to the progress view of economic history, items which we once managed perfectly happily without first enter our consciousness as exotic goods for the wealthy, but before long we all feel that it is our human right to own one. Perhaps mobile phones are the most recent example of this transition from bizarre invention to everyday necessity. Over the last 100 years, by far the most damaging example has been the car. Now we have reached a stage where, as Greens, we are pilloried for refusing each of the 1 billion Chinese citizens their human right to a car. This is a moral standard developed by General Motors and for their benefit, but we must find a way to challenge it.

This is simple once we have accepted the Contraction and Convergence framework, a system for sharing the planet's carrying capacity of carbon dioxide among its 6 billion citizens. Were this system agreed on an international basis, we would effectively move into a world where, for the purpose of production and trade, the economy would be energy limited. Decisions to produce one good would automatically remove the energy from another good. As a nation we would be sharing our energy between productive sectors and imports, which would be costed in terms of both the energy used in production and that used in transport. Such a system would resolve the issues of global poverty and climate change by limiting the amount of energy available to the global economy and sharing it fairly. It would cause a huge increase in the cost of energy-intensive goods and a parallel pressure to produce more goods as close to markets as possible, and using energy derived from renewable sources.

Once we live in such an energy-limited world, we will begin to face choices about which goods are really necessary to us. Critics of the localization agenda would suggest that we are depriving those in poor countries of the goods we take for granted. The Contraction and Convergence policy undermines the accusation of special pleading, but we should explore the concept of what we take for granted in more detail. Certain human needs may be universal, but our means for meeting them are diverse and derived from our cultures. For example, most human societies have communicated in written form, but this does not need to be using a pencil, or a biro, or a computer, if the means for producing those are not readily available. We all need to share love with members of our families, but it is only necessary to have a car to ensure this in an atomized society where individuals live far away from other family members. Imposing our concepts of what is necessary for a decent human life is part of the colonization of the mind that those in the South are doing their best to escape from.

So we have addressed the problems of cultural relativity and a fair sharing of global energy supplies. The next problem with highly technical goods is the size of the market necessary to make their production efficient. We should beware here of conventional economics definitions such as 'efficiency' and 'economies of scale'. While Iraq was subject to sanctions, Iraqi people did what humans always do when resources are scarce: they improvised and engaged in make-do-and-mend strategies. When we see their cannibalized, horse-drawn carts, we are invited to conclude 'desperate poverty: evil Saddam', but in fact a sustainable economy would cause such low-impact strategies to flourish. Mending broken goods and recycling reusable components would become economically viable, as would building goods and components for maximum life, in contrast to the built-in obsolescence of the globalized economy. We need to question the provenance of our judgement that the ersatz cart is a tragedy to be replaced by the US-manufactured SUV.

Let us take as an example of a globally produced complex product the computer. Is either its method of production or its global distribution efficient? There are probably more computers thrown away as obsolete every week in the UK than could be found in the whole public administration system of a country like Ethiopia. So much for efficient distribution. Economies of scale in the production of micro-chips have led to concentration in a small number of global sites under the control of a small range of international corporations. This represents control but not efficiency. It is the result of a process of fierce global competition to gain supremacy in this dominant sector in the Information Age. My own local economy of Wales was a major loser in that competition. The people of Wales contributed £248 million to build a state-of-the-art microchip factory for

Korean electronics giant LG on a greenfield site in Newport. While it was being built, the microchip market hit the inevitable global glut and LG merged with Samsung. The factory was never opened: the money had been wasted and the land destroyed for nothing. So much for efficiency of markets.

A final change to reorient this sector of production would be the abolition of the concept of intellectual property. What is the real reason why Ethiopia is forced to import its computers and pay world-market prices? Is it because the resources are not available or Ethiopians too benighted to make their own computers? In reality, most of these goods are produced in developing countries or the marginal depressed economies of developed countries: no corporation would pay full western rates for such unskilled work. The reason production is controlled by a small number of companies and shared between low-skill, low-pay production sites from Treforest to Indonesia is that the knowledge needed to produce the product is controlled by international law.

The argument against intellectual property is more morally pointed in the case of the global pharmaceutical market. The most glaring moral obscenity caused by control of this life-saving knowledge (the phrase 'intellectual property' should be expunged from dictionaries as logically impossible) is the deaths of innocents in poor countries because rich corporations deprive them of the right to produce medicines that could cure them. This is so strikingly immoral and the need so great that the Brazilian, South African and Indian governments have decided to flout it. We should treat all knowledge control in the same way.

Out of the global supermarket and into the twenty-first-century fair

The earlier sections of this chapter outline the various ways that the globalized marketplace has been a disaster in economic terms, and in terms of standard of living. There is also a more subtle way in which having our consumption controlled by corporations undermines our identity, especially now that our identities are found more in consumption than in production.

But the most significant threat to our future survival is the growth generated by this system of excessive production and consumption. It is time to step outside the supermarket not only because of this planetary imperative but because we deserve better. Often living a sustainable lifestyle appears to offer little except blood, sweat, toil and tears (I am thinking particularly of our commitment to allotments), but in the case of the future of consumption we can offer a life-enhancing vision. The 'end of history' only represents a threat if you are a believer in Progress. Since I am not, I have found much to value in the way our ancestors, and those in non-capitalist societies, have organized the production and distribution of goods. I find hope in the development of New Age fairs. An example was an event that took place in Milton Keynes in autumn 2002 under the name 'The Global Fair: Trading with a Conscience'. It was typical of the green fairs that are now a regular feature around the country. Items for sale include clothing, jewellery, furnishings and ideas. These events are always a bizarre mix of local crafts and ethnic items from Nepal or Guatemala, so the fair's claim that you can 'Get it Sust!' by buying 'Ethically traded and sustainable goods from around the world' may be rather dubious. It is more the energy of these events which is appealing. This is the human desire to exchange that has refused to be crushed by European directives and an unhelpful monetary regime. It is the sort of real free market which our ancestors enjoyed but which, in spite of the ideology, we have been deprived of.

Until the industrial revolution, Europe also benefited from specialist fairs, for traders in particular commodities, organized by guilds and arranged for appropriate saints' days. A green trading system would see the revival of these anorak-fests but with more sophisticated products. We already have a hint of this in some of the events you find at the NEC in Birmingham or at Olympia, where handy grandmothers meet together to compare doll's house designs or traction-engine aficionados exchange tips. In our controlled economy these expressions of identity are found only in the marginal, geekish goods, but we can imagine a system where these were the sorts of place you went to buy a computer or a hand-blender. The distance you would have to travel would depend on the size of the market. Such situations of exchange have tremendous side-benefits in terms of the exchange of information and networking between producers, as well as offering an opportunity for genuine choice between goods that can actually be compared in a way that is no longer available in the global economy. Glastonbury Festival is some sort of prototype for a twenty-first-century fair, offering specialized products, largely music and ethnic clothing, and all the incidental entertainment and hedonism of a medieval fair.

For fear of being accused of Luddism, I would also like to describe the role for the internet in my new green exchange system. The prototype for an online trading system already exists in The Ethical Junction (www.ethical-junction.org). This provides a portal for finding suppliers of ethically produced and fairly traded goods. To fulfil the needs of a green shopper it would have to add a localized dimension. On accessing the site you would need to enter your postcode so that later searches could be sorted by proximity. This function is met by another couple of websites, www.ukvillages.co.uk, which is about local suppliers, and www.nearbuyou.com, which focuses on giving you access to local suppliers in the social economy. It seems that some amalgamation of these internet portals would be a valuable contribution to strengthening local economies.

For a trading system to be successful it will have to appeal to what Janet Alty called our 'flocking and foraging' instincts. The advertising industry has exploited these for the benefit of the globalized economy. Flocking is encouraged by vast shopping malls where we mill around like disorientated sheep, and by our mutual identification of group loyalties embodied in the brand. Foraging is achieved by the dump-bin of special offers, and perhaps by the constant reorganization of goods within the supermarket. These are two reasons why we enjoy shopping which we can find more creative and enjoyable responses to. The third is the human contact which is removed by the alienating exchange of product for cash. No wonder people flock to Sunday morning car-boot sales to forage through the crap on display, which they can chat over with its former owners. The satisfaction of a car-boot sale simply cannot be explained by the money earned or the items taken home.

We can support the aspects of our local economies that continue to work, and make an effort to use and revitalize the remnants of an earlier era. Most towns still have bakeries, and often butchers and greengrocers too. You can also find a lot of information about the extent of your local economy from local directories and free newspapers. Since these are based on advertising revenue, they necessarily define an area within which people are happy to travel to buy goods, thus providing a natural definition of the local economy. Lastly, we can take hope from the various local brands and symbols that are used to define businesses and which indicate that locality has always been important in trade. In my area of mid-Wales, the sorts of locally based brands are things like Cambrian, Dragon and Ceredig, which define everything from building contractors and printers to pâtés and beers.

Conclusion

I began the discussion of trade subsidiarity by dividing goods along two axes and creating a grid, which has now been completed (see Figure 4.3). I hope it will provide some sort of guidance for personal consumption decisions, as well as suggesting ideas for policies to support the new economy we are trying to build. Some of the changes that need to be made will require political action, such as the replacement of the WTO and the end of intellectual property laws, but many can be made within our own lives, such as buying fair trade goods that are available and local craft goods as often as we can afford them. The issue of trade is about more than effacing personal guilt and reducing the impact of climate change, important though these are.

| | | RAW MATERIALS | |
		Local	**Global**
LABOUR	**Non-intensive**	Farmers' markets; self-build; domestic textiles	Fair trade; replace WTO with GAST
	Intensive	Support of local craft workers	Mending to replace obsolescence; end to intellectual property laws

Figure 4.3 People and planetary production grid: consumption patterns to minimize resource use and enhance quality of work

Local economies are good for our security of supply in a turbulent globalized world. And conversely, as Schumacher pointed out, the system of global distribution creates conflict and instability: 'people who live in highly self-sufficient local communities are less likely to get involved in large-scale violence than people whose existence depends on world-wide systems of trade'. The one valuable lesson to come out of the fuel protests of a few years back was a realization of how rapidly super-market shelves can clear once lorries are taken off the road. Given the likely instability of oil supplies in the future, we would be smart to ensure we could provide for at least our basic needs from within our own bioregions.

What saddens me most about the discussion surrounding trade is that so many well-meaning campaigners and commentators have missed the point and been taken in by the siren song of the free traders. With curious synchronicity the comment that 'when the last fish has been eaten and the last tree has died you will find that you cannot eat money' was made by Chief Seattle, who shares his name with the town where it became obvious that the existing trade game would have to be switched. This is ironic because much of the confusion about trade, and why it might be good for 'poor' nations, arises from a misunderstanding of what money is for. According to economics, one of the roles of money is to act as a medium of exchange. But in the global economy, money – that is to say, hard currency – operates as a political mechanism to permanently fix the terms of trade in the interest of the countries of the North. Since the 'poor' nations are in fact very rich in terms of raw materials, there is no other logical explanation of why they fail to grow any richer as these resources are extracted and exported (see more about this in Chapter 6). So what the countries of the South are really being offered is a switch from poker, at which they are being beaten hollow, to pontoon, but without any suggestion of reallocating chips. In fact it is worse than this because the USA, with its control over the dollar as medium of international exchange, has the equivalent of a chip-making factory out the back.

The power of money is the power of a hypnotist's watch. It is sufficient to delude the usually astute and savvy political commentator George Monbiot, who commented in the *Guardian* that 'the poor countries need money and, in particular, hard money'. Chief Seattle was not deluded: he recognized that what you need is food, clothing and housing, not money. Money can be a means of buying these items, but the relationship is not direct. The price is always subject to political pressure. This is the predominant reason why poor nations, and the poor within rich nations, would be better advised to focus on obtaining what they want rather than money, which is always the ally of the politically powerful.

What happened at Seattle was that the rich nations realized the game was up. The outrageous injustice of the trade system they had been benefiting from on a grand scale since the Second World War was no longer politically tenable. It was, as George Monbiot correctly identified, legalized theft. But we should be deeply suspicious of the apparently contrite negotiators who now emerge, wolves in sheep's clothing, to present their proposals for a new trade game. It is the presence of the pharmaceutical industry amongst their number that puts you on to this. What should we suppose they have spent the past few years doing? My money would be on stitching up a new trading system they can dominate just as ruthlessly as they dominated the last one, rather than beating their breasts and weeping for the dead children of the South.

5

Looking After your Own Doorstep: Strengthening the Local Economy

If we could think locally, we would take far better care of things than we do now. The right local questions and answers will be the right global ones. The Amish question, 'What will this do for our community?' tends toward the right answer for the world.

Wendell Berry

Amongst opponents of the environmental movement the word NIMBY – standing for 'not in my backyard' – is used pejoratively, as if there were something wrong with people who have pride in their community and seek to avoid its destruction. I would argue, rather, that this is a perfectly natural human response, and that it can be harnessed in the creation of strong local economies that will reinforce our social identities and reduce the threat we pose to the planet.

I think we are all aware of what we would not do on our own doorstep, but in Wales, where the concept of 'tidy' rules supreme, this has a particular resonance. In my home town there are women of a certain age who clean not only their own doorsteps, but a carefully measured piece of the pavement too. This may be taking localization a bit far, but pride in one's locality is a key civic virtue that should be encouraged not denigrated. It does not suit the globalizing capitalists, who have portrayed localization as a selfish response to an inevitably competitive world that will leave the poor to fester. From the subsistence perspective this is outrageous hypocrisy, since it is the global market which deprives the poor world of the ability to provide for its own, forcing them instead to provide cheap cash crops for our tables.

Recent developments in the world of football have provided an instructive lesson about global economics for many who would rather not have to engage with the dismal science. Money has moved into the game, destroyed it and disempowered its supporters. Merchandising now matters more than matches. Clubs can become bankrupt in spite of their players performing well; clubs can also lose points in the leagues because of poor performance by their boards of management. Before capitalism engaged with football the arrangement was simple: players were well paid for their high levels of skill, but poor fans could afford to attend matches because there were enough of them to generate the cash required for these high salaries. But shareholder pressure requires the extraction of the maximum possible profits (a legal requirement, as we will see later). Compared to this the interests of the loyal but poor fan count for nothing. The people's game has been stolen from them and given to shareholders who would probably rather be at Wimbledon and, if they attend football stadia at all, arrive late and sit in the hospitality box. The response by the more pioneering fans – to buy shares in their club, as in the case of Shareholders United, or even to take on the whole club, as in the case of Lincoln – is an example we should be prepared to follow in all the areas of life that are important to us. We need to take back control, and that requires taking responsibility and usually achieving ownership as well.

Colin Hines has done his best to rehabilitate the word 'protection' in terms of jobs as well as communities and local economies. We are seeking to protect local jobs, not for any selfish or narrow-minded reason, but because of a clear understanding that without local jobs and local economies there will be the loss of community and ultimately of our human identities. We are local beings. We evolved in family or tribal groups of fewer than 100 people. We have struggled to deal with the health and social problems that large cities bring with them, and we are struggling and sinking in the face of a globalized world that we are not psychologically prepared for. Globalization might suit the capitalists, but we are simply not ready for it. Our inability to cope is manifest in the rise of nationalism and the increase in depression that arises from loss of identity.

Localization is not a selfish or self-interested move; it is the inevitable consequence of facing the reality of planetary limits and social and cultural realities. This chapter provides a more detailed account of the processes that are subsumed under the term 'globalization', first from the perspective of capital and then from that of labour, and offers a brief history of the destruction of the localized economy that is the corollary of economic globalization. The following sections present the green movement's response to globalization: a system of strong and vibrant local economies, protected by a policy framework favouring local production and consumption, and based on the principles of bioregionalism. Finally, I provide a brief account of progress that has been made to build stronger and more self-reliant local economies.

Globalization, the pressure for profits and the loss of the local

Some of capitalism's most favoured apologists are keen to tell us we have always lived in a globalized world, that the communications between different sides of the planet are nothing new. Whether they mention the journeys of Viking traders, Marco Polo or the Hanseatic League, we are being persuaded that intercontinental travel and trade date far back in our shared past. This is a diversion strategy. Even the issue of the scale of global travel before this century, when most people rarely strayed beyond their town or village, is not relevant. The point is about the qualitative change in the relationship between countries and, more crucially, between countries and businesses that globalization represents. We are in a new stage of history, not because there is more stuff or more people moving across the world, but because the nation-state, which has existed for a few hundred years as the central political building block, has lost its power. The word 'globalization' describes an adaptation in capitalism which consists of it breaking the bounds of the nation-state and enjoying, for the first time, virtually untrammelled political, and hence economic, power.

This point is made succinctly by some colleagues of mine, and its origin traced back to the post-war settlement at Bretton Woods:

> The origins of globalisation in the twenty-first century lie in the institutional arrangement of Bretton Woods, set up in 1944, as a means of managing the post WW2 international political economy of the developed countries. In essence, the arrangements were an attempt to impose a reciprocal conditioning between an industrial free-market system and a nation state system . . . This resulted in nation states' domestic economies becoming increasingly subordinated to the needs of a globalising world economic system.

Another economic commentator makes a similar point about the shift in the relative power of nation-states and corporations:

> [Globalization's] common feature is to convert the state into an agency for adjusting national economic practices and policies to the perceived exigencies of the global economy. The state becomes a transmission belt from the global to the national economy, where heretofore it had acted as the bulwark defending domestic welfare from external disturbances.

So to be 'anti-globalization' is not to be xenophobic or protectionist, it is to ask fundamental questions about who the powerful players are in this new form of capitalism, and who will defend our interests as citizens.

In a report published in 1999 the Ford Foundation summarized the major problems posed by the processes of globalization:

1   Increasing polarisation and concentration of wealth;
2   Technology allowing fewer workers to produce larger quantities of goods;
3   Competitive advantage resulting in the exploitation of lower social, labour and environmental standards in other countries: the 'race to the bottom';

4   A rising tide of productivity that does not 'lift all ships' when low-paid workers cannot afford to purchase the ever-increasing quantity of goods they produce;

5   Corporations no longer anchored in the countries that can control rules about their relations with social needs;

6   The global market system removing the connection, previously provided by national governments, between democracy and capitalism.

Green critiques of globalization would add a further two points:

7   A massive increase in trade-related pollution, especially CO_2 pollution.

8   A cultural expansion resulting in an increase in the number of societies that individuals can compare themselves with, and causing increasing dissatisfaction and pressure for further consumption, e.g. the collapse of communism because of the perceived higher standards of living in the West, contemporary disgruntlement in Islamic societies.

Points 1, 3 and 4 are concerns about inequality, which I deal with elsewhere. Point 2 need not be a concern, subject to the establishment of a fairer system of distributing the rewards yielded by technological efficiency. My central concerns in this chapter are the remaining four points, i.e. those concerned with the democratic deficit and cultural confusion caused by the globalization of the economy, as well as the pressure this puts on the global ecosystem.

Under the pre-1945 settlement, an arrangement which managed to hold sway under increasing pressure in most of western Europe up to the 1970s, governments saw their role as supporting citizens against the excesses of capitalist enterprises, and they had the political power and the political incentive to do this because of the periodic return to the ballot box. We could portray this as the classic struggle within capitalism between 'labour' and 'capital', or between citizens and the power of the money system. The framework for the domination of capital that globalization represents was laid down at Bretton Woods, and corporations have used the years since to expand their power at the expense of our democratic representatives through legal protection for investment, the WTO, the deregulation of finance capital, and the increasing divorce between money and value (described in Chapter 6). While the intellectual analyses of this process have been few and far between, its effects have been felt by the people who have lost out in the power struggle. In the developed economies we feel it as pressure on the welfare state and the loss of jobs through those twin sirens of inevitable doom, downsizing and outsourcing. The effects in developing countries have been far worse, with the sorts of loss of subsistence rights and desperate poverty experienced in our own economies during the early days of industrialization.

We have noticed the loss of political power in the professed helplessness of our democratic representatives to do anything about these growing pressures.

The response has been an obvious one: if our politicians cannot do anything to help us, we will begin to help ourselves. This is the impulse behind the localization agenda. As citizens we may not understand or be able to affect what happens in Malaysia or Venezuela but we can take control over own locality: emancipation begins at home. For anybody genuinely committed to building a post-capitalist economy, it is vital that we begin now. Since Marx first found the word 'capitalism' there have been many, himself included, who predicted its catastrophic collapse. Given the inefficiencies and instabilities I chronicle throughout this book, it is extraordinary that it has survived so long. There have been periodic crises but each time the system adapts, so while the sense that we are living in a massive pyramid-selling scheme can be unsettling, I would not recommend you hold your breath on this one. But there is no harm in making sure that as much of your life as possible is sustained outside a system that looks increasingly unstable and is manifestly unjust. The alternative is a political shift towards a fair sharing of resources. This will certainly be opposed strenuously and violently, which is when we will need the protection of having some economic systems within our control.

Restless and greedy capital

The key concept of contemporary capitalism is that of 'shareholder value', a concept in urgent need of discourse manipulation if ever I heard one (emails welcome). It is now the dominant driver of our economic system, since company law actually requires that board members maximize returns to shareholders. If they undertake any activity for a motive other than profiteering, to support workers or protect the environment, for example, they could actually be prosecuted. Hence any socially beneficial activities that firms do engage in must be justified in terms of public relations. Within this legal framework, the shareholder becomes the only stakeholder with a principal claim on the firm. Other stakeholders may be engaged in dialogue, although its outcome has no legal force.

It is easy to think of corporate executives as greedy amoral bastards with no orientation except the accumulation of excess cash. And fair enough from one perspective. But it is also important to grasp how they are trapped by the structures of capitalism and particularly its money system, which forces companies to expand and to inflate their monetary value. Money, and the financial market where it is traded as though it were itself a commodity, drives the operation of corporations through a number of mechanisms. The first is fairly direct and relates to how money is created. In Chapter 6, I will explain how almost all money is created by being borrowed. So those who are prepared to borrow outrageous sums, unjustified by any assets they may have to back them up, are lauded and rewarded for their willingness to take risks. Without them the banks would not be able to bring money into existence and would not gain the face value of that money by doing so; hence the sacred status of the entrepreneur. Because this money is lent with interest due, the entrepreneur must be able to find not only the lump sum, but also the additional value of the interest, hence his or her company must grow. Capitalism's obsession with growth is not an economic inevitability; only an inevitable consequence of a money system based on interest-bearing debt. The real winners from the system are the banks themselves. They are bound to see their money returned with interest, and where the company is bankrupted by its debts they can arrange debt-for-equity swaps, where they come to own the company instead.

This is how we arrive at the paradoxical situation where the most successful companies are those that sport the largest debts. Halliburton, with its $998 million debt, is a shining example of the trend. It demonstrates the way in which global corporate capitalism operates like a massive pyramid-selling scheme, ever seeking new markets to operate the same scam, and leaving those where it has previously operated in destitution. As the economy rocked following the assault on the heart of finance capitalism in September 2001, the risks represented by Enron's massive debts (estimates vary, but $20 billion seems a conservative one, backed by only $2 billion of assets) appeared to be coming home to roost. The massive growth rates at Enron, from nowhere to the seventh largest corporation in the USA in just 15 years, are only possible on the basis of this sort of ungrounded, loan-based strategy. It was inevitably the largest collapse in US history – until the next one.

So why is inflating the value of your company – 'future value captured in the form of market capitalisation', as Anderson calls it in the creative accountant's training manual (written by three Arthur Anderson partners) – so important? It is because when critics describe unregulated global capitalism as a giant casino they are not using an analogy. What determines the share value, and therefore the equity, of a globally traded corporation is its *perceived* value. So Halliburton is only worth what people think it is worth. This is why companies like Enron and Halliburton produced questionable accounts, because by doing this they could determine the actual value of the company. The real value of companies, in terms of the assets they possess and could sell on to creditors if they crashed, is a fraction of their nominal stock-market value. So investors, including the banks and insurance companies that invest the money we may have saved, are competing with each other to bid up the price of these companies. If confidence is lost, the share value may plummet drastically.

In the global, financially liberated economy, the quickest and easiest way to make money is by gambling in this casino. You would be a fool to try to make and sell something, anything, when the market could change so quickly. It is far more rational to keep up with the pack buying the latest trendy share, and hope you smell the crash and switch your cash into something else in time. Risky as this may appear, it is less risky than global competition in manufacture, and on average yields far better returns. This appears to explain what might otherwise seem irrational behaviour on the part of corporate managers: their willingness to take unimaginable risks and their collusion with accountants to hide any indication of weakness in the company's balance sheet. One commentator has noted that this late form of capitalism

> reworks the hierarchy of management objectives as it reorients the firm: if firms have to organize process and please consumers in the product market, they must also now satisfy professional fund managers and meet the expectations of the capital market. The result is a new form of (financial) competition of all against all whereby every quoted firm must compete as an investment to meet the same standard of financial performance.

When Marx coined the word 'capitalism' he had in mind a very different economic system from the one we see today. Bourgeois capitalism was controlled by a specific and relatively new class of owner-managers, often from humble origins, who have been immortalized in popular culture from Bradley Hardcastle in the UK sitcom *Brass* to Thomas the Tank Engine's Fat Controller. In spite of the gross unfairness of the distribution of the value of their companies, it is likely that these people saw themselves as worthy wealth creators, firm but fair. They did at least exhibit some commitment to their local communities and felt a responsibility for providing employment, no matter how exploitative. We might suggest that then, as now, those who controlled capital displayed more or less concern for the well-being of their employees and the environment; the difference was the visibility of their behaviour. The exploitative mill-owner portrayed in Victorian novels by Gaskell and Dickens was an obvious local target, quite distinct from the CEO of the corporation that owns today's workplaces. This sort of capitalism has died in the globalized economy where only shareholder value matters.

Andy Pike presents a narrative of the decline and death of one such bourgeois capitalist enterprise: the Vaux Brewery by the river Wear on Teesside. The brewery, founded in 1837, was an important provider of employment in a depressed local economy, but it was also a symbol of pride in the area and gave workers and community members alike a sense of identity. The brewery's owners were not philanthropists, but they demonstrated a commitment to the local economy that would have been impossible for a transnational corporation:

> By the late 1990s, Vaux had been managed for three generations by members of the Nicholson family. Their particular style of paternal, regionally rooted capitalism was underpinned by a patrician and high Tory political culture. Such dynastic family management is embedded within the North East's historic class structures with the landed aristocracy, industrial pioneers and national state functionaries often paternalistic in their outlook and management style.

The Nicholsons struggled to maintain control of the brewery, but this became impossible in the face of 'brewing's increasing capital and scale intensity [which] generated strong investment capital demand that could not be met by retained earnings or North East regional investors'. In his memoirs Nicholson identifies the culture clash between traditional and globalizing capitalists. Pike comments that 'The post-"Big Bang" political economy and culture of speculative short-termism, fee-seeking and deal-making by "plain spivs" (Nicholson, 2003: 154) was increasingly at odds with the Chairman's "gentlemanly capitalism".'

Nicholson's account suggests that, while profit-seeking remained the key objective of the company, there was a commitment to some basic ethical standard and to employees in the local economy. The need for increased levels of capital investment led to a loss of control over the company (now a diversified hotel and entertainment group called Swallow) from the Nicholson family to institutional investors. The patrician owners tried to rally a defence campaign, appealing to regional identity across the boundaries of ownership and control, but the campaign failed and the brewery was closed in 1999. The pressure from the stock market for 'shareholder value' overcame the commitment to the local economy, with its associated ethical stance:

> Closure uprooted Vaux's longheld traditions and culture as an 'ethical company' that would normally 'seek solutions which while preserving

shareholder value, avoid factory closures where the business can be sold instead'.

With a history dating back to Cuthbert Baus in 1837, the closure meant the end of a longstanding association between the brewery and the city . . . Amid contested assessment of 'shareholder value' and profitability, the Swallow board controversially decided to reject the Management Buy-Out (MBO) led by the local brewery management in favour of the closure and asset disposal advocated by their advisors and supported by their major institutional shareholders based in the City of London.

Loss of control was inevitable because the modern globalized economy demands capital investment on a scale impossible to the individual entrepreneur. Corporations can only survive by consolidating into larger groups that can carry larger debts. Effective control is passed to the financial institutions. More importantly, given the focus of this chapter, control of the economy moves outside the local economy into the global financial market. There is no longer any space in the economic sphere for considerations regarding employment or community. This has led economic geographers to portray a global economy without attachment to place, and an autonomous financial system, even 'the end of geography', or economic geography at least. From the perspective of capital, the locality no longer matters.

Freebooting and insecure labour

The capitalist's dream of a vast pool of unemployed labour and of groups of workers bidding each other down in a competition for poorly paid work has become a reality in the global marketplace. This was surely one of the causes of the corporate drive towards the enlargement of the European Union, leading to a situation where poorly paid, but often highly skilled, workers in central and eastern Europe can mop up the remains of European manufacturing industry employment – and, with the emphasis on the Services Directive of the EU Lisbon Agenda, service sector employment too. Such economically powerful figures as Digby Jones of the CBI and Chancellor Gordon Brown are no longer ashamed of arguing that European workers must price themselves into jobs against the sorts of wage levels seen in Brazil or China. A senior Indian adviser at CII agrees, considering that the West should 'compete, not whine':

> The reality, however, is that their own people are not competent and are high-cost vis-à-vis their counterparts in the developing countries . . . When competitiveness is the sole concern, patriotism and nationalism get secondary priority.

The sort of competition that relatively comfortable and affluent western workers are being drawn into becomes clear from a consideration of the relative wage rates of workers in different national economies, as presented in Table 5.1. With the need to acquire a monetary income 20 or 50 times that of workers in poorer countries to support the lifestyle they have grown used to, there is no future for employees in the West in this competition.

Table 5.1 Comparison of hourly pay rates in various poorer countries with those in France, 2000

Country	Hourly rate (French francs)
Madagascar	1.2
Philippines	4.0
Thailand	3.5
Vietnam	1.5
France	55.0

Source: Mendizabal and Errasti (2005).

Towards the end of the twentieth century, the argument was about drawing a distinction between skilled and unskilled labour. Those in the West would continue to undertake skilled labour, and command a wage premium, leaving the unskilled labour for those in the South:

> At any given time, each country produces the goods which lie within the narrow band of factor intensities in which its current factor endowments give it comparative advantage, while also consuming a wide range of other goods imported from countries at higher and lower levels of development . . . reduction of barriers to trade would thus result in the North producing only skill-intensive goods, the South only labour-intensive goods.

Aside from the inherent racism of this 'international division of labour', it has also proved an inaccurate reflection of reality. Concerns about the reduction in wage levels that a huge additional workforce would inevitably cause were swept aside. Wood was even confident enough to claim that, not only would there be more skilled jobs, but unskilled jobs would receive higher returns. A more accurate picture would be likely to divide the world between unskilled work being carried out by a billion Chinese workers, and skilled work being carried out by a billion Indian workers. Peripheral, meaningless and marginal employment is still carried out in western societies, mainly focusing around sales and personal services. Financial fiddles are operated to provide sufficient money to those workers through job subsidies to ensure that they accept the twenty-first-century

Table 5.2 Recent movement of skilled employment to India

Company	Date	No. of jobs	Type of work
Welsh Assembly	June 2003	n/a	Computer mapping
Lloyds TSB	Oct. 2003	1,000	Enquiries
HSBC	June 2003	9,000	Banking
Aviva (inc. Norwich Union)	Dec. 2003	2,500	Insurance
Abbey	Jan. 2004	400	Banking
NHS	Feb. 2004	n/a (£896m)	Data processing
Bearingpoint (formerly KPMG Consulting)	Feb. 2004	2,000	Software writing
Standard Life	Apr. 2004	50 (initially)	Health insurance
Norwich Union	June 2004	700	IT and business systems
National Rail Enquiries	July 2004	1,000	Rail enquiries

Note: As an inhabitant of Aberystwyth, I have personally wept tears of frustration at the decision to move National Rail Enquiries to India.
Source: Panvel clipping services: *Farmers' Guardian, Metro, Sunday Times, Times of India, Business India, Daily Mail.*

division of labour with docility. Rather than a system for the production and distribution of goods and services, in the West work has become a system for the unequal distribution of money best summed up by the Czech adage: 'We pretend to work; they pretend to pay us.' The waste of time and human resources this represents is discussed further in Chapter 7.

Services

Amongst Indian commentators of a neo-liberal bent, these developments are greeted with delight, although it should be noted that voters in the world's largest democracy are not so sanguine about the consequences of globalization for their society, as was made clear by the result of the 2004 election – when Prime Minister Vajpayee and his enthusiastically pro-globalization government were defeated by the votes of the rural poor in favour of the Congress Party. The delight shown by the Indian press as the call centres expand contrasts with the gloomy tone of British newspapers. Journalists also demonstrate hostility to attempts by unions to defend British jobs. In what they term an 'outsourcing backlash', they report 'a growing trend for "British and proud of it" companies such as Nationwide Bank [Building Society], Northern Rock and HBOS to wave the British flag and loudly reject the chance to outsource to India.'

India has been particularly successful in the IT sector, with Bangalore becoming know as silicon valley. According to Nasscom, the Indian trade body, sales of software were up by 26 per cent in 2002, with outsourcing accounting for a quarter of sales. Overall, India has seen its IT services sector grow by 17 per cent in a year, compared with 4 per cent global growth. Perhaps it was a racist underestimation of the abilities of Indian workers that led to the conclusion that skilled jobs in the West would be safe. In fact, moving on from computing, Indian doctors are now seeking to compete with European ones. A whole range of pathology tests are likely to be carried out in India, where costs are 25 to 30 per cent lower. Table 5.2 gives some examples of recent off-shoring decisions by British companies.

Two of the prominent mutual players in our economy have, unsurprisingly, bucked the outsourcing trend and stated their determination to continue to employ workers in the UK. These are the Nationwide Building Society and Co-operative Financial Services, which recently recruited 500 call-centre staff in its north-west headquarters.

Manufacturing

The only prediction by economists that proved correct was that the situation would be worse in manufacturing. As figures from the Trades Union Congress indicate, it is far worse (see Table 5.3). This takes total manufacturing job losses since April 1997 to just over 770,000, a fall of 18.6 per cent. On current trends, the sector will have lost nearly a fifth of its workforce by the end of 2004. The loss of manufacturing employment in a longer perspective is shown in Figure 5.1, which illustrates the drastic decline since 1978 for both men and women.

The British government itself is cutting costs by signing contracts with Chinese manufacturers to produce uniforms for British soldiers: contracts with 60 British companies were terminated in 2004 and a £50 million deal signed with a firm that subcontracts much of its production to China. Between 1996 and 2001 Hornby moved its manufacturing to China. Losses of £4.5 million became profits of £5.4 million by March 2003, and Hornby's share price rose threefold. China is now producing its own wideboys, like the Mr Feng described in an article by Rupert Wingfield Hayes. He has made his fortune by producing cigarette lighters, in the shadow of the tobacco industry's move into the less health-conscious and larger markets of the poorer countries. 'In Japan this costs about $25,' he

Table 5.3 Employment loss in manufacturing, 2004

Sector	Employees	Change over year to March 2004	
	(March 2004, 000s)	*No.*	*%*
Total	3,390	−99,000	−2.8
Electrical engineering	378	−20,000	−5.0
Textiles	169	−19,000	−10.1
Ceramics, metals	560	−15,000	−2.6
Transport equipment	350	−13,000	−3.6
Chemicals	223	−9,000	−4.0
Machinery	303	−7,000	−2.3
Paper, print, publishing	429	−5,000	−1.1
Plastics and rubber	211	−4,000	−1.9
Food, drink, tobacco	458	−4,000	−0.9
Other manufacturing	308	−3,000	−1.0

Source: Office for National Statistics.

Table 5.4 Changes in manufacturing employment in various European countries, 1997–2002 (000s)

All in work	All manufacturing	High-tech manufacturing
Spain	+509	+152
Italy	+417	+147
France	+146	+71
Germany	+116	+298
UK	−575	−154

Source: EU Commission.

gloated to the journalist, 'I can make it for $1!' His workers, sucked into the cities from the countryside, are paid $90 per month. There is no competing with these 900 million workers; in the competitive international labour market, western workers are entirely superfluous. Wingfield Hayes quotes the conclusion of one Chinese economist: 'Just think of it this way, if all the industrial jobs in Europe and America moved to China tomorrow, we'd still have plenty of people left over!'

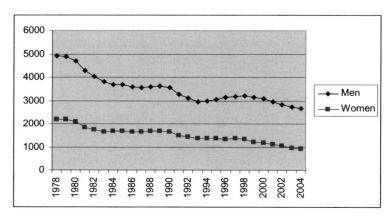

Source: *Workforce Jobs by Industry 1959–2004* (ONS, 2005).

Figure 5.1 Decline in manufacturing employment, 1978–2004

However, this is only half the picture, since figures show that the so-called uncompetitive European economies are actually managing to hold on to manufacturing jobs much better than the UK and the USA. The TUC concludes that a more active involvement with the labour market by government and greater levels of employment protection have resulted in better performance by the other EU members. Table 5.4 shows that the losses can be better sustained because they follow a period of manufacturing growth, so that the 1997–2002 figures for manufacturing employment are positive, compared to large-scale losses in the UK. We can conclude that not only does the creation of a competitive market lead to poor working conditions and pay levels, but it also fails to secure jobs. It is only the UK and US workers who are being forced to compete with Chinese workers; those in countries where the social welfare model persists are protected. This applies to high-tech as well as traditional manufacturing.

Retail

Food is our most basic need, and this may explain why the few shops that remain in most high streets are food shops like bakers and butchers. The stranglehold of the supermarket has pushed most grocers over the brink, but their alimentary manoeuvres are not limited to control of the UK food market: they too have global ambitions. Retail is the latest sector to experience an expansion boom into what are termed 'emerging markets' – markets where outsourcing of other forms of employment has created a pool of consumers far larger than in the existing markets, which are themselves saturated with over-supplied shoppers. Multinational retailers expanded by 33 per cent in these new markets in 2003/4, making new entries into 16 countries. The market analysts A. T. Kearney note that the top 30 global food retailers extended their 'empires' into 85 different countries in 2003, having had outlets in only 15 countries a decade earlier. Their figures, reproduced in Table 5.5, show that eastern Europe and India are the most attractive targets. Key corporate players include the USA's Wal-Mart, Tesco, with its base in the UK, and French company Auchan.

Table 5.5 Expansion of multinational retailers in emerging markets

Country	2004 rank	2003 rank
Russia	1	1
India	2	5
China	3	3
Slovenia	4	14
Croatia	5	n/a
Latvia	6	19
Vietnam	7	0
Turkey	8	6
Slovakia	9	2
Thailand	10	18

Source: Data from A. T. Kearney, reported by Burt.

Shareholders at Tesco's 2004 annual general meeting heard that Tesco controlled 27 per cent of the UK retail market, making a profit of £1.6 billion on sales of £27 billion. The same day MPs received a report detailing Tesco's failure on ethical trading with overseas and domestic suppliers, illustrating 'how Tesco's abuse of power impacts on people and communities . . . by putting small traders out of business, killing off local high streets, bullying suppliers, and damaging the environment through its never-ending demand for cheap food'. The global food economy is putting farmers under the same sorts of pressure that manufacturing workers have endured for decades. In 2003 farmers' incomes in the UK fell by 47 per cent, leaving them earning £2.90 per hour, while Tesco chief executive Sir Terry Leahy earned £2.977 million, or 250 times more per hour.

Bioregionalism: an ecologically grounded approach to the economy

Let us start again at the beginning and see how we might decide to organize a system of production and distribution along rational lines: in other words, let us throw the profit motive out of the window. In its place we will put two simple alternative objectives: the maximization of human well-being and the protection of the planet. This takes us along a wholly different route and towards some quite different conclusions about how economies should be arranged.

Economics is about resources and so we might begin with a consideration of which resources are the most important, and think about ensuring a secure supply. This is the starting-point of a system of economic organization called bioregionalism. Bioregions are natural social units determined by ecology rather than economics, and that can be largely self-sufficient in terms of basic resources such as water, food, products and services. Bioregionalism has at its heart two of the central principles of green economics: balance and cycles. Ecology demands that we recognize our part in a complex web of natural systems, and this should reflect the places we choose to live and how and where we choose to access our resources. This is what we mean by living in balance with nature. Respecting the natural cycles of life is often referred to as 'closing the loop', so that within our bioregional economy we are responsible for all our waste and we have a neutral impact on the natural cycles that maintain the earth in balance, primarily the carbon cycle.

Your bioregion is effectively your backyard. It is the part of the planet you are responsible for. Bioregionalism means living a rooted life, being aware of where your resources come from and where your wastes go. It is the opposite of a life lived in the limited knowledge that food comes from Tesco, leaving everything to the global corporations that are only too willing to take on this responsibility in return for their profits. Unlike political boundaries, bioregional boundaries are flexible, but should be guided by the principle of subsidiarity in the case of any individual resource or service. Within the bioregional approach, beginning with the local is a principle that trumps principles such as price or choice.

Bioregions begin with ecology but they also interact with culture. The most poignant loss for many as a result of globalization is any sense of themselves as rooted in a local culture, whether in terms of the food they eat or their national costumes. We are being homogenized into suit-wearing consumers of an unvaried diet of TV dinners and reality gameshows. Bioregionalism offers us all the opportunity to use the economic sphere to regain our sense of self, and our sense of community with others.

For citizens in the global supermarket and the global labour market, the movement away from the local is unsettling. Evidence for this can be found in the strong support for initiatives to support local producers, like Buy British campaigns and the local produce sections of supermarkets. Such campaigns are often dismissed as xenophobic and Little-Englanderish, although in reality it is the loss of identity resulting from globalization that is creating an increased appeal in identity politics such as that based on nationalism and race. The most powerful response to the wish to reconnect with the local through our economic activity has been the development of the local food economy, which Helena

Norberg-Hodge described as 'bringing the food economy home'. The local food movement has taken on a life of its own outside the green movement. An example is the Foundation for Local Food Initiatives, a cooperative providing consultancy services to the local food sector.

Perhaps the most stylish and media-savvy of the proponents of a strengthened local economy is José Bové, leader of the French Confédération Paysanne, or peasants' confederation. He has been involved in media stunts such as filling the Champs-Elysées with wheat and releasing sheep into central Paris, as well as numerous demonstrations destroying both GM crops and supermarket supplies imported from overseas when local produce is available. Despite his official persona as a sheep farmer and maker of Roquefort cheese from Larzac, Tarn, he has a long history of political activism, cutting his teeth in opposition to the building of a US military base which would destroy his farm. He is now skilfully using the understanding of the political system these experiences gave him to put pressure on the weak point of the globalized economy, and the point he has chosen is food. Hence his identification of McDonald's with *malbouffe* (bad food) and his imprisonment for trashing an outlet in Millau.

In the Anglo-Saxon world, politicians profess a helplessness in the face of global competition, but others are less supine. The most effective pressure for a relocalization of national economies has come from those with the most pressing agenda: the Greens. Since trade-related pollution is the fastest-growing contributor to global CO_2 emissions, those with a concern for the environment have developed a platform of policies to manage the market in favour of the local. Foremost among these is Colin Hines, whose *Localisation: A Global Manifesto* makes a strong argument for government action to strengthen and protect local economies: 'The essence of these policies is to allow nations, local government and communities to regain control over their local economies; to make them as diverse as possible; and to rebuild stability into community life.'

The policies called for in this 'manifesto' amount to a platform of guidance for the direction of the economy, while leaving individual actors free to make choices about production and consumption decisions. In other words, it is rigging the market in favour of the planet and citizens, whereas the capitalist market is rigged in favour of corporations and their shareholders. The most important policies are systems of tariffs, subsidies and import and export quotas, to encourage local production. Such policies would support the system of trade subsidiarity I propose in Chapter 4, and would be essential to counteract the climate-change impact of the present trade system. Hines also suggests a policy of 'site here to sell here': in other words, producers would be required to make goods within defined economic areas, balancing the needs of consumers in those areas with the needs of employees. On the capital side he proposes the grounding of capital through exchange controls, limits on consumer credit, and the imposition of taxes on speculative financial transactions. Government support for industry would be switched from corporate welfare towards tax breaks for local investment.

The focus throughout Hines's work is on protection. We have no need to be defensive about our desire to protect our local economies, so long as we allow others the freedom to protect theirs. We owe no duty to the out-moded theories of dead free-trade economists. A system of internally strong local economies would be able to interact without one exploiting and dominating any other. It is also a far more secure way of guaranteeing our supply of basic necessities than the globalized trade system. We are now pitifully dependent on imported food. Figures from the Office of National Statistics show that food imports into the UK rose by 24.6 per cent between 1992 and 2002 and that the annual balance of payments deficit in food moved from £4.7 billion to £9.8 billion during the same period. The government is unconcerned; a statement from DEFRA in July 2003 noted that 'National food security is neither necessary nor is it desirable.' This attitude seems irresponsible in view of the increasing competition for the oil on which food transport relies, as well as the reduction in transportation that will be required to tackle climate change.

Public procurement offers an important opportunity to support local economies and one that is being taken up by Labour politicians in spite of its flying in the face of the spirit, if not the letter, of EU competition legislation. The thinking behind this is that public money should be kept in the local economy wherever possible, and since public bodies spend so much money, they should buy locally wherever possible. The UK government spends over £13 billion a year on procurement. Expenditure by local authorities in England is estimated at around £40 billion. There are various initiatives in Wales, including Powys Food Links, which supplies locally grown organic meat and vegetables to hospitals and schools in Llandrindod Wells, and the arrangement between Hybu Cig Cymru (the Welsh red meat development body) and three large hospitals in north Wales. Competition rules can usually be evaded by reducing the size of the contracts (they only apply to contracts worth more than £150,000), which can also help small, locally based suppliers.

An interesting perspective on the movement actually taking place in our local economies is given by the 10-year study of changes in entries to the *Yellow Pages* directories of local businesses (see Table 5.6). They dis-covered a rapid decline in traditional food and hardware categories, with a corresponding increase in professions 'catering for beauty and body image, or alternative therapy and stress relief'. Under the heading 'butcher, baker, candlestick-maker?', they note that greengrocers suf-fered the largest percentage decrease of 59 per cent over the ten years, closely followed by butchers (40 per cent), hardware retailers (34 per cent) and bakers (20 per cent). However, entries in the candles classification had boomed by 208 per cent, an intriguing but unsurprising reflection of twenty-first-century lifestyles.

Table 5.6 Key classification changes in the Yell directory, 1992–2002

Classifications registering highest growth		Classifications registering greatest decline	
Classification	% increase	Classification	% decrease
Aromatherapy	5,200	Greengrocers	59
Cosmetic surgery	1,780	Butchers	40
Dieting and weight control	1,445	Coppersmiths	35
Make-up artists/services	1,007	Hardware retailers	34
Reflexology	829	Farmers	29
Alexander Technique	724	Insurance brokers	26
Tutoring	601	Gamekeepers	21
Mobile phones	546	Bakers	20
Recycling	356	Clinics	18
Saunas and sunbeds	299	Carpenters and joiners	16

Source: Yell, *The Alternative Census: A Ten-Year Social and Economic Analysis of the Changing Shape of the UK* (Reading: Yell, 2004).

We can draw both negative and positive conclusions from the figures displayed in Tables 5.6 and 5.7, about what is going on in our local high streets. The first conclusion is the increasing dominance of supermarkets, pushing the traditional small shopkeeper and farmer out of business. However, the areas of growth suggest an increased interest in self-care and health, which would certainly be important factors in a green economy. And it is worth noting that, apart from mobile phones and saunas, which are high-energy industries with negative health impacts, the other expanding categories are the sorts of personal service with low CO_2 outputs that we would seek to see expand in a sustainable economy. When confronted with the question 'Do you really want to end economic growth?' I have often responded that it depends what growth you are interested in. You won't be able to drive your car as much or have a new sofa so often, but you can have as much massage and as many trips to the local theatre as you like. The market already seems to be moving in that direction. It is also worth noting that the only category listed amongst the fastest growing new entrants that is not a service is the farm shop.

Table 5.7 Fastest-growing new entrants to the Yell directory, 1992–2002

Classification	% increase since entering Yellow Pages	Year of entry
Shiatsu practitioners	3,100	1996
Nutritionists	969	2000
Fitness equipment	759	2000
Yoga	635	2000
Farm shops	623	1996
Health centres	283	2000
Image consultants	242	1996
Internet web design	75	2000

Source: Yell, *The Alternative Census: A Ten-Year Social and Economic Analysis of the Changing Shape of the UK* (Reading: Yell, 2004).

Conclusion: local community rests on the local economy

I discussed in Chapter 4 the concept of trade subsidiarity and the system for deciding where different goods should be produced within a market system functioning according to the framework created by localization policies. There are pressing environmental and equity reasons for following up these policies; their benign social effects are less frequently discussed. There has been much concern expressed in academic and political circles about the loss of community involvement and the death of civic spirit, but no link is made between this and the divorce between work, identity and community that is an inevitable consequence of the globalized production and distribution system. I must now reveal my weakness for Adam Bede, as an icon of the rooted worker, whose foundation in meaningful work allows him to be a rock of his local community. I am not advocating a return to eighteenth-century technology but rather drawing to attention the nature of relationships in a pre-capitalist village where a person was known for his or her work, which was a central part of each person's identity. I would ask you to imagine how such a person would feel compared to a person who works in an MFI factory such as the one in Runcorn, or sells its sofas on a characterless, out-of-town wasteland.

I illustrate this point with some photos of my home town, Aberystwyth. Figure 5.2 contrasts a local woodworker with the MFI shop as two alternative locations to buy furniture. Figures 5.3 and 5.4 are pairs of contrasting sales outlets in the service sector, contrasting supermarket shopping with shopping in local shops. The pride and ego-reinforcement of the local shopkeepers is obvious in the beauty which they create in their shops; contrast this with the utilitarian design of Safeway, with its overpowering array of advertising boards, and the extreme impersonality of McDonald's, where the market exchange has become devoid of any human contact, as money and food are exchanged through a plate-glass window.

Others are making the connection between the competitive global economy and the breakdown of society. Take this quotation from the Relationships Foundation:

> Global competitive pressures have forced the UK banking sector to merge or perish. As a result, financial institutions have reaped economies of scale and been able to adapt better to new developments such as 24 hour trading and the onset of on-line banking. For most customers, it means better facilities and convenience in their day to day dealings with money. The downside, however, has been branch closures, as well as centralisation of decision-making which leave little room for local discretion. The concepts of mutuality and accountability, present in many of the financial institutions with strong local ties, are also in danger of becoming a thing of the past.

It goes on to detail the ways in which globalization has caused a deterioration in the quality of family life and job security, in workplace relationships and, by extension, all relationships. As Helen Petrie puts it, 'many of us are moving from a world in which we knew neighbours, friends and colleagues into virtual worlds where interaction is distant'. To the global economy we are units of production, our feelings to be acknowledged and understood only so that they can be manipulated to increase our efficiency. As the following statistics make clear, this has had a disastrous effect on our social lives:

- Some 40% of households are now said to share a meal less than once a month.
- More than half the population believe they would feel lonely without a television.
- Nearly a third of young adults would not know their neighbours if they saw them (compared to nearly 75% of over-55s, who regularly chat to their neighbours).
- Two-thirds of 6- to 17-year-olds have a TV in their bedroom (making watching TV mainly a solitary activity).

Figure 5.2 A local woodworker contrasted with the impersonality of the MFI frontage

We are a social species. These pressures reducing our human interactions are part of the reason for the epidemic of dis-ease identified in Chapter 1. Strengthened local economies would offer us reinforced identities. We would once again be able to describe our jobs in ways that other people could understand and without embarrassment. We could enjoy a sense of

Figure 5.3 Two local shops in Aberystwyth

pride as we saw others in our community visibly benefiting from our job well done. I do not underestimate the importance of these social benefits of revitalized local economies, but the economic consequences are perhaps more important. In an era of increasing competition for dwindling oil supplies, and growing instability in financial markets, it is just plain

Figure 5.4 The impersonality of Safeway supermarket and McDonald's

stupid to rely on the supply of our basic resources by markets over which we have no control and to expect them to be transported over thousands of miles. Localization is not only a necessity for our well-being and that of the planet, it may also be a necessity for our survival.

6

Money: How it Works; Whom it Serves

> Capitalism is the use of money to make money for those who have money.
>
> David Korten

Money is one of the most marginalized issues of our time. Most people never ask themselves or others questions about where money comes from, what it is, or who controls it. This is a shame, since money quite clearly lies plum at the centre of an economic system that is not called capitalism by coincidence.

This question has become even more pressing in the post-globalization version of capitalism, where money no longer operates as a tool facilitating trade in products, but is used to make money directly by various confidence tricks in a system which is now commonly referred to as 'the casino economy'. The creation of money by banks was originally intended to facilitate the exchange of goods. However, from the start a range of financial scams have been perpetrated which remove this need to get your hands dirty making things.

It is no coincidence that globalization, as represented by the vast expansion of trade in goods, occurred simultaneously with the liberalization of financial markets. Countries which had once attempted to maintain political control over finance through setting interest rates, controlling the activities of banks, and through credit and exchange controls were persuaded that further capitalist progress required the market to take on these functions. Money can now be used merely to generate more money for those who have it, leaving not production but finance to play the central role in the global economy:

> The finance industry lies at the heart of globalisation. Of the total international transactions of a trillion or so dollars each day, 95 per cent are purely financial. Globalisation in not about trade; it is about money.

> The financial system now completely dominates the real economy of goods and services.

Money is useful for the obvious reason that it enables you to pay for a luxurious lifestyle, but more importantly to those who control capital, money gives them a claim over future production, so that over time they are enabled to accumulate an unfair share of a community's resources and power:

> In reality, people who save and invest money do not save goods. They merely transfer their claim from the original commodities in existence to those produced and sold in a future period. Furthermore, they expect an increased share of them as a reward for investment. Crucially, the money which they use to spend or invest is constantly created and destroyed by the banking system for its own financial advantage.

There are few subjects in modern life about which so many lies are told and so many misunderstandings encouraged, both politically and personally, than about money. It is, in fact, neither the root of all evil nor what makes the world go around. It is a neat but deceitful political tool that enables those with power under a capitalist system to exercise that power to generate an unfair advantage for themselves. For readers who have not delved into the inner workings of the financial system before, I should warn you: you are in for an exhilarating but bumpy ride. You should not be surprised to find yourself thinking 'I just can't believe it'. I have frequently felt that way myself when embarking on a similar journey. The disbelief is similar to that experienced when watching a confidence trickster, but be assured that, just because the show is good and you have believed it for a long while, that does not mean that it is true.

Whence it came; where it went

If you ask people where money comes from, they will probably tell you: from a bank. Dig deeper and you will find that people believe that the money they take out of the bank has been deposited there by somebody: by the person herself, in which case it is simply a withdrawal, or by somebody else, in which case it is a loan. This is the first big myth of money, because the truth is that all or nearly all (depending on your theorist of choice) the money you take from the bank has been created out of thin air by the bank itself.

When you begin teaching students about the economics of banking, you teach a fiction known as 'fractional reserve banking', and many who have never taken economics as an academic discipline or worked in a bank have a hazy notion about this system. It is understood, because of Hollywood movies about 'runs on the bank', that the bank does not actually hold, or need to hold, as much money as it lends to people. Because it is highly unlikely that everybody will come and ask for all their money, all at the same time, the banks can consider themselves to be acting with probity if they retain only a proportion as 'reserves', this proportion being understood to be around 10 per cent. Let us for the time being take this story as a reasonable account of how banks create money; it is the one that is reproduced in most economics textbooks. The first stage is the deposit of some money by a punter, let us say £100. Because banks have learned from historical experience that only one in ten of such punters will want her or his money back at any given time, they feel quite secure in lending £900 on the basis of this deposit, effectively inflating its nominal value, and thus reducing its real value, tenfold.

The second myth about money that is universally believed is that it is, and needs to be, backed by something of real value. Governments create money and this money has credibility because the government has a sufficient store of gold in its vaults to support its value. Like the reserve banking story, according to this fiction governments can create more money than the gold they have, but only up to a certain limit. This story was true for some time, but it was found that the uncontrollable growth of the capitalist economy rapidly outstripped the gold available to support it and maintaining a 'gold standard' stifled economic growth.

Eagle-eyed and sharp-minded readers will have noticed that there is an inconsistency between the two stories told so far, in that they disagree about who is responsible for creating the money. They have in common the idea that, while there should be something of real value backing up a currency at least in part, who owns this collateral and who therefore creates the money could be either the bank or the government. This is how things were, both banks and government were entitled to create money; governments created money as fiat issues, whereas banks created it in return for a debt. Some state money was backed by gold, some by confidence alone, generating four kinds of recognizable money in a modern economy: commodity money, managed money, fiat money and bank money (see Figure 6.1).

So there are several different types of money, distinguishable by the nature of their back-up and by who controls them. Banks can create money on the basis of deposits, as credit. Governments can create money by selling bonds, or just by making a decision to create currency. It may be efficient to leave the job of generating credit for economic activity to banks, so long as they operate within political controls, but it will also be necessary to have money created by government both as credit, to fund public works, and as currency, to facilitate economic activity without the creation of parallel debts. The balance between these different types of money is a political decision. As Figure 6.2 shows, throughout recent history, and increasingly since the Second World War, government has relinquished its role in money creation in favour of banks. The recent economic history of the developed economies has been a shift in the balance towards debt-based bank money and away from public money. This has had the inevitable consequence of increasing the proportion of money

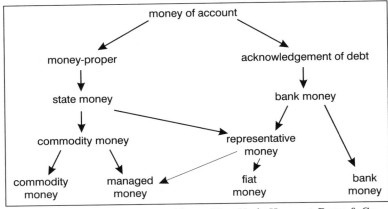

Source: J. M. Keynes, *Treatise on Money* (New York: Harcourt, Brace & Co., 1930).

Figure 6.1 Keynes's illustration of the classification of money

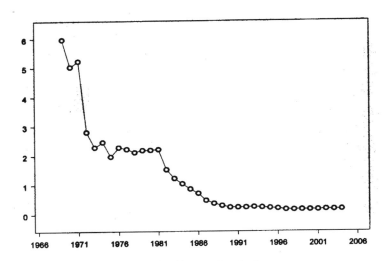

Source: Data from Bank of England interactive database.

Figure 6.2 Ratio of debt money to government money, 1969–2004

paid to bank shareholders and producing a squeeze on the money available for public investment.

A bank charter is literally a licence to print money. Since the system of requiring a certain proportion of assets to be kept on reserve has gradually

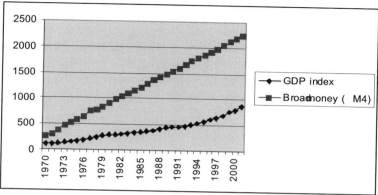

Note: 'broad money' includes all possible types of credit as well as hard cash; M4 value has been divided by 100 to achieve appropriate scaling and was originally in £m units.

Sources: GDP data from ONS; M4 data from Bank of England.

Figure 6.3 Growth in broad money compared with growth in the economy (GDP), UK, 1970–2001

been eroded, the only control on banks' ability to produce money as credit is our willingness to borrow, hence the constant stream of junk mail and TV advertising offers of credit. When the banks lend us money, the debt is listed and the money sought and retrieved, but at that point it belongs to the bank. They have used our willingness to borrow as an opportunity to create a debt; when we repay the debt, the money they have taken from us belongs to them. No wonder we are seeing record bank profits: they are simply creating their profits out of our debts.

No surprise also that we see spiralling levels of personal, business and public debt. Neoclassical economists see no problem with this. On their planet, the creation of money in this way will be balanced out by a corresponding amount of economic growth. Apart from the obvious fact that money supply is growing far more rapidly than economic activity (as shown in Figure 6.3) from a green perspective this growth itself is a problem. So the most important first step towards creating the steady-state economy that will not put intolerable pressure on the carrying capacity of the planet is to change the system of money creation that generates the need for growth.

The discussion so far has been in terms of a national currency, but currencies are also exchanged and used to pay for exchanges of goods and services between national economies. This role is now played primarily by the dollar, which has acquired the status of international reserve currency since the agreement establishing the financial structure to dominate

Box 6.1 Schemes and dreams on the Mosquito Coast

The establishment of the Bank of England was balanced by the creation of the national debt, clearly illustrating the link between money and debt creation. Initially, the bank was established privately by Scottish entrepreneur William Paterson, who persuaded the government to raise £1,200,000 by selling the national debt to citizens who would redeem their share with interest in a fixed number of years. The scheme was accepted in 1694 and from then until the following year Paterson served as a director, when he fell out with the other members of the Court (or board) and was sacked. Paterson was an entrepreneur and the Bank of England was merely one of his many schemes to create money from thin air. He is probably most famous for the subsequent disastrous Darien project. In 1693 he set up the 'Company of Scotland Trading to Africa and the Indies', which sold shares in a proposed colony on Darien on the Panama isthmus. The Scots were keen to take advantage of expanding international trade and so there was no shortage of investors: about half a million pounds, half Scotland's national capital, was invested. Darien was in fact the original Mosquito Coast and most of the settlers died within the year. The scheme was also sabotaged by English traders and the English governor of Jamaica, who did not want any competition. Thanks to Paterson, the Scottish economy was nearly bankrupted, preventing Scottish entrepreneurs from competing with the 'British' empire, and we have lived with the national debt for the past 300 years and more.

Galbraith's conclusion on banking seems most apt:

> Much discussion of money involves a heavy overlay of priestly incantation. Some of this is deliberate. Those who talk of money and teach about it and make their living by it gain prestige, esteem and pecuniary return, as does a doctor or witchdoctor, from cultivating the belief that they are in a privileged association with the occult.
>
> *Money: Whence it Came, Where it Went*, p. 5

global capitalism after the Second World War. Under the Bretton Woods Agreement, the USA also extracted the right to have its currency – the dollar – considered the equivalent, in terms of economic weight, of gold reserves. In the post-war exhaustion, low morale and financial desperation of the other world powers, the USA pulled off this extraordinary confidence trick which has enabled its dominance for the past 50 years but left us all with a teetering economic system. The coda to the story is that the USA proved itself incapable of maintaining the value of the dollar and, in the face of the need for massive liquidity resulting from the costs of war in Vietnam, Nixon 'closed the gold window' on 15 August 1971.

This meant that dollars were now themselves no longer linked to the reserves in Fort Knox, but floating free, and foreign central banks could no longer exchange their dollars for gold.

Global capitalism relies on one country's currency to provide credibility for the system as a whole. Initially this role was undertaken by gold itself, as a commodity of real value, but the movement towards fiat money, which went hand in hand with the capitalist expansion, meant that currencies rather than gold played this role. The reserve currencies – sterling, the dollar, the yen and the euro – are all used to underwrite economic activity, but just as in banking there is a central bank, so in the currency system there is a central currency and this is the currency of the most powerful player in the global economy – the global hegemon. It is mainly its own credibility and that of its economy and military structure that guarantees the functioning of the international economy, but it needs its own back-up in the form of gold reserves.

During its days of empire, the UK played the role of preferred currency. At that time US bankers supported the pound – a fact that alienated those outside the charmed circle, who could not understand why US gold was being used to support a foreign competitive economy. Similar questions were raised when Chancellor Gordon Brown sold 415 tonnes of the UK's 715 tonnes of gold reserves in May 1999, reducing the official reserve percentage held in gold from 16.7 to 7 per cent, and substituting currency, a mixture of dollars, euros and yen. This is a record low level of gold holdings compared with the 2,000–2,500 tonnes held between 1958 and 1965, most of which were sold during Britain's financial crises of the late 1960s and early 1970s.

What we can learn from monetary disasters?

I understand that this sort of discussion is hard to take. As Galbraith so eloquently put it: 'The process by which banks create money is so simple that the mind is repelled. Where something so important is involved, a deeper mystery seems only decent.' But as is so often the case in economics, as well as home economics, the proof of the pudding is in the eating. So for those who are not yet convinced by this account of the nature and instability of the money-banking system, some examples from history can be used to illustrate the theory in practice. Such periodic disasters are inevitable, indeed symptomatic of capitalism as an economic system. They are the boom-and-bust cycles that are generated because the capital that lies at the heart of the system is created in such an illogical and unstable way. In the words of Galbraith again: 'As banking developed from the seventeenth century on, so, with the support of other circumstance, did the cycles of euphoria and panic. Their length came to accord roughly with the time it took people to forget the last disaster.'

The role of a monetary system should be to facilitate an equitable exchange of products and work. At any point where this exchange becomes unbalanced, the natural response should be to adjust the quantity or speed of circulation of money until the three factors – work, products and money – come back into balance. But the owners of money are likely to resist this adjustment if they are using money as a store of value, since it may reduce their wealth. Other powerful vested interests operating within a capitalist economy can then prevent a rebalancing adjustment and inadvertently exacerbate the problem until what began as a monetary imbalance becomes an economic catastrophe. Accounts of three such well-known events follow.

The first is the Great Depression in the USA. The problem undoubtedly began in the stock market, where overvaluation of companies, resulting from speculative trading, caused a classic bubble in value and a subsequent collapse in the value of shares. In this case the trouble was exacerbated by trading in (or gambling on) the future value of stocks and by trading 'on the margin': that is, buying stocks on credit using other shares as collateral. Once the bubble burst, speculators needed to find the money to pay off the value of the loans they had taken on to pay for the worthless shares, and they did this by either withdrawing savings or taking out loans from banks. This took the crisis beyond the markets and into the banking sector, leading to the collapse of many banks and a withdrawal of money from the real economy. Wages could not be paid, or inputs to production bought, or final goods bought. This was now a classic slump, where there are people wanting to work and people needing to buy the products of that work, but there is no money to lubricate the process.

Roosevelt's response to the Depression which followed inevitably from the financially generated bust was to print the money to pay wages, and then to create work of social value and pay those wages in exchange for it. You might ask why he did not just pass the money on to those who needed it, but that would have broken the link, essential to capitalism, between money and work. It would have fundamentally undermined the ideology of capitalism that says, if you want money you must work for it. Hence in the illogical logic of this ideology, it was better to build public works projects, like the roads to nowhere constructed in rural Ireland during the potato famines.

The most famous monetary collapse in a developed industrial economy is that in Germany between the wars. This began as a drain of money from the economy through the system of reparations. As Germany's economy weakened, global capital began to speculate against the currency, driving its value lower still. The government responded by printing more of the currency, which only led to a spiralling decline in its value, until Germany reached the situation we are so familiar with from contemporary newsreels of people taking prams-full of money to buy loaves of bread. The Reichsmark had gone into the First World War worth 1 gold mark and was worth half that much at the end of the war. By November 1923 it took one billion Reichsmarks to buy a gold mark, meaning that the Reichsmark was only worth one-five-hundred-millionth of its former value. The disastrous consequences of this for the economic life of the nation are clear.

Once confidence in a currency is so severely damaged, the only feasible response is to create a new currency, which was a process managed by the Finance Minister, Hjalmar Schacht. In November 1923 he created a new parallel currency called the Rentenmark; to create confidence it was backed by land, in this case the most solid asset of the German economy. The Rentenmarks allowed economic transactions to take place within the economy, although they were not legal tender, had no fixed relation to the Reichsmark they replaced, and could not be used for international payments. This made the Rentenmarks speculation proof. Bizarrely, much of the speculation against the currency that had destroyed it had actually been funded by loans from German banks. In *The Magic of Money*, Schacht explains how the Reichsbank made loans to support the speculation against the German currency. Thus the government, which has always been blamed for economic mismanagement and for printing too much paper money, was not primarily responsible for the inflation. By 1924 the Rentenmark and Reichsmark were being treated equally and the Rentenmark could be withdrawn.

The lessons of the German hyperinflation are twofold: first, that financial speculators' only motive is to make profits and that they are unconcerned about the social and political consequences of their speculative activity; but, nonetheless, governments can use political power to control this speculation if they wish, exposing the myth of powerlessness.

A less well-known example is the financial collapse in Argentina in 2001/2. It is a slightly different story because it takes place in the context of a vulnerable economy which is not at the top table of international capitalist planning. Like many non-reserve-currency economies, Argentina suffers from being under-monetized: in other words, there is less money in that country relative to the level of economic activity than in the USA or UK. This makes it vulnerable to citizens exchanging their pesos for foreign reserve currencies or sending them overseas. This vulnerability was exacerbated by the pegging of the currency to the dollar, which meant that once the dollar's value began to rise on the foreign exchanges from 1995 onwards, Argentina's exports became more expensive and less attractive than those of competitor countries, whose currencies could devalue against the dollar. The financial crisis in Mexico in 1994, followed by those of the 'Asian tigers', Russia and Brazil from 1997 to 1999, undermined confidence in Argentina's ability to pay its sizeable external debt.

In late 2001, members of Argentina's wealthy class began to take fright. The USA was having difficulty repaying its own massive foreign debt because of an over-valued dollar; this was true of Argentina in spades. The peg that had seemed to be Argentina's salvation was translated into the final nail in its coffin. Those who could withdrew their pesos, exchanged them for dollars and sent them overseas. This led to a classic bank failure on a national scale in December 2001. The government froze bank accounts, leading to severe political instability with five different presidents in a fortnight.

Before long Argentina was in exactly the situation of the USA during the Depression, with insufficient money circulating to allow economic transactions to take place, and people wanting to work with nothing to pay them, while factories with their raw materials inside stood idle. While we have looked down our neo-imperialist noses at this economic mismanagement, we might be wiser to draw lessons about the instability of our own monetary system, as more than one economic commentator has noted:

> So, the Argentinian economy has collapsed and social and financial chaos reigns. We shall read a great deal about it, but you can be sure very few analysts, if any, will mention the actual and fundamental cause of this disaster. To do so is too horrifying, for what has destroyed Argentina, is the same cause at work all over the world today. Argentina's fate is the world's fate – and that is too drastic a conclusion for any analyst who wants to be paid for his work.

Argentina's politicians appear to have learned from their bruising experience of the global financial markets. In January 2005 the country offered its foreign creditors 25 cents per dollar for the debts. This is effectively a default, but 700,000 bondholders may have to settle for it. The experience may offer a lesson to other indebted national economies around the world.

The conventional explanation for these disasters is the same in each case: such cyclical events are inevitable within capitalist economics, but if the market is allowed to operate freely, the economy will recover. In each of the cases reported here this account is inaccurate, since the disasters wrought by capitalist economics were solved politically. More to the point, we are quite at liberty to reject an economic system whose apologists advise us to take such cyclical disasters – along with the personal tragedies they bring – on the chin and make a decision to build our economies on more secure and stable foundations. It should be noted that the solution to the bust in each case was not to abandon the economic system which had created the problem – that would have gone against the interests of the powerful players within capitalism. So the system of working for wages and relying on the instability of the interaction between production, money and work was not brought into a state of balance, because to do that would have excluded the possibility of generating profits which are paid to those who have power and wealth without contributing work.

There are many other examples of the use of money to achieve political ends, primarily to gain control of resources and wipe out competitors. This was seen most clearly in the series of financial collapses that began in Thailand in 1997 and soon engulfed Indonesia, Malaysia and South

Box 6.2 John Law's incredible land bank

John Law was a Scottish entrepreneur and financier. Given this, it seems almost superfluous to add that he was also addicted to gambling, as well as being a rake and a drunk. Law went to France in 1716 where he became adviser to the regent, the Duc D'Orléans, who was having to deal with the indebtedness left by his brother Louis XIV's lifetime of excess. The duke granted Law a Charter to establish a bank issuing notes backed initially by precious metals but later by shares in an ill-fated development scheme in the French American colonies, known as the Compagnie d'Occident. The shares boomed, as French investors competed to have their piece of the apparently gold-rich soil of Louisiana and Mississippi. But Law was not even investing the money received in the scheme, rather he was lending it to the regent to pay expenses and debts. Many thus paid used the notes to buy more stock in the Compagnie, generating a classic bubble. The crash came when a French nobleman demanded, as was his right, to have his notes exchanged for gold. This led to a rush by others to do likewise and the collapse of the bank with massive losses by all investors. The Duc de Saint-Simon's epitaph on the scheme is a salutary lesson:

> If to the solid merits of such a bank are added, as indeed they were, the mirage of a Mississippi scheme, a joint-stock company, a technical language, a trickster's method of extracting money from Peter in order to pay Paul, the entire establishment possessing neither gold-mines nor the philosopher's stone, must necessarily end in ruin, leaving a tiny minority enriched by the total ruin of all the rest of the people. That, in fact, is what actually happened.

Source: Galbraith, *Money: Where it Came; Whence it Went.*

Korea before spreading outwards to affect Russia, Brazil and Argentina. Thailand had led the way in liberalizing its financial markets and encouraging foreign investment. Its fellow 'Asian tigers' followed suit, leading to a financial boom in south-east Asia, where huge profits were made by foreign investors. The boom was inevitably followed by bust, as speculators grew concerned about over-valuation of their assets and took flight. These were not economic collapses; it was clear that these countries were following classic neoliberal policies with great success: 'The 1997–99 contagion . . . spreading from Bangkok to Brazil, was financial in its transmission mechanism, unlike the trade-linked contagion of the earlier decades.' It is financial investors who used their political influence to bring about capital market liberalization and who now gain from speculating in one currency after another.

One might go a step further and argue that such speculation is also intended to reduce the value of the assets of these countries, whether businesses or national resources, making them more available for expropriation at a lower price. Corporations have already been found to have used foreign debt to force poor countries to sell valuable assets like water. Speculating against these economies reduces the price of these assets to the global investment sharks.

The power of international finance is also used to achieve direct political aims, particularly the annihilation of regimes hostile to global capitalism. The USA used its economic muscle to undermine Cuba by imposing a trade embargo. During the Cold War, Castro could use his support from the Soviet bloc and the deal with Comecon (Council for Mutual Economic Assistance) over Cuban sugar to earn foreign exchange for trade, but following the collapse of the Soviet Union, Cuba was increasingly vulnerable and had to introduce the dollar as legal tender in 1993. Castro introduced a 10 per cent commission on the transfer of dollars into pesos for Cuban citizens in autumn 2004, presumably as part of a policy to switch to the euro as the reserve currency of choice.

During the Spanish Civil War, the global financial community used its power to work against the democratically elected government of Spain, which was considered hostile to capitalism as a result of its commitment to worker control at the local level. There was a massive flight of capital out of the country, some $250 million at 1931 value, which was exported in contravention of exchange controls. Multi-millionaire and Falangist supporter Juan March worked against the peseta on the foreign exchanges as well as bankrolling Franco's coup. During the war, finance was used to undermine the democratic forces, including an unofficial trade embargo arranged by the pro-Falange governors of the Bank of Spain. The forces of capital were threatened in Spain, and in the face of this the democratic government had no chance, although the price of capitalist support was 40 years of dictatorship for Spain and 6 years of world war with its millions of lost lives.

The politics of money

If this account of money creation and control is correct, as I believe it to be, there is one obvious question raised: why should governments allow themselves to be controlled by banks and financial speculators? Why has government relinquished its power in such an important area, so that, instead of creating money to pay for what we need, we have to, as individuals and as government, keep borrowing it back from banks and paying their shareholders for the privilege? Capitalism is a system for the transfer of wealth from poor to rich, and this is achieved most efficiently through the financial system, including the public finances. The rich and powerful make sure that they maintain power over those systems, making any suggestion that we live in democracy a farce. Governments are afraid to implement policies that prevent this siphoning away of our wealth because of the likely retaliation from the financial markets. The lessons of Black Monday have been well learned by politicians the world over. In an era of financial deregulation, the democratic power of politicians is virtually non-existent.

The conjuror must create a feint to keep our attention away from the deception. In the case of the public finances, this feint is the taxation system. The most resounding debate in recent years is about the precise rate of just one tax: that on incomes. This is a classic example of divide and conquer amongst the not-rich, because the rich do not need to pay taxes. This perennial political argument creates a situation where we resent each other because of our slightly lower or slightly higher contributions to tax or needs from the welfare system. Meanwhile the rich, whose assets, especially land, are virtually exempt from taxation, use the services paid for from taxation, but employ accountants to prevent them paying any themselves.

Another negative result of the money system is that we are losing the value of our work, as well as the satisfaction in our work, because the system of production is outside our control. I cover this in more detail in the following chapter, but it is worth pointing out here that if we are working and other people are not working then our work is subsidising their lifestyle. Capitalism is the system that enables them to do this. Entrepreneurs, or wealth creators, are lauded by society, yet those whose work they benefit from are much less well rewarded. Imagine that a man walking down the street sees another man with £100 in his hand. He hits him over the head and takes the money. He is a criminal and must be put in gaol. But now imagine that he gives the man a job, pays him £100 and makes another £100 profit from his work. He is now a wealth creator and lauded by society. The moral situation is the same. This is how the system of work enables a transfer of money from poor to rich. The transfer is not justified morally or because of a differential in effort; it is facilitated because one person has more power, by virtue of their control of enough money to establish a business.

The third and most subtle way that the money system works to the benefit of the rich is through the public debt. Criticism of the national debt is a common thread in radical economics. For poor countries, national debts force them to engage with an unfair trading system to generate enough foreign currency earnings to pay the interest. They are tied into a system of debt-bondage with which the rich countries replaced their more unsightly imperialist policies. The national debts of rich countries are less immediately troubling, since if you have a reserve currency at your disposal you can accrue as much debt as you need. In this setting the debts are rather a pump that operates to transfer money from the poor to the rich. If you have money to spare, you can invest it in the national debt by

buying government bonds, the mechanism by which governments sell debt in themselves to generate money for public spending. The earnings on these bonds are paid for by the government through taxation of those who have to work because they do not have enough money to live by making investments, including in bonds. Since the rich do not pay taxes, this is another mechanism for transferring our money to them. Hence the national debt of the UK is making the rich richer and the poor poorer, just as the national debt of Tanzania or Peru is.

This is not a just or satisfactory system. The obvious answer is to return to a system of state-created money to pay for works of national importance. Here we enter less marginal territory because there have been two Early Day Motions in the House of Commons in recent years calling for just this to be done, and receiving upwards of 30 votes.

A common response to the suggestion that the government should print money is that this would cause inflation. We have seen huge monetary inflation in recent years, as credit controls have ended and people have taken on increasing levels of debt, yet price inflation has been virtually eliminated. What we are suggesting, at minimum, is the substitution of money created for the public by the government for money created as debt by banks. So long as government reclaims its right to control the amount of private credit in the economy, there is no need for an increase in the quantity of money in circulation, just the nature of its ownership.

As well as huge popular movements for taking the power to create money from banks and back to the people, there have also been some well-placed supporters. Dr William Temple, Archbishop of Canterbury during the war (1942–4), wrote that

> It cannot be justified in modern conditions that the Banks should, in order to meet national needs, create credit which earns interest for themselves. The State must resume the right to the control and issue and cancellation of every kind of money. Till that is done, a body within the community will control what is vital to the community, and that is a false principle.

This high-level political pressure led to the establishment of the Radcliffe Committee on Credit and Currency, which finally reported in 1959. The evidence collected had the advantage of forcing the Bank of England to confirm the nature of its money creation, purely as credit in its own books, but no attempt was made to change this.

Instead we have an economy whose money is almost all created as debt, which must then be borne either as public debt or as private debt. For many in the UK, constant and growing debt has become a fact of life. This habit is learned early, with students now being encouraged to take on substantial and long-term debts when they are barely out of school. The average student now owes £12,000 when leaving college. Debt amongst the UK population as a whole is also growing at a record rate. Total lending rose by £9.4 billion in December 2002, the highest monthly increase since records began in 1993.

In a managed monetary system, the primary question must be: how much money should we have in circulation in a steady-state economy? It seems right to relate the quantity of money to something explanatory about the economy it relates to, to prevent an excess of money or a deficiency. The correct amount would clearly relate to the economic activity in that economy.

Another perennial question in the debate about money is whether it should be linked to something of ultimate value or created by faith alone. The confusion over this question appears to derive from a confusion of the scientific thinking required to solve a purely technical problem with the spiritual unease created by the notion of faith-based money. This may explain the Islamic proposal for a gold-backed dinar as a competitor to corrupt western currencies for global trade. It may also explain why Jesus told his followers that they could not worship both God and Mammon. In the present capitalist economy, money is created as 'credit' by the banks and, since there is no backing for this creation in terms of gold, it is appropriate that the word has the same root as 'credibility' or belief. The money exists because we believe it does. We do not need gold to back up this belief; in fact that would only achieve the limitation of economic activity, mediated by money, to the amount of the gold that had been discovered, which makes no sense:

> the credit structure was historically based upon gold, the existence of which bears no relation to human requirements for goods and services. In the past, gold production, quite illogically, exerted a disproportionate effect on the mechanism of prices and credit.

To conclude this section we need to determine the qualities we would require of a money system in a sustainable and just economy operating within a steady-state paradigm. First, money should be created by and controlled by the citizens in that economy; all should have equal power over this most important tool of an economy. Secondly, we need to break the link between money and growth by ending the system of creation of money by banks as debt, and the payment of interest for those debts, since both of these force

---

Box 6.3 The South Sea Bubble

In 1719 the South Sea Company offered to take over the government debt (then standing at £31 million), in return for trading concessions, offering an official £3 million lump sum as a sweetener, as well as substantial unofficial bribes. It outbid the Bank of England and acquired the debt in 1720. These costs were met by share issues, and although the company had virtually no value, a policy of talking up its prospects and the speculative fever this caused led to an increase in their value from the initial £120 to £950 in July of the same year. Directors of the company increased share values by purchasing their own shares. Once word seeped out that the directors had sold all their stock, there was panic selling by investors, most of whom, including Sir Isaac Newton and Jonathan Swift, lost sizeable fortunes.

The South Sea Bubble set off trading frenzy amongst all classes in London, and founding a joint-stock company by selling new shares became a very profitable business. Shares could be sold in vague projects such as the improvement of the Greenland fishery and the importation of walnut trees from Virginia. Not only were the proposed projects intangible, to put it politely, but also the shares were grossly overvalued relative to the actual assets of the company. This is a pattern which was evident prior to the 1929 Wall Street Crash and before the dot.com bubble burst, and is exemplified perfectly in current stock-market values, which are overvalued by such techniques as counting unbilled receivables as assets – the Anderson trick used by Enron.

Source: Garber, P. M., *Famous First Bubbles: The Fundamentals of Early Manias* (MIT Press, 2000).

---

the expansion of the economy beyond planetary limits: 'The effect of this method of creating money is that the economy has to grow in order to avoid collapsing . . . the growth imperative imposed by the debt-money system is a positive feedback mechanism – a vicious spiral.'

Thirdly, money should be created by fiat, without being linked in any way to the existence of some valuable commodity. As a principle this is sound, since it is illogical to relate the amount of money in circulation, and hence the amount of economic activity that can take place, to the random discovery of a rare resource. However, since money does have the power to control economic activity in this way, it may be possible to use that to the benefit of mankind by linking the most powerful type of money – that used for trade between national economies – to the most precious human resource: the climate. Ideas for such a linkage are presented in a later section. Since money is created by fiat, it follows that the quantity of money can be determined by the creating body. Taking into account the velocity of circulation in any given economy, the quantity of money should be tailored to reflect the optimum level of economic activity within the steady state of that economy.

DIY solutions to the money problem

For many the first response to understanding the negative role that conventional money plays in local economic development was to establish a LETS system. LETS (local exchange trading schemes) are systems where a community of people, generally in a limited local area, exchange goods with each other using cheques as payment. They invent a fictional currency usually related to a local feature, such as the bobbin in Manchester or the Rheidol (a local river) in Aberystwyth, but the currency is only ever virtual. LETS received huge interest and energy when they first emerged, but in practice they have suffered from various limitations. First, a LETS currency can never compete with a national currency in an economy where there is sufficient of the latter. Secondly, the relationships within LETS are different from those in the market, and members have found it difficult to find a cultural middle path between favours for free and work for money. Thirdly, those who have skills have still tended to prefer to sell them in the market where they can, often leaving the LETS short of solicitors or plumbers but with plenty of aromatherapists and dog-walkers. This is not to undermine the importance of LETS. In many areas they have hugely increased the well-being of members, and perhaps most importantly, have forced people to reconsider what money is, which is the necessary first step to building support for radical change in our financial system.

The rest of this section gives you examples of creative ways in which people around the world are responding to the problems with money. The only limitation is your own imagination and your ability to work together as a community.

Make your own money in Argentina

Following the collapse of the Argentinian financial system described above, the country suffered a money vacuum. The rich had sent their money to their Swiss bank accounts, while foreign creditors had sucked out everything else. Argentinians responded as creative human beings would have done the world over: they made their own money. They did this through 'barter clubs', first set up by three ecological activists in 1989. The Red Global de Trueque (RGT: global barter network) aimed to 'utilize resources and knowledge according to principles of sustainability' and promote 'the exchange of goods and services without

> **Box 6.4 Speculation in the mining sector**
>
> From end-1995 until early-1996 a Canadian mining company called Bre-X Minerals experienced a spectacular rise in its share price. The share price went from little more than a few Canadian cents to more than C$25 per share. The reason was that the company had announced a large find of gold reserves in Indonesia, promising to be the largest new find of gold in the twentieth century. Estimates of the gold reserves increased over time and subsequent reports of mining consultants and the Indonesian Mines Ministry indeed confirmed the existence of the gold reserves. Financial firms such as Lehman Brothers and J. P. Morgan strongly recommended to buy the shares of Bre-X. The share price increased accordingly. Trouble started when the chief geologist of Bre-X went missing and was presumed dead. It turned out that the mining reports were based on 'salted' samples and the gold reserves non-existent. The share price of Bre-X Minerals collapsed in the early months of 1997. Using the benefit of hindsight, some 'experts' may label the Bre-X Minerals case a typical example of irrational investor behaviour in the stock market. However, the fact remains that ex ante, based on what appeared to be qualified and independent reports, rational stock market investors had valid reasons to expect large future profits from this proposed mining operation. They therefore increased the share price of Bre-X, which, according to fundamental finance theory, should currently reflect the expected discounted value of future cash flows.
>
> This sort of stock market speculation explains why Shell persistently overvalued its reserves, since these were virtually the corporation's only tangible assets and any downgrading would cause a collapse in the share price.
>
> *Source*: Erasmus School of Economics, Erasmus University, Rotterdam.

being restricted by access to money'. It began as a LETS scheme but reluctantly moved to the creation of *arboles* (trees) as a form of paper currency for the purposes of flexibility and convenience. For the pioneers of this and similar systems of local complementary currency the principles of locality and membership were important in maintaining control over the currency, and ensuring its benefit for the local economy. The systems ceased to be 'barter' once the currency was produced and are now fully fledged alternative money systems.

Argentina's provincial governments had an independently powerful role and did not support the monetary restrictions imposed by the centre. They began both to engage with the community currencies and to create state-level currencies of their own. Practitioners in the field of economic regeneration will recognize the process of political takeover in the example of Eduardo Hekker, Secretary of Economic Development for Buenos Aires city government, who 'argued that the state should support [the network] with technical assistance including credit and training which would allow it to become a large scale incubator of small enterprises seeking an insertion in the formal market and transforming themselves into successful competitive businesses'. This is a starkly patronizing position to adopt towards a grassroots organization that has functioned effectively for five years, undermining the suggestion that any technical assistance is required. It also imposes a certain view of the path of economic development – towards larger scale and greater profits – which may well be in opposition to the values of those involved in the scheme. The state involvement was consolidated with the signing of an agreement by the Secretary of Small and Medium Industries of the national government to offer training, technical advice and funding in December 2000.

Making love in Japan

Japan is an example of a society which appears to have been successfully capitalist without ever being convinced by the culture that is necessary to support the economic system. Neoclassical economists have long bewailed the Japanese penchant for saving rather than spending – risk-averse behaviour that leads to insufficient demand. Worse still, Japanese citizens are refusing to borrow, a dangerous decision in a financial system that relies on debt for money to be created. Horrified US economists watch debts being repaid despite rock-bottom interest rates. Outstanding bank loans have fallen year-on-year in Japan for 45 months in a row, 'sucking $741 billion in credit out of the system'. Perhaps the explanation might be that Japan is tired of being involved in a capitalist system in which it was always adding more value to the lives of US citizens than to those of its own and where it would always be more vulnerable in the times of bust than its transpacific neighbour.

What economists would call a 'failure of demand' occurred in Japan, leading to the capitalist nightmare of a failure of growth, with historically low rates of return on Japanese bonds. But greens who have visited the country say that well-being still appears high in Japan and that it may indeed be moving towards being a prototype of a steady-state economy. One way that well-being is being maintained is through the desertion of the global financial system and the creation instead of locally based money systems. Japan is now the world leader in the creation of community currencies, to provide liquidity in economies that are being abandoned by the global financial system.

An example is a project run in Yamato, Kanagawa, using a local electronic currency based on credit cards. Cards were given to 73,000 residents, each with 10,000 monetary units called 'love' already encoded.

The loves can be used in exchange for discount at local shops or to buy second-hand goods advertised on the city government's website. Participants in the scheme were able to increase their love credit through engaging in voluntary social welfare activities, advertised on the website. The idea of the scheme is to find a way to match up needs and abilities of local people to increase well-being. It is based in Japan's strong culture of community and mutual support, backed up by its advanced internet capacity.

German currency solutions

One of the few advantages for Germany in the disastrous intra-war inflation discussed above was a deep and, it seems, lasting scepticism about the reliability of conventional money. So it is unsurprising that some of the most interesting experiments in community currencies are arising in Germany, especially in response to the inadequacy of the euro to lubricate economic activity efficiently given its corporate and monetarist bias. Germany has around 50 local currency initiatives: by being geographically limited they increase the value of the local multiplier and thus strengthen the local economy.

The Chiemgauer was launched in the Salzburg town of Chiemgau in 2003 and is accepted by around 150 shops and service providers including the optician and pizzeria. Chiemgauers to the value of €60,000 were spent in the first year of the scheme, which was started by a local economics teacher. To add credibility the currency is backed one-for-one by euros, which are deposited in a local bank before Chiemgauers are issued. They can be exchanged back but for a 5% fee. The Chiemgauer uses Silvio Gesell's concept of demurrage to increase its velocity of circulation. Gesell observed that part of the reason for the German deflation was that money was not circulating rapidly enough because people believed it would increase in value if they held on to it. His concept of demurrage is like negative interest, so that money slowly loses its value over time, increasing the number of times it is spent in a fixed period. This is achieved by effecting a staged reduction in its face value over time. It initially has validity of 3 months, after which its value can only be extended by purchasing a stamp costing 2% of its value. Since it earns no interest, there is no incentive to hoard or invest, meaning that the currency will instead be spent, increasing economic activity. Money generated from the extension and exchange charges is used to fund local social projects.

Michael Linton's open money system

In the distant realms of money engineering there is a distinct split between those who are working for complementary currencies, and those who would regain political control of our national money. Further out still is a thinker who is questioning the whole concept of money that is politically controlled – Michael Linton. Although he lives in London, I met Michael in Canada, which is appropriate because it was in that country that he began designing currency systems as part of the boom in new economy ideas that flourished on Vancouver Island in the 1970s. The best known is the 'LETSystem', for which Michael is most famous.

Michael told me all about his grand new designs in a Thai restaurant in Montreal, after we had shared a few beers and a joke about the fact that the Canadian $20 bill has a picture of the common loon on one side and the Queen on the other. Money works because a community of individuals wishing to exchange place confidence in it. In the case of the dollar or yen, that confidence derives from a state imprimatur. In the case of a LETS, it grows out of confidence in each other. In Michael's new open money system, this confidence will extend progressively outwards through the region and eventually across the globe.

As Michael points out, where you live is an important part of who you are, so your local LETS will continue to represent a large share of your trading. But it is only part of who you are. We all have other interests, skills and networks. Each one of these needs a currency to facilitate interaction between its members. I have experience working as a copy-editor for academic books, but I do not use this skill in the formal economy. I may, however, consider taking on similar work for the new medium of exchange, let's call them 'pubs'. So I will have ceased to be an Aberystwyth-based editor but will have become an international publishing worker with contacts in Japan, India and Namibia. I will exchange with other writers and publishers across the globe. Perhaps I will also join the opera-lovers' currency system, buying accommodation in Kiev or Sydney (for Pavs, perhaps?), or the cooperative activists' currency, swapping skills with others in Canada or Kuala Lumpur. We will all build up new systems of overlapping global identities to replace the threatening identities of nation and consumption that we use as shields against the alienating force of the globalized economy.

It may help to grasp this idea by thinking of it by analogy with the internet. The present money system operates more like telephone calls: an exchange between a limited network which is controlled by an outside agency that profits from the exchange. Open money will operate more like the internet. People are free to trade with whomever they choose on a global basis. They will create their own currencies to suit their own needs without control from any authority. A currency Darwinism will decide which currencies flourish on the basis of their popularity, just as the internet does with websites.

There are two obvious questions that such a scheme needs to answer. First, how would traders be sure they could trust the person they wished to exchange with? In a LETS system you tend to know the people you trade with, and word usually gets around in the community about who does not provide an adequate service. With open money a similar system of reputation would be likely to build up, and perhaps this could be facilitated via the operation of online feedback along the lines of the Amazon book review system. Michael points out that it is not really a question of trust, but rather of performance. If the trading partner delivers, then I pay. My partner has to decide whether he has enough comfort or confidence in the value of the currency, not in me personally. So what about the odd occasion when we wanted to trade in a market whose currency we do not trade in regularly, such as when I need to find a builder but have only Pavs, pubs or Owens? This situation requires the possibility of trade between the currencies, which Michael sees as being facilitated by an eBay-style online trading system. Currencies themselves could be swapped at a rate of exchange agreed between the traders.

Like many a good idea, when I first thought about all this I decided Michael was completely mad. My mind was, in Galbraith's famous words, repelled. But I have been thinking on the fringe long enough to know that rational minds often treat the best ideas this way, so I let this one swill around my jet-lagged head for a while. This led me on to consider the many collateral advantages that open money might generate, as most creative human developments have a tendency to. I can already imagine its impact on our identities, which will at once become more diffuse and more defined, counteracting the alienating effect of globalization. It will have other unforeseen psychological consequences for those who are attributed little value by the conventional market; and its political impact in terms of major withdrawals from the banking system can only be dreamed of.

For those of you with a respectable job and a monthly cash income in a state currency paid into a bank account, all of this may seem like economics for Zogons. But many people in the green movement carry out valuable work for no reward because it is not valued by the conventional economy. Open money could facilitate these exchanges, reducing the risk of disillusion and activist burnout. With open money, currencies will be created by us to meet our needs; the only limit is your imagination.

A mutual response to banking: Sweden's JAK bank

The system of interest that is an inevitable part of the capitalist banking system is a danger to the planet because it requires growth in the real economy to keep pace, leading to a constant expansion of money, which needs to be matched by a constant expansion in physical economic activity. From Sweden, that utopian source of solutions to so many of our social and economic problems, comes an approach to banking that addresses this problem: interest-free banking that is internally balanced and so does not require trespass on the planet's resources. JAK bank represents a mutual approach to the need to borrow money that is reminiscent

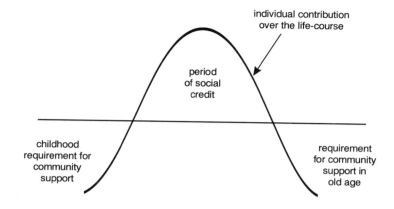

Figure 6.4 Illustration of the ability to provide for one's individual needs over the productive life-course

of the early building societies and of savings schemes that people in poor communities continue to use to this day. All these systems rely on the principle that there is strength in numbers. One person may never be able to afford to raise the capital to buy a house or even a car, but by pooling their resources they can ensure that each person can raise such a large lump sum in turn.

These schemes have the enormous advantage that no money is lost from the system. In contrast, interest-based systems rely on the lure of a certain percentage per year to attract depositors, who are people who have spare money. This interest must be paid by the borrowers, and often amounts to more than the value of the initial loan. Hence, any interest-based system results in the transfer of resources from poor to rich. In the JAK system, saving and borrowing are seen as a way of balancing your needs across your own life, with support from other members. This is illustrated in Figure 6.4, which centres around a single person's lifetime income generation, illustrated as an inverted U-shaped curve. As a child you are below the self-sufficiency line, reliant on others' earnings, and you return to this state in old age. During the middle phase, when you are healthy and productive, you have more income than you need and this needs to be saved for later use. In the JAK system you need to imagine other curves overlapping horizontally with this basic curve, since these represent people at other stages of their lives who can supplement your income, and whose income you supplement during your middle years.

Rather than interest attracting new depositors, in the JAK system it is the 'after-savings' that keep the system in balance and remove the need to

---

Box 6.5 Tulip mania

The tulip madness that took over the Netherlands as finance capitalism was cutting its teeth there can be traced back to the import of the first tulip bulbs from Turkey in 1559. The Dutch were mad for these beautiful flowers, which rapidly became status symbols – the more unusual the colour or pattern, the more valuable the bulb. Throughout the first decades of the seventeenth century their value rose exponentially. By the height of the mania in 1635, a single tulip bulb was worth the equivalent today of £35,000. Tulips were exchanged on the stock exchange and again ordinary people were sucked into the speculative madness, allowing the wealthy to extract their money from them. In February 1637 the bubble burst, when confidence was destroyed by some investors drawing the obvious conclusion that these values could not be sustained.

Source: C. Mackay, *Extraordinary Popular Delusions and the Madness of Crowds* (New York: Faber, 1986).

---

use interest to attract depositors. Members of the bank are effectively borrowing each other's money. Those who have a need first, borrow first, but they must ensure that there is money in the fund to meet others' needs to borrow; they do this by paying back extra money as they pay back their loan. Without these after-savings the fund would very soon find itself over-extended and have to refuse future loans.

A comparison of banking costs under a JAK-style system and under a conventional banking model, with an average interest rate of 7 per cent and based on a loan of £200,000 over 30 years, indicates that more than half the average payment under a conventional interest-style loan goes in paying money to depositors (around £770 per month, compared with the £550 that goes to repay the loan). While the monthly repayments are about the same in both cases, with the JAK bank part of this is after-savings which still belong to the borrower. The real difference comes at the end of the term, when the JAK borrower receives a lump-sum equivalent to the value of the loan.

Although it is important to note that this is a response to the rapaciousness of the banking system, not a solution to the creation and control of money, thinking about banking in this way is liberating. After recovering from the initial disorientation of imagining a world without interest, you begin to see that relying on one another feels considerably safer than relying on the international money system. You also begin to see how the system of interest itself creates the insecurity of that system as surely as it is driving the planet towards destruction.

And now for the big idea

The big idea is the creation of the EBCU (environment-backed currency unit) to replace the dollar as the world's trading and reserve currency. It will be established as a neutral international currency along the lines of the 'bancor' proposed by Keynes at Bretton Woods, but with the added advantage of being based on the right to produce carbon dioxide. It will simultaneously sew up the problems of global poverty and climate change and solve them at a stroke. The poverty of the South can be explained in terms of its inadequate consumption of the global economy's energy; the over-consumption of the rich, developed countries can be explained in the same way. Table 6.1 shows how the shares of carbon dioxide of poor countries do not match their shares of world population. The comparison of India and the USA is the most striking: a direct swap of carbon dioxide would resolve around a fifth of the inequality at a stroke. India is responsible for 5% of the global output of CO_2 but has nearly 20% of the world's population; the USA, by contrast, is responsible for 25% of emissions but has only 5% of world population.

Table 6.1 Shares of population and shares of carbon dioxide emissions: a sample of rich and poor countries

Country	% population	% CO2
USA	4.77	24.4
Sweden	0.15	0.21
UK	0.99	2.39
Malawi	0.19	0.003
Malaysia	0.38	0.55
India	17.08	4.78

Source: CO_2 emissions data are from Oakridge National Laboratory for 1999; population figures are from the UN for 2000.

The Intergovernmental Panel on Climate Change (IPCC) is a UN panel of experts who have exhaustively analysed available data about the consequences of carbon dioxide emissions to estimate the 'carrying capacity' of the planet: that is, how much CO_2 it is reasonably safe for us to emit. The Global Commons Institute (GCI) in London has developed a model for sharing this total amount fairly between the world's people on a per capita basis, and then for reducing this amount rapidly over time; the model is called Contraction and Convergence (C&C). If we work with the year 2000, the sums work out rather neatly, since the model suggests around 6 billion tonnes of carbon can be produced, and the planet has around 6 billion people, which allows us 1 tonne each. Table 6.2

compares the amount of carbon dioxide we produce now with the amount we would be able to produce in a C&C framework.

Again it is clear from the table how the poorer the country is, the less of its share of carbon dioxide it is producing and the more it needs an input of energy from the richer nations. At present we measure economic energy in terms of money, usually dollars. In an economy that respected planetary limits we would measure activity in terms of energy, since this is the scarcest planetary resource. As green economists we need to move towards an economy which uses energy as both a way of measuring the economy and, ultimately, the basis for its means of exchange or money.

Table 6.2 CO_2 entitlement under a per capita regime and actual emissions: a sample of rich and poor countries

Country	CO_2 entitlement	Actual CO_2 emissions in 1999	CO_2 per capita
Algeria	31.59	24.76	0.80
Cameroon	15.57	1.28	0.08
Denmark	5.46	13.55	2.54
India	1,050.13	293.94	0.29
Jamaica	17.31	2.79	0.16
Kuwait	2.63	13.09	5.10
Senegal	9.90	1.02	0.11
UK	60.99	147.20	2.47
USA	292.90	1,499.85	5.26

Note: CO_2 is measured as mega-tonnes of carbon. There are two possible ways to measure CO_2, either as a gas or in terms of the solid carbon. We have used the latter unit because of the neatness of the 6 billion tones and 6 billion people of the C&C model. The ratio between the two units is simply the ratio of their molecular weights, i.e. 44/12, so that 1 tonne of carbon is equivalent to 3.67 tonnes of CO_2.
Source: Emissions data from Oakridge National Research Laboratory, USA, for 1999; population data from UN for 2000.

So what we need is a mechanism for facilitating these carbon dioxide exchanges between rich and poor countries. It is obvious that if we just created the market today, the USA would be able to purchase all the licences it wanted and nothing would change. This is because the US dollar is the main global trade and reserve currency. To enable fair trade in carbon dioxide we would need to create a new global currency: the EBCU, an idea proposed by Richard Douthwaite in his 1999 book *The Ecology of Money*.

At the Bretton Woods Conference in 1944, the British delegation, headed by J. M. Keynes, proposed a neutral currency for global trade. When trade is based on a currency that is also the national currency of a state's economy, the system inevitably gives that state considerable financial power, but also distorts its domestic economy. Keynes proposed that an international currency should be created to facilitate global trade; he called this the 'bancor', meaning 'bank gold'. Douthwaite's proposal is similar, but in this case the currency is based on the planet's scarcest resource: its ability to absorb carbon dioxide. The bancor was to be created and controlled by an International Clearing Union. This would ensure that a balance of international trade was established by fining countries which carried either trading deficits or trading surpluses. Thus countries with a surplus would have an incentive to trade with countries in deficit to create a balance of global trade. The ICU would also allocate the new currency on a global per capita basis between all the people of the world.

The EBCU proposal is raising interesting questions about what the economic impact would be of a world with a strict carbon limit. In such a world the energy intensity of one's products and the way one produces electricity become the most important decisions, as they should be if we are to counteract climate change. The distance that goods travel before they are sold is also important, since the carbon dioxide produced by the transport process would also need to be covered by EBCUs. Because of the complexity of measuring them and pressure from the global corporations, international air- and sea-transport emissions were excluded from the Kyoto limits, although domestic air and all road freight is counted. With the inexorable increase in goods transportation that globalization brings with it, trade represents the fastest-growing source of CO_2 emissions.

Conclusion

The history of money is nothing like as dry and mathematical as you might have expected. It is a rollercoaster ride of hope, greed, expectation and disappointment. We see people selling virtually valueless items – such as tulip bulbs, or rights over foreign swamps, or pieces of paper legitimated by Kenny boy of Enron – for huge sums of money. More than any other aspect of the study of economics, it gives the lie to the myth of rational economic man.

Overall we may conclude that this is not a very clever way to organize something as important to all of us as our money system. All the histories of money agree that the money system within capitalism is based on faith alone. Each guarantor of money has had its period of popularity until the money generated outstripped the confidence and it collapsed. It happened with tulips in Holland in 1637, when capitalism was just taking off, and then in England with the South Sea Bubble in 1720, when capitalism transferred its allegiance to the British rather than the Dutch East India Company. It happened in the USA in the 1920s, when the Fed was foolishly trying to back up an unrealistic gold policy in the UK, and in the 1990s with the insane overvaluation of dot.com companies. And it will go on happening for ever. Like all good cons, it is not the product that is important, hence the bizarre and worthless quality of the 'goods' that created these booms. It is the schmuck's belief in the conman that matters. While we continue to behave like schmucks, we will continue to have a destructive and periodically catastrophic financial system.

The money that we use every day has been created in an inequitable and secretive way and is not subject to the democratic controls we would expect of something so important in a democratic society. For this reason I would recommend that those dedicating their lives to moving towards a humane and sustainable economy should extract themselves from the money system as far as possible. I am not suggesting a retreat to survivalist communities such as Tinker's Bubble for all of us, but it is worth replacing your current attitude towards money with a more questioning and suspicious one. It is at the point where you deal in money that you are allowing the pernicious economic system most to control you. Using mutual or ethical banking and mortgage services is some sort of response, but a more powerful one is undermining the power of money altogether by operating outside the money system as much as possible. Pointless acts of kindness and the gift economy are reserved for Chapter 8, but to conclude this chapter I would like to recommend a tactical compromise with the money system rather than slavish adherence.

Capitalism is a pyramid-selling scheme that is backed up by the financial system. Money will grow out of control. Economists may not be honest enough to admit all of this (although Galbraith gets pretty close), but they do not deny that booms and slumps are symptomatic of capitalism. The powerful are happy to accept such an unstable system because, when the crash comes, they will be the first to know and have the power to insulate themselves against it. But in terms of you and me, such a money system is just a guarantee of future disaster for ourselves and those we love. It is not difficult to conceive of a stable and just financial structure. The only reason we do not have one is that the unfair and unstable structure we are clinging to at present works to the benefit of those who have the power to change it.

politicians

7

Taking the Labour out of Work: Reconnecting Producers and Consumers

> The wages of work is cash.
> The wages of cash is want more cash.
> The wages of want more cash is vicious competition.
> The wages of vicious competition is – the world we live in.
>
> D. H. Lawrence

Something has gone very wrong in the workplace. In Chapter 1 I presented various data to indicate that we in the developed and wealthy societies are unhappy. Something ails us that we cannot quite define, but it certainly cannot help that we detest our work so much that we spend most of the year dreaming of our two weeks in the sun and the retirement to follow.

I offer as evidence of this desperately inefficient time-management strategy an advert for Thomson holidays during which we watch a lone, poolside sunbather repeatedly shifting his sun-lounger to catch every possible ray, while we are informed that 'for every afternoon in the sun you have to work three weeks and two days'. There are a number of points about the image conveyed by this advert that are both symbolic and deeply troubling. First, *the man is on his own*. Are we to assume that he prefers spending his holidays alone, that his perfect escape is to a place where there is only his own company? Second, he is sitting by a swimming pool and yet *he never swims*. Like so many lives, the really enjoyable activity is missed because the central character, economic man, is distracted by the sun-lounger or his drink or the shadow, or whatever. But most importantly, he is enjoying not being at work because *he does not like his work*. His holiday represents an escape from his life, which is made unpleasant because of work he undertakes from pressure rather than from choice.

This is the greatest offence that capitalism does to a species that has as one of its central psychological drives the need to carry out useful work in conjunction with others. We are persuaded to miss the point, to spend our lives working for holidays and retirement rather than demanding employment that is intrinsically rewarding. I have written about this at great length elsewhere, so for the purposes of this chapter I shall focus on reminding readers of how life felt when people controlled their own work, before the coming of capitalism and the sort of work that is all, in one way or another, wage slavery.

A couple of times while seeking financial support for my PhD research into work in the South Wales Valleys, I have been made aware of the ignorance of the nature of working people's lives by the middle-class people who make decisions about them, and the complacency they have when considering the work of others. The shock they feel when their cosy work structures are removed by the new management practices is the only good I have to say for them. As an example of the attitude I despise, during an interview with one grant-making body I tried to justify my decision to consult local workers in the South Wales Valleys to ensure that they might not be forced to do jobs they detested. The very debonair and neatly groomed man who chaired the panel looked at me pityingly and told me that he sometimes did not want to come into work in the morning. He did not know that I had worked in the office next door to his, which was in a Georgian building in Oxford with a leafy garden attached, and knew how pleasant conditions were for an Oxford academic. The contrast with the life of Valleys workers, to which he was sublimely indifferent, filled me with rage. More recently, my application for a funding grant was rejected on the basis that 'Whilst the idea of "participatory employment policy-making" is quite interesting, it is open to the accusation of being somewhat utopian.' In my response I pointed out that even in medieval Europe, according to a Muttenberg ordinance, 'every one must be pleased with his work'.

> We are laughed at when we say that work must be pleasant, but – 'every one must be pleased with his work', a medieval Muttenberg ordinance says, 'and no one shall, while doing nothing, appropriate for himself what others have produced by application and work, because laws must be a shield for application and work'.

This chapter is guided by the belief that 'everyone must be pleased with her/his work'. If that principle is not followed in an economy, the economy is not working properly. We can, and should, do better than an economy where miserable people work in pointless occupations for three weeks and two days just to spend a lonely afternoon by a swimming pool. Work as it is constituted within capitalism is not only economically inefficient and socially destructive, it is also spiritually offensive: 'Soul-destroying, meaningless, mechanical, monotonous, moronic work is an insult to human nature which must necessarily and inevitably produce either escapism or aggression, and . . . no amount of "bread and circuses" can compensate for the damage done' is how Schumacher made this point.

To put this labour-market failure into perspective, this chapter presents a few historical insights into employment. I begin with a brief exploration of Marx and his views on work, before arriving at the heart of the matter: the organization of work by guilds of skilled craftsman. As a Green I am very wary of using the insights of history in case I am accused of wanting to go back to the horse-and-cart. In this chapter I take the risk because the organization of production by specialists rather than by salesmen is so clearly a superior system, and because ignorance of history, especially social history, is a key explanation for our failure of imagination when it comes to reorganizing our economy.

Marx's concept of alienation

A famous critique of the nature of work within a market system is to be found in the writings of Karl Marx. One of his central concerns was the social and psychological effect on the individual of life within the market. As expressed by Terry Eagleton, Marx's view was that 'Under market conditions, individuals confront each other as abstract, interchangeable entities; working people become commodities, selling their labour power to the highest bidder; and the capitalist does not care what he produces as long as he makes a profit.' So there is nothing original in the critique of the anti-globalization protestors, although they may not recognize the source of their complaint.

Marx reserved a special place for work in his analysis: he considered it to be the central expression of what he referred to as our 'species-being'. It is because what we do as a species is to work that the mutation of work into its capitalist form is so socially and psychologically damaging. It is this process which Marx refers to as 'alienation', meaning that the items which people produce with their work are appropriated by the minority of people who own the means of production: that is, the employers or, in today's terms, the global corporations. As Marx puts it in his *Early Writings*:

> This fact simply means that the object that labour produces, its product, stands opposed to it as something alien, as a power independent of the pro- ducer. The product of labour is labour embodied and made material in an object, it is the objectification of labour . . . In the sphere of political econ- omy this realization of labour appears as a loss of reality for the worker.

Interestingly, in connection with our wish to devise sustainable methods for the distribution of goods, Marx related this sense of alienation to our relationship with nature:

> Estranged labour not only (1) estranges nature from man and (2) es- tranges man from himself, from his own active function, from his vital activity; because of this it also estranges man from his species. It turns his species-life into a means for his individual life.

Box 7.1 LG: a cautionary tale about modern work

Wales is the classic case study of the failure of inward investment as a response to regional unemployment in the globalized economy. The most prominent disastrous investment was at LG, trumpeted at the time of its announcement as the largest inward investment ever into Europe. The project was in two parts and involved the construction of an integrated monitor plant and a microchip wafer-manufacturing plant on a greenfield site near Newport. The cost was £1,664 million for the promised creation of 6,100 jobs. The size of public-sector support was also a record at £248 million: that is, slightly in excess of £40,600 per job. The TV assembly plant functioned between 1998 and 2003, the larger semiconductor part of the planned scheme was cancelled, and in May 2003 it was announced that only 350 employees would be kept on. Most of the £250 million of development grants had disappeared into LG's international debts, while the actual size of subsidy per job had risen to £124,000.

   The fiasco of LG demonstrates the economic fallacy of relying on foreign corporations, but the social consequences have not been evaluated. This is the story of one unemployed worker who was employed by LG in 1999:

> The workforce performed the same job for up to 12 hours per shift, on a continental shift pattern. What I did observe in this period was the turnover in staff. What you should understand is the mind-set of such a place. From a management perspective all that matters is 'the line' and its output. Any notion of loving your workers and treating them fairly is for the middle classes and office workers. From the workers, it was how much pay and what can you get away with? The main fear for British management after any long break, such as summer shutdown or Christmas, was just how much of the workforce would return?
>
> The [wage] structure was, as I remember it, basic plus 40%, 25% and 15% shift premium. So, 12 hr, 3 × 8 hr or double day. I got basic + 40% so I was well paid, relatively, for what I did and the hell I was working in. The reason for the lower wage in south Wales is that social costs are far less than in Europe. I cannot comment on low wages in Wales in general. But in south-east Wales I ended up on £16,400.
>
> Certainly from the comments both inside the plant and outside, the £200 million was not spent totally on the plant, either building it, or equipping it. The buildings both inside and out rapidly became shabby. The equipment broke down and never seemed to be properly repaired. Strange approach, for a company that's here for the longer term. Again from rumour and speculation, I do not think the plant ever made a profit. At major management briefs, which the whole

workforce attended, we were always shown financial detail and how much in loans the parent company owed. There was speculation by the workforce on how we could stay afloat and that the company had asked the Welsh Development Agency for more funds.

From the middle of 2003 . . . there were rumours circulating of impending cuts or closure. Maintenance of production machinery was cut. People who left who provided support functions on the shift were not replaced. Staff numbers per section on production were cut. Naturally LG protected itself by having plants like this in Mexico, China and other low-cost locations. The plant convenor was of the personal opinion that no glass product would be made in west Europe in 5 years. To shore up market share the Koreans joined forces with Philips of the Netherlands, with the new HQ in the Far East.

So were there any benefits? Personally it kept me off the unemployed register and gave me insight into the world of global manufacturing. Possibly witnessing the end of mass manufacturing. For the local agency, which was tasked with supplying staff for the site, it was a bonanza. It was rumoured that the money made from LG enabled them to have a purpose-built premises on a new business park opposite the LG complex.

Finally, in the business section of *The Times*, 10 July 2004, p. 55, LG Philips reported a net profit of £328 million.

Source: Many thanks to the anonymous contributor for this insight.

In other words, the process of work and the creation of products that are bought and sold by others destroys the individual sense of self and radically undermines our identity.

I took this point on in a paper I presented to a conference on identity in 1996. My central point was that the process of alienation and loss of identity has been extended by the globalization of the international economy. I supported my argument by drawing a comparison between work in an MFI furniture factory and the work carried out by Adam Bede, the eponymous carpenter-hero of George Eliot's novel. Adam Bede's work links him directly to the other members of his community. He makes an intricate kitchen cabinet for the employer of the woman he loves, in the hope that this will catch his beloved's eye and win her heart. How distant this portrayal of identity and relationship in work is from the life of the person who tends the machine that turns the thing, that makes the pin, that joins the leg to the bed, that they sell on the industrial estate. He or she has no idea where the item will be sold or used, never mind by whom. And similarly, when we shop we have little idea where or by whom the items we buy were made. We lose our sense of connection and the producer loses their sense of identity.

In response to this loss of identity, and particularly for those who are too poor to adopt brand-based consumer identities as discussed by Baudrillard, we see a rise in identity groups based on gender and ethnic identities. This unfortunate response to globalization has long been predicted and yet appears to surprise and horrify the Establishment when it expresses itself in large numbers of votes for politicians who base their appeal on the offer of an identity. In spite of radicals' and environmentalists' warnings of the imminent depletion of natural resources or the collapse of the financial system, it seems that the most dire threat to globalized capitalism is actually posed by the loss of identity created by the meaningless and exploitative systems of both production and consumption that it feeds off. So the survival of liberal democracy requires a solution to the problem of the alienating market system. According to Oliver James, therapist and social critic, so does our happiness as a society. His best-selling book identified the competitive ethos of capitalism as playing a central role in increasing rates of unhappiness and clinical depression.

What economists mean by a free market and by monopoly

This chapter focuses on the system for work organization that preceded the capitalist work form: the medieval guild system. Conventional economists, when they have considered the guild system at all, have criticized it as a system based on monopoly. According to a critic writing at the high-point of capitalism, guilds

> shackled free commercial intercourse . . . blindly aimed to reduce free competition to a minimum, regarded what we now consider legitimate speculation as a crime, deflected from the town every powerful current of trade, mercilessly obliterated the spirit of mercantile enterprise, and crushed out every stimulus to extensive production. The municipal atmosphere was surcharged with the spirit of rigid protection.

Yet according to a recent reanalysis of the evidence on medieval guilds, these apparent 'monopolists'

> seldom regulated wholesale trade, often allowed other 'monopolists' to enter their markets, frequently sold merchandise similar to, in the same market as, and competing for customers' attention with merchandise of other 'monopolists', and never possessed authority over venues outside of their hometowns where they sold most of their merchandise.

Guilds have been portrayed as a threat by economic historians not because they operated systems of monopoly or opposed freedom but because they represent a system of interaction between production and distribution that worked for the benefit of society and the producer rather than for the advantage of the capitalist, and that prioritized the quality of the product and social justice above profit.

Before discussing the contribution that may be made to a new system of distribution by insights from medieval production systems, some time should be spent outlining the framework within which the discussion takes place: that is, providing an outline of the existing distribution system as viewed by economists. Arguments for the superiority of the market system of distribution are based on several assumptions that cannot be validated in the modern, global economy (see Chapter 2). The concept suggests that buyers and sellers freely choose to come to 'the market' to exchange their goods at a mutually beneficial price. It is important to notice that these buyers and sellers might once have been producers and consumers, but it is very unlikely that this will any longer be the case. This chapter looks back to the time when the producers of goods did organize the selling of their own products through the guild. As will be explained later, one of the central roles of the guild was to exclude middlemen who did not produce but merely extracted some of the value of the product made by somebody else. By contrast, in the modern economy, this extracted, non-earned wealth sustains most of those in employment, whether they are advertisers, chief executives, or shop assistants.

The important question in an economic analysis of markets is: who has the power to determine the price of the product sold, and its quantity? Economists are generally less concerned with the 'quality' of the product, simply building in a usually unrealistic assumption that all examples of a given good are 'homogeneous': that is, the same. In the neoclassical explication of the ideal type of market, which operates under a system of 'perfect competition', neither the buyer nor the seller is able to influence the price. This is a consequence of the large number of buyers and sellers. So if the seller sets the price for an item too high, buyers will be able to find somebody else selling it cheaper and can buy it from them. This explains the economic objection to any kind of price fixing, which we will see later was another central function of the guild. But it fails to take into account the tendency for producers to consolidate into fewer, large groups – a tendency that has become particularly pronounced over the past 30 years. In a situation where there are, for example, five large supermarket chains, or four clearing banks, it costs the managers of these concerns little to ensure that their prices are relatively comparable and it would be against the interests of all to cut prices drastically, even if that might attract more customers.

It is also important to note that, in the late form of capitalism, profit matters to the exclusion of all else, including the product. I am afraid that whenever I think about this the example that comes to mind is always ladies' knickers, so I hope you will bear with me if you have never bought these. There was a time when Marks & Spencer just made good knickers and you could always buy them there. They may have been a little bit more expensive than other people's, but the extra was worth paying because the knickers were comfortable and lasted. In the underwear department, these are important considerations. But I challenge you to find a decent pair of underwear in today's high street. If we consumers rule, why can't we find a pair of quality knickers? I have created a special underwear test (which I have patented, to retain my intellectual property, as the Cato Drawers-and-Window Test). This involves holding your underwear up to a source of light to check the strength of the weave. You will be shocked by the result. We are living with knickers our grandmothers would have rejected as shoddy and worthy only of cleaning windows. Neoclassical economics would suggest that there is a market opportunity here for somebody who produced a decent pair of underwear. I would certainly pay a premium price. But instead all suppliers of these items are competing on price, outsourcing production to Vietnam or the Philippines, using only the cheapest materials, so that knickers are see-through and fall apart within months. This is the way the best profits are made, and the best knickers are no longer of any concern.

On a more serious note, this is an inevitable consequence of the concentration on shareholder value. M&S has come under pressure from shareholders, in part because it was one of the companies which tried to show commitment to an indigenous workforce in the UK. Shareholder value forces managers to squeeze the last penny out of the production cycle, sacrificing quality to profits. The traditional economic production method

> is not a realizable project for industrial and commercial company managers whose corporations are caught on a fundamental contradiction between what the capital market requires and the product market allows (at least without special-case advantages of immateriality or intellectual property rights). The result so far is a redoubling of management effort with an intensification of all forms of restructuring (such as horizontal merger, divestment and downsizing) which in different ways swap high and low ROCE [return on capital employed] activities, reduce the capital base and sweat out labour for usually transient gains.

The discussion of medieval guilds that follows shows how they balanced the needs of producers and consumers, and the strictures of price and quality, far better than the global market of the twenty-first century: 'The masters did not provide much testimony on how they viewed the question of competition; the calculus of different factors seems to have weighed in favour of emphasizing quality and individual craftsmanship at the expense of competing on the basis of price.'

In a modern context, we can imagine the development of cooperatives towards the same ideal, where 'sharing power in a democratic setting can reconcile these interests [the competing interests of stakeholders] by focusing on the common purpose of all co-operatives – creating wealth by producing excellent goods and services that enhance the quality of life for all'.

Lessons from the dark ages of capitalism

When I was at school, the clever girls studied political history. They had the opportunity to learn the names of a great many men and the precise dates when they ordered other groups of unnamed men to kill each other. The stupid girls studied economic and social history, which was perhaps considered more relevant to future housewives and their domestic economy, or perhaps was intended to provide more refined titbits for dinner-table conversation (notwithstanding the changing of the Pastons' underwear). Whether through good fortune or chronic low self-esteem, I chose social and economic history, which was one of the best choices I ever made. The history of these islands is replete with lessons to inform anyone seeking to improve the present human situation, of which medieval guilds are one. In this section I explore the role they played in the medieval economy and society, and suggest drawing some lessons from the experience to inform the sustainable distribution system we may propose to replace the global market.

It is hard to establish any exact dates for the inception of craft guilds. The first documentary evidence that is available is from the twelfth century, although it makes it obvious that guilds already had a long history at that time. Their development was a natural consequence of the need for organization in the steadily growing European cities, within which the marketplace enjoyed special protection. The most thorough source of information concerning guilds in England was provided by the fortunate discovery of the Census of 1388 in the basement of the Chancery in London in the middle of the nineteenth century. This provides a full picture of the central role played by guilds in the economic life of England at that time. The following sections summarize the various roles played by guilds.

Economic role

The concern of the craft guilds was to preserve the skill of their particular method of production; rather than competition between themselves they cooperated to ensure the highest standard of product. Three methods that 'entrepreneurs' of today specifically favour as a method of gaining maximum profits were specifically banned by the guilds, namely:

- forestalling (buying up merchandise before it reached the market, i.e. acting as middlemen and extracting value without producing anything);
- engrossing (stockpiling to force prices up);
- regrating (buying and reselling where prices might be higher).

Since one of the methods used by a monopolist to extract economic rent is to raise prices by restricting supply, it is clear that guilds were acting directly against monopolistic practices. In fact ideas about fairness and justice lay at the heart of guilds' concerns. Laws forbade the creation of barriers to entry and exchange, and banned the manipulation of prices and quantity by suppliers.

A prominent advocate of the medieval guild system was Prince Petr Kropotkin, who viewed it as an example of the sort of system of mutual aid he thought should replace centralized state bureaucracy. Here is his glowing account of the economic function of the guild:

> The craft guild was then a common seller of its produce and a common buyer of the raw materials, and its members were merchants and manual workers at the same time . . . An idea of 'justice' to the community, of 'right' towards both producer and consumer, which would seem so extravagant now, penetrated production and exchange. The tanner's, the cooper's, or the shoemaker's work must be 'just', fair, they wrote in those times. Wood, leather or thread which are used by the artisan must be 'right'; bread must be baked 'in justice', and so on. Transport this language into our present life, and it would seem affected and unnatural; but it was natural and unaffected then, because the mediaeval artisan did not produce for an unknown buyer, or to throw his goods into an unknown market. He produced for his guild first; for a brotherhood of men who knew each other, knew the technics of the craft, and, in naming the price of each product, could appreciate the skill displayed in its fabrication or the labour bestowed on it.

He draws special attention to the influence such a system of organization had on the attitude towards work, and the way work relations influenced social relations generally:

> Therefore, the predominance taken by the old craft guilds from the very beginnings of the free city life guaranteed to manual labour the high position which it afterwards occupied in the city. In fact, in a mediaeval city manual labour was no token of inferiority; it bore, on the contrary, traces of the high respect it had been kept in the village community. Manual labour in a 'mystery' was considered as a pious duty towards the citizen: a public function as honourable as any other.

Other significant economic powers of the guilds included:

- setting quality standards for production: those not meeting them could be expelled;

- setting the price paid for materials and labour and for final product;
- when necessary, fixing production quotas for members to ensure sufficient production to meet needs and prevent competition between members;
- guaranteeing loans for members who needed to buy equipment or premises;
- operating a system of risk sharing and pooling of assets – for example, in the case of expensive export ventures.

The issue of quality control is an important one. In a competitive market, producers will try to find ways to 'undercut' other producers, either by using cheap materials, or by making the item rapidly and poorly. This is the reason it is so difficult to buy quality products in today's global market, even if you are prepared to pay more for them. By contrast, the members of the guilds prided themselves on the quality of their work. Obviously the issue of quality was closely linked to that of price. In the medieval guilds, the concept of 'the just price' was paramount and it was the guild's duty to fix this, subject to an acceptable quality of product.

Such a system of price fixing would be anathema to the capitalist market, and might indeed lead to distributive inefficiencies. But this is not to suggest that producers should lose all control over their product and its quality. Since markets are socially determined institutions, we might choose to learn from this pre-capitalist form of production control while still allowing the market to play a primary role in the distribution of goods in exchange for money.

Educational role

It seems logical that an organization responsible for the quality of production of a particular item should also take on the role of training, but the educational remit of the medieval guild extended much further than that, in a time before any general provision of education. Guilds controlled membership and in order to join a young man (or, more rarely, woman) had to serve a seven-year apprenticeship and then work as a 'journeyman' or a daily paid worker. In order to become a guild 'master', he or she had to produce a piece of work of sufficiently high standard, known as a 'masterpiece'. Guilds monitored the apprenticeship system and inspected the working conditions of both apprentices and journeymen, but their educational role also extended beyond the technical expertise of their craft. They also established minimum general educational standards for apprentices, who were expected to learn to read and write, to master basic arithmetic and to have religious instruction. The skills of the particular trade were passed on from the older person to the younger, and along with them the more diffuse 'mysteries'. Yet it is clear that an important social function was also taking place, something that might nowadays be referred to as mentoring. The rite of passage into the adult world that is so difficult for citizens in industrialized societies, and especially for boys, was largely undertaken by the guild master.

Political role

Guilds played an important role in the administration of medieval cities. The City council was made up of representatives of the various guilds, who also paid taxes for their right to exercise control over their craft. The guilds were responsible for the town's security, both by taking on the up-keep of a particular section of the defensive wall and by providing men for the town militia. When the German emperor Barbarossa attempted to take the city of Legnano in 1177, he was defeated when the members of the butchers' guild of Milan attacked his army with the tools of their trade, including cleavers, large cutting knives and pole-axes. The guilds also provided equipment and manpower for local fire defence and guard duty. They underpinned the city's administration by supporting local magistrates and by providing members to serve in the local courts.

It is important to consider these various roles of the guilds together, rather than focusing exclusively on their economic role. Part of the problem of the global economy is that corporations are able to operate both their buying and selling activities in a footloose manner, paying no regard to the social and political consequences in the countries that they operate in. In the UK the growth of the organization Business in the Community is a recognition of the need to address this dislocation, as are the numerous examples of corporate sponsorship, but these initiatives are a far cry from genuine grass-roots connection such as that offered by guilds of producers. The movement from the guild system to the wage system was not an easy one. We may wonder about the social and psychological repercussions of the decline of guilds. How were men and women who had found their identities in carrying out useful production within a cultural framework defined by the guild to change to a condition of wage slavery? It may be no coincidence that the decline of the guild system was shortly followed by the development of Puritan sects whose ideology of work in one's own station was an invaluable support to the new employers.

The guild socialists

The system of guilds was swept away by the rapid expansion of a money- and trade-based economy during the Renaissance, so it is not surprising that early critics of capitalism looked to the economic organization that predated it and especially at the medieval guild. Building on the work of William Morris, Robert Owen and John Ruskin, at the turn of the twentieth century a group of socialists – especially A. J. Penty, A. R. Orage and C. H. Douglas – did exactly that through the movement for guild socialism. It seems fair to say that at this time there was a struggle for the soul of socialism. This struggle is often portrayed as between the revolutionaries, who wanted to overthrow existing political structures through violent rebellion, and the revisionists, who wished to use an extended franchise and education to move towards a fairer society without violence. But this account of history leaves out one of the heated debates of the time which has since been portrayed as a path to nowhere: the idea of cutting the link between income from employment and survival. This was the debate which, in the early years of socialism, was led by the guild socialists:

> In essence, guild socialists opposed wage slavery. They sought an end to the commodification of labour, whether under the capitalist or the collectivist state. Hence they sought economic democracy as a means to a classless society, rather than industrial democracy for the working class alone. A core concept of guild socialism was the promotion of 'all corporate work to the level of vocation', uniting in real fraternity all whose industrial destinies are intermingled. From the outset, guild socialists demanded nothing from industrial capitalism. Rather, they explored the potential for the construction of a viable alternative.

The guild socialists shared much with the modern green movement, particularly an understanding that the economic system, and the system of work at its heart, is destroying both the planet and the spiritual life of humankind. Their harking back to medieval structures was based in a conviction that the values of simplicity and respect for craftsmanship were lost at the onset of capitalism. It was the 'denial of the opportunity for creative labour that represented the quintessence of capitalism's inequity for it was this that robbed humanity of what was necessary to be fully human'. They rejected the focus on price at the expense of quality and the loss of status of people as producers in favour of people as consumers, and they linked both these trends to the growth in shoddy products, 'the cheapness of which is paid for by the lives of their producers and the degradation of their users'. For the guild socialists, state socialism as represented by the electoral politics of the Labour Party was a means to the end of an empowered, locally based society: 'a transition period during which people would be getting rid of habits of mind bred by the long ages of tyranny and commercial competition and be learning that it is in the interest of each that all should thrive'.

These ideas have found new life in the revival of the cooperative movement, discussed in Chapter 3, and in the green movement. Nothing proves the need for such ideas better than the futile weapon of the strike, which is still the primary tool of the trade union and labour movement. This futility is best demonstrated by the ritual threats to strike by impotent union leaders whose factories are closing so that jobs can be relocated in China. One can almost imagine the corporate manager's sarcastic comment: 'Ooh, I'm scared.' Use of the strike is a proof of weakness; it represents working people advertising the fact that their only power is by virtue of their labour. Far from challenging their status as wage slaves, they are actively participating in its entrenchment. 'Although the Marxian analysis of capitalism informed socialism in general, the emergence of a Labour Party based on a single class of the wage-earners was bitterly resented by many socialists as leading to the perpetuation of capitalist–labour relations, and hence of capitalism itself.' Kropotkin shared this analysis, criticizing 'the political emphasis of Labour politicians on the right to work, as preceding the right to well-being. Surplus value existed because men, women and children were forced of dire necessity to sell their labour for a fraction of its productive value. From such a perspective, the right to work was a strange demand for socialists.'

The guild socialists perceived the trade unions not as exercising lobbying power on political parties but as directly controlling production. They would be integrated within an industry, rather than focusing on strict class and craft distinctions. They argued that medieval workers maintained control over their work and its quality, rather than being subject to any employer. This was of infinitely more value than accepting existing power relations and then arguing for a better share with the ultimate threat of merely withdrawing labour, and hence self-starvation. They agreed with the argument put forward here that the market system focuses solely on price, to the detriment of the quality of product and of the producer and consumer alike: 'the demoralizing tyranny of an uninstructed majority interested only in the cheapness of what they seek to purchase'. They also rejected the distinction between producer and consumer, on the logical premise that we all play both roles in a developed society and that any attempt to reorganize an economy from one perspective or the other leads to a pointless conflict. We are divided from and ruled by one another in our simultaneous roles as producer and consumer.

At the time, this thinking was dismissed as naïve and idealistic, partly because of its commitment to the spiritual importance of satisfying work under one's own control. In fact this offers the perfect response to Marx's problem of alienation, but the hard-nosed rejection of anything non-materialistic has continued to blind socialists to this reality right up to the present. The defeat of the proponents of a utopia based on good work by those who consider utopia itself a pejorative term has led to a world where the meaningless consumer existence and the right to a new sofa every year is considered progress enough.

The fall and rise of the craft guilds?

The system of control by artisans which the guilds represented was incompatible with the rise of capitalism, which required the surplus value generated by the makers of goods to be reinvested for the creation of future profits or paid to the owners of capital. The beginning of this process of expropriation and reinvestment of surplus occurred with the expansion of the wool trade around the turn of the thirteenth century: between the 1280s and the first decade of the fourteenth century the number of commercial transactions in wool almost doubled in England. The wool was exported to Flanders to be turned into cloth; the trade itself and the finance for it were based in the northern Italian city states, especially Florence:

> Already by the end of the Middle Ages something which we might call capitalism had appeared in Flanders and Florence; that is to say that industry and a system of finance were being organized by the rich owners in order that they might become more rich. This system, with all that it implied, had by the seventeenth century largely replaced the stable order of the Middle Ages.

This early form of capitalism is usually referred to as 'merchant capitalism' to distinguish it from the industrial capitalism that followed. The weakening of state power relative to economic power is already becoming evident by 1353, with the king's reliance on the taxation of trade in wool to fund his wars in France. This is now considered one of 'several important aspects of London life', of which the strength of the merchant patriciate was another.

In a striking parallel with the present situation, Nelson writes that 'After 1350 markets began to grow smaller, and the powerful long-distance merchants had to lower their costs in order to compete.' This led to the 'putting-out system', especially common in the weaving trade, where producers rented equipment and worked on a piecework system for merchants, who made the profit from their labour. Later equipment came to be concentrated in factories, where workers were simply hired on a wage basis, the final end of the system of independent work and skilled artisans cooperating through producer organizations. The manufacturing guilds fought the development of these proto-capitalist forms: historical texts offer some evidence that they did not go down without a struggle. In the mid-fifteenth century the traditional system of rotating the powerful position of Lord Mayor of London around the various craft guilds of the city was challenged. In 1439 and 1440 Ralph Holland, the contender from the tailors and drapers guild, was passed over for the position of mayor. In 1440 John Paddesley, a goldsmith, was chosen instead. The guilds organized resistance to this loss of status and power; armed gangs of artisans took to the streets:

In London a political struggle was at play between artisans and merchants, between those who produced and those who bought, distributed and sold at great profit. Through a subtle interplay of their wealth and court patronage, the guilds of tailors and drapers tussled over primacy as governors of their city.

The money was on the side of the merchant capitalists and the goldsmiths who bank-rolled them, and the king took the same side because he needed money loaned by the bankers or taxed from the merchants to pay for his foreign wars. It was this constellation of interests that overpowered the guilds and turned the independent skilled workers of the 'dark ages' into the wage slaves of industrial capitalism. Despite their narrowly defined economic success, the merchants neglected entirely the social, political and educational roles that the craft guilds had played, which led directly to the deterioration of social standards in the later Middle Ages, greatly exacerbated by the industrial revolution. The abandonment of production controls also had severe economic consequences, with the development of the boom-and-bust production cycle which modern economists consider an inevitable part of economic life, but which is only really an inevitable part of the capitalist production system.

The end of the power of guilds in the economic sphere paralleled the growth in power of the merchants and their developing role as proto-capitalists – those who owned the means of production and organized the distribution of products without actually being involved in production themselves. Workers ceased to be the owners of the product and eventually came to own only their labour-power, which they were forced to sell to ensure their survival. Part of the role of the guilds was later filled by trade unions, but the nature of unions and their range of concerns is testimony to the fact that people who were independent producers are now sellers of their own labour in a 'market' for human physical effort. As unions have been challenged with growing legal and political opposition in recent years, and as employers have moved production to regions of the world with low labour standards, most production takes place under the exclusive power of the corporation.

So what lessons can we take forward from this experience of the medieval guilds? First, in spite of the erosion of the religious faith which supported it, the lesson about the importance of spiritual well-being in the economic sphere is well made. A second lesson is the importance of maintaining ownership and control of our economic activity and our skills. This is what the guild system guaranteed above all. And through this ownership came a regard for good workmanship and higher-quality products. Identity in work was strong, as was the sharing of skills within the group. This had many social spin-offs in the Middle Ages, and the re-development of a similar system could challenge many of the problems created by capitalist work systems in terms of isolation, alienation and depression, at the individual level, and loss of civic pride and community spirit, at the group level. Schumacher expressed the tragedy of the loss of these more rooted work systems: 'Social cohesion, co-operation, mutual respect, and above all self-respect, courage in the face of adversity, and the ability to bear hardship . . . no amount of economic growth can compensate for such losses.'

There is not space in this book to discuss fully ideas for the respiritualization and rehumanization of work, but it is worth mentioning Schumacher's development of the concept of 'right livelihood', one of the requirements of the Noble Eightfold Path of Buddhist teaching. This defines a threefold purpose of work: to utilize and develop the faculties; to overcome an egocentric tendency by joining in a common task; and to produce goods and services that contribute to a 'becoming existence'. Such a spiritually grounded ideal of work would surely help to counter the prevalent feeling of despair and alienation we find amongst the employed and the unemployed alike in our *soi-disant* advanced capitalist society.

Stone Age economics: citizens' income, self-provisioning and income pooling

The purpose of the system of work under capitalism is twofold: we work to earn money to buy stuff, and we make the stuff that we later buy. Our satisfaction is defined in terms of that stuff. Product development and innovation jointly ensure that there is always new stuff to be bought, and built-in obsolescence and advertising jointly convince us that we need, or feel that we need, more stuff. Thus capitalism consumes energy and resources and generates wants and work. We are more dissatisfied than our primitive ancestors, whose societies have been described as the original affluent societies and whose approach to production and exchange is described in terms of 'Stone Age economics':

> There are two possible courses to affluence. Wants may be 'easily satisfied' either by producing much or desiring little. The familiar conception, the Galbraithean way, makes assumptions peculiarly appropriate to market economies: that man's wants are great, not to say infinite, whereas his means are limited, although improvable: thus, the gap between means and ends can be narrowed by industrial productivity, at least to the point that 'urgent goods' become plentiful. But there is also a Zen road to affluence, departing from premises somewhat different from our own: that human material wants are finite and few, and technical means unchanging but on the whole adequate. Adopting the Zen strategy, a people can enjoy an unparalleled material plenty – with a low standard of living.

This conclusion is based on anthropological observation of hunter-gatherer societies, whose people are always well provided with food and who spend far more time in leisure activities and far less in work than members of industrialized societies: a group of native Australians from Fish Creek spent an average of 5 hours per day gathering and preparing food (their 'work') while the Hadza of Tanzania, who have not been pushed into more marginal land, spend less than 2 hours per day on average on this activity.

Much of this chapter has been devoted to a consideration of work arrangements in medieval times. In spite of our preconception that life was 'nasty brutish and short', we find that then days were defined not by the absence of work, as we define our 'bank holidays', but rather by the absence of a religious festival, the *dies non festivus*, which was a day when you unfortunately had to work. E. P. Thompson describes the difficulty the early capitalists found in organizing their workforces to obey the clock and to abandon Saint Monday, the day spent recovering from the excesses of the weekend rather than working.

The movement from feudalism to the industrial society was the final removal of any rights of subsistence without paid labour. The medieval peasant enjoyed various rights to graze cattle on common land, collect firewood, glean following harvesting, and so on. Most people who lived on the land also had some plot on which they could grow food for their own survival, making them able to subsist without paid work. This system was swept away with the enclosures, which turned land into a profitable asset: as Simon Schama has pointed out, sheep were more valuable than tenants, and capitalist logic justified the eviction of people from their homes and the elimination of their ability to subsist. This is a new kind of disempowerment:

> Capitalism is the first economic system in history that does not give access to resources as of right to the citizens of a country. Resources, goods and services are available only to those who have money, not to those who live within the boundary of a national economy.

The dependence on money income began gradually, with the loss of resources to grow food and build or heat homes. From having enjoyed considerable rights and freedoms UK citizens became paid labourers, in the burgeoning factories of industrial Britain.

Many of the first-generation migrants to the industrial cities continued the tradition of subsistence by keeping a pig or a few chickens in their yard, and the culture of subsistence was carried forward by the allotment movement, which arose at the time of movement from land to cities, from the late eighteenth century onwards. This ideal of self-reliance has been eroded by generations of wage slaves and the increasing commodification of our food supply, so that a large proportion of our population can now no longer even cook food. Contrary to the myth of independence and choice, the market economy has in fact made us utterly dependent:

Where wage labor expands, its shadow, industrial serfdom, also grows. Wage labor, as the dominant form of production, and housework, as the ideal type of its unpaid complement, are both forms of activity without precedent in history or anthropology. They thrive only where the absolute and, later, the industrial state destroyed the social conditions for subsistence living. They spread, as small-scale, diversified, vernacular communities have been made sociologically and legally impossible – into a world where individuals, throughout their lives, live only through dependence on education, health services, transportation and other packages provided through the multiple mechanical feeders of industrial institutions.

This is not to argue that production for exchange is a new phenomenon, just that within capitalism it takes on a special significance, where growth is measured solely as the growth of capital and, if you consume what you have produced, you are considered not to have produced.

In other societies, remnants of subsistence remain, although they are under pressure from the encroachment of the market. If you have ever puzzled about how the people of Russia can survive on such low and falling income-per-head figures, it is because of a systematic underestimation of the importance of subsistence to the Russian economy under communism via the system of dachas. These 'country estates', as they are often portrayed, were continued by Stalin, who was aware of the vulnerability of centralized food distribution. Citizens were required to grow food on their allocated piece of land, usually owned by a family rather than an individual, and only cultivated during the relatively short Russian growing season. The produce of this land could be preserved to keep alive many Russian people outside the market economy, whose rapid introduction following 1990 led to such chaos.

The process of enclosure and the exclusion of people from the land is continuing today in the developing world:

> The same thing is happening now in other parts of the world – to the arctic peoples being deprived of their means of livelihood by the pipeline operations of oil and gas companies, to the equatorial forest peoples being deprived of theirs by multinational loggers and ranchers, and to Asian and African peasants being deprived of their livelihood by big dams and other development projects sponsored by national governments and the World Bank.

The response to the denial of subsistence and the sucking of provision into the marketplace is to reclaim your right to provide for yourself by boycotting processed foods and making for yourself. You can begin by giving Auntie Bessie her marching orders and cooking your own Yorkshire puddings. Nothing is easier to make than batter, and once you have it mastered you can also make yourself pancakes whenever you want. For those who already know how to cook for themselves, the next step is thinking where the food comes from, prioritizing food grown locally and by farmers' cooperatives, or even growing your own food, either in your garden or by finding an allotment.

Your next step might be to think about making your own clothes and renovating or even building your own home, perhaps in cooperation with others. You may have heard of the latest movement to have the capitalists quaking in their boots: guerrilla knitting. The political content relates to the need to re-empower ourselves rather than buying all clothes off the peg, but there is also a great deal of humour and camaraderie in this attempt to reinforce and revive important self-provisioning skills. Self-build is better established and has a longer history. The focus here is on environmentally sensitive building, as well as enabling those who are cut out of the housing 'market' because of speculative buying and selling to provide their own homes for themselves and their friends.

A solution to the subsistence problem in terms of money is to cut the link between earning and survival by introducing a payment to each citizen as their share of the national income, or 'common wealth'. The proposal for a basic weekly income from the state as of right, generally referred to as a citizens' income, would 'break down the market-imposed boundary between paid work – i.e. employment – and unpaid work such as domestic labour'. Robertson has gone further, proposing a change to the taxation and benefits system that shifts the burden of taxation away from unemployment on to pollution and land, generating enough to pay for the introduction of a citizens' income (of around £55 per week) over a 10-year period.

A DIY version of the citizens' income can be achieved through an income pooling scheme, such as the Snowball group in the east Midlands which has been running for 20 years. The members – five adults and one child – pool their earnings and redistribute them according to need. Snowball meets every two weeks, when each member declares his or her income and need for spending. The two highest earners are a part-time management consultant on £322 per week and a youth worker. The experience has been educational, as one member explains: 'I am quite clear that what anybody earns is no measure of the person or their worth to society.' The benefit of the system is that members do not have to be in continuous full-time employment, allowing them a chance to develop alternative life paths.

Conclusion

Work is a key part of the capitalist power system. It is a means of extracting our energy and turning it into profits for somebody else. This explains the disgust for those who would rather couch out and enjoy the sunshine amongst capitalist apologists such as Niall Ferguson. He decries continental Europeans' longer holidays and shorter working weeks and days, as well as the higher levels of unemployment and industrial action in mainland Europe. Overall the average 'American', US citizen we assume, worked nearly 2,000 hours per year, compared with a mere 1,535 by the average German, some 22 per cent fewer hours. This sort of hysteria at the failure of the work ethic gives the clue to who might be the beneficiaries of the work system, and it is certainly not those who do the most work. More interesting is the fact that the quality of the work carried out is of less importance than its quantity. In spite of their reputation for short weeks and long lunch-breaks, the French have the highest output per man-hour amongst OECD countries, while productivity levels in long-hours UK workplaces are much lower than in continental Europe.

Most of the work that most people in advanced industrialized societies are engaged in is pointless. Worse than this, it is consuming scarce energy, producing CO_2 and using up resources without achieving much in terms of human well-being. The whole process seems so illogical that some years ago I was forced to conclude that the system only exists to justify a grossly unequal allocation of material value. After all, if a single mother with three children has to survive on less than £1,000 per month while the bosses of corporations earn that much in less than an hour, the immorality is obvious. But Mr Fat Cat can always claim to have worked hard for the money and we must accept this as justification.

Within the carbon-limited economy of the twenty-first century, we cannot afford to be so wasteful. The built-in obsolescence of late capitalism must be replaced by an ethic of reduce–reuse–recycle. And we must also challenge the social waste, the waste of creativity and human spirit which call-centre jobs represent. We must develop jobs for ourselves that allow us to feel pride in our work and its products; such work could become part of our 'right livelihood'. It could be organized through a modern version of the medieval guilds, and would be owned and controlled by ourselves as members of cooperatives. We should not see work as an end in itself, and should do our best to minimize the work needed, rather than creating work. Only somebody who was set to benefit from the work of others would want to do something that would seem so insane to the members of a society we might label 'primitive'.

8

Together We Can Do Better Than This

Life is short; play more
Microsoft X-box advertisement

The main achievement of the apologists for capitalism lies in having convinced its opponents of the inevitability of the system, so that we feel coy or embarrassed about suggesting we would like our economy organized according to a different pattern. They have not been backward in coming forward with overpowering assertions as to the inevitability of the market system. Caroline Lucas, a valued colleague in the quest to create a sustainable alternative to capitalism, discussed this 'huge public relations exercise' in the annual Schumacher lecture she gave in 2002:

> According to Renato Ruggiero, former Director General of the WTO, trying to stop globalisation is 'tantamount to trying to stop the rotation of the earth'. For Bill Clinton, globalisation is 'not a policy choice, it's a fact'. Tony Blair has called it 'irreversible and irresistible'. It's clear that these descriptions of globalisation are deliberately designed to pre-empt any radical alternatives being proposed. And yet, to seriously suggest that fundamentally challenging the dominant economic paradigm is somehow equivalent to trying to reverse inexorable cosmic laws is a pathetically crude political device that I think all of us should reject.

Rather than Galileo being punished for questioning the laws of physics, we can now feel ourselves to be heretics for questioning the hegemonic economic system of capitalism. Such arguments are also marshalled to indicate the inherent weakness and illogicality of any who might oppose the onward march of capitalism. In this vein, Michael Portillo described the anti-globalization movement as 'a largely incoherent, Canute-like attempt to resist the inevitable'.

The reality is very different, and if there is one message I would like you to take away from this book, it is that capitalism is a recent and insecure template for organizing economic life. It has been the dominant economic system in the West for only some 200 years, and has gone through some pretty shaky times during those two centuries:

The assumption of the naturalness and inevitability of capitalism masks its rather insecure history. It was not until the latter half of the nineteenth century that the model became secure in the UK through the combination of legislation and colonialism. By the early twentieth century it was undermined by a global recession only to re-emerge within the nursery of post-war reconstruction. By the 1960s and 1970s the cracks were showing once more. In the mid 1970s in the UK and the US an ideological coup was staged by neo-liberals largely through the Chicago School. That model is now under threat from anti-globalisation forces, the instability of stock market and currency values and the threat of global recession.

Before the advent of capitalism the understanding of what was morally and socially acceptable in terms of economic activity was utterly different. The charging of interest on loans was outlawed by the Church, as were many other forms of profiteering, then referred to as 'usury':

> Such awareness of the ethics of business coincides with contemporary pastoral treatises, which listed types of usury, analysing the many injustices and sin inherent in the habitual forms of exchange, profit-sharing, lending and investment. One such text opens with the words: 'usury shows itself in many manners' and lists twelve types of lucre.

This description of the moral strictures imposed on 'business' refers to a period in the late Middle Ages on the cusp of capitalist expansion, at a time when economic activity was still subject to religious authority: 'the world of economics was subject to moral law; in particular usury, the lending of money on condition of receiving extra money on repayment, was regarded as a sin; so was avarice, or the desire for gain itself'. The TINA mantra so beloved of Thatcherism (There Is No Alternative) is precisely intended to prevent us thinking of alternative ways of running the economy. This is why emancipating yourself from mental slavery, in the words of Bob Marley, is a subversive act in itself.

The first section of this final chapter will discuss in rather more detail a number of ways in which we have been inveigled into going along with a system that works against most of our interests most of the time, and how you can gradually extract as many parts of your life as possible. Then I introduce you to some friends you might not know you have: others who have seen the errors of capitalism from its earliest days to the present. The following section offers some hopeful signs from the discipline of economics before I challenge you to play your part in replacing global capitalism.

As a whole, this chapter is intended as an invitation to join me and the new virtual friends you will become acquainted with later in this chapter in the most important project of all. I dare say that if you have stayed with me this far, you are already committed to several individual causes, protecting the rainforest or trafficked women or starving children. If you have ever wondered why these worthy causes keep proliferating in spite of the investment of so much energy by so many good people I would have to join Bill Clinton in telling you that 'It's the economy, stupid.' This is the conclusion I reached several years ago, and I have found it far more efficient and more fun to go direct for the source of the problems that have always depressed and enraged me. I hope I can tempt you to share in this important work.

Capitalism as religion

Capitalism is a powerful economic system, but more importantly it is also a system of ideas. We grow up with such ideas in childhood and reinforce them in our dealings with each other. The ideas are communicated, maintained and elaborated through a system of mantras, which operate to control our thinking and to tie us in to a nasty, selfish way of behaving in society. I've listed some of the most popular in Box 8.1, with some suggested replacements. On the principle that it would be a good idea not to do the opposition's work for them, I would suggest you begin to eliminate these from your vocabulary, and challenge them when used by others. Some of these are rather insidious. For example, if you believe that there is no such thing as a free lunch, it makes you feel like a 'loser' (a tremendous capitalist concept) every time you give something away, such as a lunch for your friends. Your act of generosity immediately becomes a gesture that requires reciprocation. Against the backdrop of this mantra, gift becomes exchange. Kindness is lost to capitalism. I am making a collection of these as a consciousness-raising exercise, so please send others on a postcard or by email.

The way to reject the mantras is through active intellectual subversion. If you find one of the mantras pops into your head, or that you are responding to it in your behaviour, you need to switch it for something that has the opposite consequence. I once saw a poster for a band called 'Shocking Insanesburys'; the name is subversive in itself, since the comfortable task of supermarket shopping has been ideologically challenged. The band-name is more accurate for the nature of consumption in modern capitalism, which is no longer about satisfying desires but rather about bringing the competitiveness of production into our homes. A stampede at a newly opened Ikea outlet (see the story in Box 8.2) demonstrates the desperation people feel about establishing their identity through consumption.

The fetishization of home furnishing has reached such a pitch that people no longer invite friends into their homes for the shame of what they might find there – last year's style of sofa would be social death. Fashion was always capitalism's favourite child, but it has now been allowed to run around all areas of our lives, throwing tantrums if we dare to

Box 8.1 Countering capitalist mantras

There is no such thing as a free lunch.	Food is for sharing.
You can't get something for nothing.	Unless you are a shareholder or landowner.
Everybody has a price.	Generosity is its own reward.
Time is money.	My time is my own.
If you're so clever, how come you ain't rich?	If you're so rich, how come you ain't happy?
Nothing in life is free.	The best things in life are free.
Money makes the world go round.	Love makes the world go round.
We need to protect our wealth.	We need to rely on the love of others.
If it isn't hurting, it isn't working.	If I can't dance, I don't want to be part of your revolution.

express our individuality rather than buying the latest designer label. The brand has become an expression of who we are, and those who can only afford the cheaper brands are themselves branded as losers. To avoid this shame a friend insists on pronouncing Lidl as *lidèle*, imbuing the pile-it-high-sell-it-cheap supermarket with a continental air that saves his blushes.

This is all unnecessary sacrifice at the altar of the growth fetish, that *sanctum sanctorum* of neoclassical economics exposed so brilliantly by Richard Douthwaite in *The Growth Illusion*. In spite of the money, energy and intelligence spent persuading you of the need for elaborate consumption patterns, this particular mindgame – elsewhere I have called it 'Sen and the art of market-cycle maintenance' – is easily defeated. You can get together with your friends, green friends are particularly useful for this, and establish your own ethic of consumption based around minimizing carbon and maximizing self-expression.

As for another favourite capitalist mantra, I can state on the basis of an experiment I conducted that I have disproved the hypothesis that there is no such thing as a free lunch. A couple of years ago, I was invited to a 'seminar' arranged by a financial services company. I had a few qualms about having my lunch provided by a major global investment corporation, largely relating to the length of the spoon that would be required, but

Box 8.2 Sofa madness

At one minute past midnight last night, Ikea's new flagship store opened in north London, and managers expected that around 2,000 bargain-hunters would quietly file in. The British, after all, have a reputation for being decorous queuers. But Ikea had not predicted that up to 6,000 people would descend on the new store, in Edmonton, with a stampede to get in resulting in a frightening crush.

Thousands had been lured by bargains – some of which were only available until 3 a.m. even though a 24-hour opening was planned – such as 500 leather sofas for only £45. Cars were abandoned on the roadside as shoppers attempted to reach the store in time to secure the best offers.

Six people were taken to hospital, including a man in his 20s who was stabbed nearby at around 1.30 a.m. He was said to be in a stable condition, and it was not clear whether the incident was related to the opening.

According to a senior fire officer, 'There were crush injuries and people suffering from shock from the pushing and shoving.' Nine ambulances attended the scene.

Source: M. Oliver, 'Slowly but steadily, madness descended', *Guardian*, 10 February 2005.

I reassured myself with the thought that I could treat the occasion as an experiment to explore whether there is, in fact, such a thing as a free lunch. I was highly interested in who my fellow seminaries might be – these people whose money the corporations use to desecrate the planet and maim and destroy millions of lives. It was hard not to baulk at the overtly 'civilized' tone of the surroundings, but by the time the lunch finally arrived I was well aware that several others were also in the church-mouse brigade and just there to enjoy it. And what about the lunch? It was actually rather good and I haven't had to pay anything yet. I noted clearly on my questionnaire that I did not want to meet anybody from the company to discuss my financial affairs, and waited with interest to see whether it worked, knowing I could probably dispel the hounds with a few back copies of my bank statements if the need arose.

The growth in individualist pensions and investments has diffused the location of blame for the gross exploitation that typifies the globalized economy. Just as the message of *Our Common Future* was that we were all responsible for planetary destruction, we are now told that we are financing the activities of the corporations through our pension funds or savings and are hence so deeply implicated that we can no longer make moral statements of outrage. My experiment with the free lunch and the encounter with a financial services salesman taught me how this method of co-option works. Like much of the propaganda in support of capitalism, it is based on fear. Our shiny-toed salesman began by earnestly explaining the need to 'protect our wealth' against an unidentified threat, and outlined the 'dangers' our financial strategy had to 'overcome'. Other threats, such as the inability to pay for long-term care – an 'increasing concern' – and the 'wasting' and 'squandering' of wealth (for example, by spending it), were peppered throughout the presentation, just to keep alive that sense of insecurity that would make us feel the need for his generous expertise.

Our financial friend seemed keen to assure us of two things: we were unsafe but he was an expert who could guarantee our safety in the future. I had the feeling that I wasn't the only person in the room who had grasped the fact that he needed to prove the second point in order to justify the salary that had paid for that expensive suit he was wearing, which had been accounted for from the fees of other investors just like us. I was, perhaps, the only person who knew that a recent competition to choose the share portfolio making the best returns over a year – run by a financial paper – was won by a friend of mine and her A-level economics class. Their winning formula? Basing their choice of shares on the same shares' performance in the previous quarter. She does not have an expensive suit.

It appears that such salesmen of capitalism have not been entirely successful. Despite the many years of propaganda, we have not abandoned care for our fellow man or woman. We still overwhelmingly support a health service paid for from taxation and would rather a decent pension for all was organized along the same lines than be left to the wolves of the financial markets. In Chapter 3, I described at length the closure of the Vaux Brewery on Teesside. Part of the reason for its closure was the need to increase 'shareholder value' in the parent company, justified on the basis that shares in that company needed to generate an income to pay the pension funds of retired workers just like those at Vaux. At a liaison meeting he had organized to try to save the brewery, the Bishop of Durham said 'I doubt whether a trade union pensioner would want to know that his pension was made more secure at the expense of jobs in the north-east of England.'

Money is at the heart of the economic system called capitalism, and this is the place where you can begin to extract your own life from that destructive and damaging system. Box 8.3 offers some further ideas for challenging capitalism in your everyday life in practical ways. Most of this chapter is about thinking your way out of the capitalist value system, but there are also practical steps you can take. It is important not to be daunted and to maintain your awareness that, as you extract your energy and money, along with millions of others, you are weakening the system.

As well as reviving the old hippy commitment to 'pointless acts of kindness' (paying the toll for the person behind you is a particularly

---

Box 8.3 Ten ways to challenge capitalism that wouldn't frighten your grandmother

1   Arrange to buy your vegetables through the nearest organic box scheme.
2   Switch all your bank accounts to the Nationwide or another mutual building society.
3   Shop at the Cooperative – better still, join your local coop.
4   If you work in the private sector, cut your hours of work at least by half.
5   Cook more at home, for yourself and your friends.
6   Don't vote, unless the party you vote for has stated anti-capitalist economic policies.
7   Whenever you are talking to somebody involved in business, ask them if their business is a cooperative, and have something to back yourself up if they ask why you asked this question.
8   Get an allotment.
9   Cut down on your coffee intake, and make sure that what you do buy has been fairly traded.
10 Before you buy anything, ask yourself how much you know about who made it and how, and move towards products where you have more information and closer ties.

---

subversive one of these), two additional concepts that are valuable in undermining the capitalist worldview are the *gift economy* and the *ethic of plenty*. If the mantra of capitalist economics is 'everything has a price', we can create a powerful subversion strategy by giving away things we could sell. By refusing to accept money in exchange for something that could be sold, we are beginning to create a gift economy. Anybody who has brought up a baby has direct first-hand experience of the gift economy. As soon as you are out of hospital, female friends and relatives arrive with their old baby clothes until you find yourself overwhelmed with them. It is one way in which women prove their instinctive willingness to give freely to each other. Women's natural skill in creating a gift economy may relate to their inferior power in the money economy. Research indicates that those with smaller financial resources are far more willing to give to those in greater need than themselves.

The virtual gift economy is now under way, thanks to the worldwide spread of the concept of 'freecycling'. This is an extension of the concept of recycling of consumer goods that we probably already support through the local furniture recycling centre. It offers three advantages that are essential to a green economy: reducing waste through the reuse of bulky consumer goods; reducing energy use through the removal of the need to produce new goods; and meeting the needs of people with inadequate money for those goods. The internet version was launched in Tucson, Arizona in May 2003 and has spread worldwide. Each local group has a moderator who can update details of members and goods available for gift. You may well already have a local group, or may feel like starting one in your area. You can find details at www.freecycle.org. Freecycling is very much focused on operating outside the money economy and so is an important part of the new gift economy.

The ethic of plenty is more problematic because it is important to think of the 'wealth beyond measure' of Paul Ekins' famous early book on green economics, rather than the addictive consumption of our capitalist economy. The pressure to consume actually arises from our sense of scarcity; if we felt trusting of nature's bounty, we would not feel so desperate to store up valuable items in this world. You can find evidence for this in the hoarding behaviour of those who lived through the war, the last time we experienced real scarcity in the UK. The change of mindset required to feel that you have sufficient when others are enjoying higher material standards of living is a challenge we must all take on. Elsewhere I have explored the way in which the combination of the concept of 'relative deprivation' and the advertising industry create a world where we will always feel the need for more. The maintenance of this feeling of scarcity is necessary to encourage the increasing consumption that economic growth requires:

> Modern capitalist societies, however richly endowed, dedicate themselves to the proposition of scarcity. Inadequacy of economic means is the first principle of the world's wealthiest peoples. The market-industrial system institutes scarcity, in a manner completely unparalleled and to a degree nowhere else approximated. Where production and distribution are arranged through the behaviour of prices, and all livelihoods depend on getting and spending, insufficiency of material means becomes the explicit, calculable starting point of all economic activity.

Enough is a vital concept: if we have enough, we are not deprived. To learn this we need to begin to share the mindset of subsistence societies, like those reported by Marshall Sahlins. Working more hours and buying more things will never bring us sufficiency, just an endless cycle of more unsatisfied wants, and more work to earn the money to satisfy them.

Three assumptions underlie the ethic of scarcity:

- There is shortage and if I do not immediately take my share, there will not be enough for me. This understanding is partly one of the many unacknowledged consequences of the wartime rationing experienced by the older generation who have bequeathed us their fears, but is reinforced constantly by advertising urging us to buy now before stocks expire.

- You must take what you can now and then keep it. Giving to somebody else will mean you are left short of something you need. This leads to hoarding of unnecessary items which might be useful to somebody else.
- You will be left without and there will be dire consequences because nobody will help you.

In other words, it is an ethic based on fear. To turn these around we need to create our own ethic of plenty with the following assumptions:

- There is plenty for all our needs: nature is bountiful when we treat her with respect and care.
- Sharing is good for the giver as well as the receiver and moves us towards the kind of world we want to live in.
- You can trust others to look after you: we are better at looking after each other than selfishly competing.

But most important in the move towards the ethic of plenty is to be clear what sort of things you want plenty of. I suggest that every time you feel afraid about providing yourself with the necessities of life, or you feel mean-spirited, you visualize the cornucopia of Greek myth. That is what your mother, Gaia, provides you with, so as the bumper sticker says: 'Love your Mother'.

You'll never walk alone

When spending your life building the replacement for capitalism, it is easy to feel lonely. I began this chapter by pointing out that the prime success of the market system, and conversely its prime weakness, is the fact that it has convinced us that There Is No Alternative. To achieve this, the contributions of those who believed in, fought for and in some cases died for a better alternative have been eliminated from official histories. We all collude in this practice every day when we fail to remember our ancestors in the struggle against this oppressive and exploitative system. So in this section I am going to introduce you to some friends who have shared in the project. Some of these are familiar friends, but others have been stripped of their radical credentials for ideological reasons and you might be rather surprised to find they were as hotly opposed to capitalism as we are.

Percy Bysshe Shelley (1792–1827)

My first and personal favourite is one of our foremost national poets, Shelley. He has been rather eclipsed by Keats in recent school syllabuses, but he remains a towering literary figure. Yet the fact that his work and his life were dominated by revolutionary fire and rage against social injustice has been airbrushed away. Even his death in a 'boating accident', while a social and quite possibly political exile in Italy, has been portrayed as the mishap of a romantic fool, while a government-sponsored assassination seems much more probable. Thanks mainly to Matthew Arnold, doyenne of the respectable Victorian literary establishment, Shelley the political firebrand has been reduced to the big girl's blouse of the *Blackadder* TV series.

Shelley was famously sent down from Oxford for his atheistic views and his first important political poem, 'Queen Mab' (1813), is directed at the Christian attempt to exploit people on earth by promising them a heavenly paradise in return for their obedience. Instead the poem suggests the creation of an earthly paradise and was rampantly libertarian in tone and content. Shelley had the poem printed at vast expense on high-quality paper in the hope of attracting the aristocracy, whose children at least might read it. The theme of 'Queen Mab' gave no immediate hint of the revolutionary content. Although Shelley has been championed by some socialists, his prescription for change, which he thought should be 'gradual – albeit total', seems to have more in common with a green political strategy. He also supported civil disobedience in contrast to an extended representative democracy, which he believed could always be corrupted by the powerful. He shared the green view of the role of the intellectual in undermining the governing assumptions of an unjust society, discovering the truth and then daring to speak it. 'In historical moments when the political and cultural are deeply interconnected, when cultural signs and symbols are essential to the preservation of power, when the government would call upon any and all "ideological state apparatuses" from religion to reactionary reviews, then cultural intervention has political and social consequences.'

Shelley lived in the tumult of the early days of capitalism, while the industrial cities were growing out of control and independent artisans were losing their livelihoods under pressure from the get-rich-quick factory owners. It was the era of Ned Ludd, and a work of his with contemporary resonance is a pamphlet he wrote on the death of Princess Charlotte, the cause of histrionic public mourning, which bemoaned the execution of three Luddites for opposing the destructive march of progress. As well as prefiguring anti-capitalism, Shelley also opposed the imperialism of the English state in Ireland, which he visited during his teens and during one of its periodic famines, caused by the extraction of its resources by English lords and the control of its economy for the benefit of English interests.

Inevitably in view of his other interests, Shelley displayed a strong interest in economics, a nascent discipline at the time, and the way it was used to maintain the interests of the rich and powerful. His ability to cut through the verbiage of banking practices is impressive, although perhaps the lack of development of the economics discipline and its chicanery assisted him here. By 1820 Shelley had already made arguments like those presented in Chapter 6 about the way the monetary and banking system is used to channel money from the poor to the rich. His *Philosophical View of Reform* argued that 'the public debt is a system for transferring income from the labouring segment of the population' to those who had money to lend to government and would thus accrue interest, and who profited from government expenditure in wars. He related this process to the debasement of currency through the printing of paper money, an argument parallel to that used by monetary reformers for Nixon breaking the link between dollars and gold to fund the Vietnam War some 150 years later. Shelley notes the link between power and money once a real link with gold is broken: 'All great transactions of personal property in England are managed by signs and that is by the authority of the possessor expressed upon paper, thus representing in a compendious form his right to so much gold, which represents his right to so much labour.' The system thus enables those with power to use money to extract labour from others. Such a system does indeed increase 'the national industry', but Shelley correctly identifies that this means 'to increase the labours of the poor and those luxuries of the rich which they supply . . . to augment indefinitely the proportion of those who enjoy the profit of the labour of others as compared with those who exercise this labour.' His radical conclusion is that the consequences of this new system, which we would now have the benefit of calling 'capitalism', 'have been the establishment of a new aristocracy, which has its basis in fraud as the old one has its basis in force'.

Song – To the Men of England (1819)

Men of England, wherefore plough
For the lords who lay ye low?
Wherefore weave with toil and care
The rich robes your tyrants wear?
. . .

Have ye leisure, comfort, calm,
Shelter, food, love's gentle balm?
Or what is it ye buy so dear
With your pain and with your fear?

The seed ye sow another reaps;
The wealth ye find another keeps;
The robes ye weave another wears;
The arms ye forge another bears.

Percy Bysshe Shelley

Shelley himself wrote extensively on a very modern theme: the way scientific and technological advances are used not to create the earthly paradise for all, but to generate profits for the few:

> The cultivation of those sciences which have enlarged the limits of the empire of man over the external world, has, for want of the poetical faculty, proportionally circumscribed those of the internal world; and man, having enslaved the elements, remains himself a slave. To what but a cultivation of the mechanical arts in a degree disproportioned to the presence of the creative faculty, which is the basis of all knowledge, is to be attributed the abuse of all invention for abridging and combining labour, to the exasperation of the inequality of mankind? From what other cause has it arisen that the discoveries which should have lightened, have added a weight to the curse imposed on Adam? Poetry, and the principle of Self, of which money is the visible incarnation, are the God and Mammon of the world.

If we substitute a word like 'imagination' for what Shelley called 'the poetical faculty', this quotation has immediate relevance to our political project.

Jonathan Swift (1667–1745)

Swift is at first sight a much less promising revolutionary. Unlike Shelley he was subtle – hence his use of parody, satire and allegory – with one eye always on the possibility of position and preferment. Unlike Shelley he met no sticky end but lived to a good age and was granted the living of Dean of St Patrick's Cathedral, Dublin. But as an Anglo-Irish Protestant he was a double outsider, giving him a unique perspective on the English exploitation of the homeland that he struggled to come to terms with, and a rage that only the colonial experience seems able to generate. As a pattern for living with oppression and surviving, and using black humour to expose its viciousness even to its perpetrators, Swift has no equal.

Like our other friends, his shade lives on associated with that most benign of forms, the children's story, for this is how *Gulliver's Travels* is usually read, it taking degree-level education to begin to unpick its now outdated satire. Even there, however, we see a clear statement of Swift's political interest in Gulliver's statement that '*Poor* Nations are hungry, and *rich* Nations are proud.'

Swift's central target was the exploitative, what we would now call imperialist, relationship between England and Ireland. In *The Story of an Injured Lady* (written in 1707), he describes the economic abuse at the heart of the relationship by analogy with an abusive sexual relationship. He describes the unequal power relationship between the two countries: 'If your little Finger be sore, and you think a Poultice made of our *Vitals* will give it any Ease, speak the Word, and it shall be done; the Interest of our whole Kingdom is, at any Time, ready to strike to that of your poorest

Fishing Town.' The sacrificing of Ireland's interests to those of England was seen most clearly in the political control of trade to benefit the developing capitalist economy of England. Swift's arguments to this effect in a pamphlet he wrote in 1720 are similar to those used by Gandhi nearly two centuries later; in Swift's case it was the wool trade, in Gandhi's the cotton trade. His suggestion that Irish women favour domestic textiles to protect the Irish poor was an exact parallel to Gandhi's arguments about *khadi*.

His most famous polemical attack on the relationship between England and Ireland is the viciously satirical *Modest Proposal*, which is a classic parody of economistic thinking proposing the sale and consumption of Irish children. The scheme is minutely planned and costed, with its 'projector' enumerating the six advantages: a reduction in the number of troublesome papists; an increase in income for tenants who can thus pay higher rents; an increase in GDP; a reduction in the expense of child-rearing; variation in the board of fare; and an inducement to marriage. With the domestic needs for meat met within Ireland, beef and pork would now be available to be traded for English tables. The whole discussion is horrifying but it is also a brilliant parody of the rational economic calculus that is equally valid today, when we read justifications of the export of luxury food crops for western tables while children in the countries where they are grown are starving. Like modern economics it works because the projector never questions his own insane and immoral assumptions.

Swift was writing nearly a hundred years before Shelley and at a time when the financial system which was needed to support the development of capitalism was just being developed. He was fortunate enough to view at first hand the instability of this way of generating money, as he lived through the boom and bust of the South Sea Bubble (1711–20). He did not share Shelley's insightful analysis of the power structure lying behind the monetary system, but he did recognize that the shortage of coin in Ireland was related to the link between Irish currency and English currency and the unequal power between the two, just as Argentina has found its currency vulnerable because of its link with the dollar.

William Morris (1834–96)

William Morris is best remembered now for his designs for wallpaper and soft-furniture coverings and also for his statement that you should keep nothing in your house that you do not consider either useful or beautiful. Thus has another radical thinker been neutered and turned into a creator of marketing slogans. In fact if you search for this quotation on the internet, you are most likely to find it recommending homeware items on eBay. For one of the founders of British socialism, this is a travesty as well as a tragedy that would no doubt have Morris himself spinning in his grave.

Morris began his professional life as a craftsman, specializing in interior decoration and the creation of designs derived from the medieval revival movement popular at that time, perhaps as a response to the final destruction of its social forms by the dominance of industrial capitalism. His thinking is the foundation for the green political economy we are building today in its commitment to social justice, to the right to subsist without paid work, to the revaluation of craft, to the importance of quality in all things to replace the market-oriented obsession with quantity. Morris was interested in beauty, but it was not a physical beauty disembodied from social and economic realities. For Morris the origin of beauty was nature, and its disfigurement by injustice must be fought as vehemently as its loss in contemporary design.

For many commentators, Morris was one of the founding fathers of English socialism, more influential in its early days than Marx and Engels. Morris was cynical about the wage system, and shared many of the criticisms made in Chapter 7 of the conflation of 'work' and 'labour':

> Most of those who are well-to-do cheer on the happy worker with congratulations and praises, if he is only 'industrious' enough and deprives himself of all pleasure and holidays in the sacred cause of labour. In short, it has become an article of the creed of modern morality that all labour is good in itself – a convenient belief to those who live on the labour of others. But as to those on whom they live, I recommend them not to take it on trust, but to look into the matter a little deeper.

He was equally swingeing in his attacks upon the imperialist capitalism of the British Empire:

> Whatever England, once so beautiful, may become, it will be good enough for us if we set no hope before us but the continuance of a population of slaves and slave-holders for the country which we pretend to love, while we use it and the sham love for it as a stalking-horse for robbery of the poor at home and abroad.

Morris was a formative influence on the guild socialist movement, whose ideas were explored and developed in Chapter 7. He believed in an economics of emancipation, a revaluation of human creativity and ingenuity, and the importance of a fundamental respect for nature. He was, as we should be, proud to be called a utopian, aiming to build the perfect society rather than just putting up with the shoddy one capitalism has handed to us.

Mahatma Gandhi (1869–1948)

It is impossible to do justice to the breadth of wisdom and knowledge in the thinking of Gandhi in the small space available here. Gandhi's political achievements have made it impossible for him to be dismissed from history easily. Churchill's derogatory reference to him as a 'seditious middle temple lawyer, now posing as a fakir . . . striding half-naked up the steps of the vice-regal palace' actually indicates that Churchill feared Gandhi, whose understanding of power was far deeper than his own. Of all Gandhi's sayings the one I find most valuable is: 'First they ignore you; then they laugh at you; then they fight you; then you win.' Here he had the last laugh over Winston. Another useful one to bear in mind is 'Strength does not come from physical capacity. It comes from an indomitable will.' At the time that Gandhi developed a strategy to defeat the British Empire, it was an economic system far more powerful than capitalism is today, and the nature of its collapse provides both inspiration and support to our cause.

In terms of the themes explored in this book, Gandhi's most relevant contribution is his concept of *swadeshi*, or self-reliance, which offers a prototype for the localization of the economy called for in Chapter 5. Gandhi lived his whole life at the sharp end of British capitalism and he understood it from the inside out. Using the insights of a subsistence economy, he saw the importance of a system of production and consumption of goods that was locally based and human-focused rather than dominated by the market. His salt marches and campaign for homespun cloth or *khadi* (the origin of the spinning wheel on India's national flag) were designed to achieve not just national independence but local and personal independence too:

> *Swadeshi* carries a great and profound meaning. It does not mean merely the use of what is produced in one's own country. That meaning is certainly there in swadeshi. But there is another meaning implied in it which is far greater and much more important. Swadeshi means 'reliance on our own strength'. 'Our strength' means the strength of our body, our mind and our soul.

The actions against the salt and cotton industries were not random gestures: they were well-aimed non-violent tactics to challenge the economic system that oppressed India. Here Gandhi has given us another most useful concept, *satyagraha*, or non-violent resistance. This tactic of analysing the problem, identifying its power and using a creative tactic to expose the oppressive nature of that power is at the heart of the actions against road building or war making followed by the green movement. Underlying this action is the need for *sarvodaya*, or a complete non-violent social transformation. As we transform our lives, change our ways of engaging in economic activity, and challenge the mental slavery of capitalism, we will be creating the new economy we want to see.

In spite of his having read none of the classic texts of western economics, Gandhi was asked to tackle the issue of economics directly in 1916, when he gave an address to a room of professional economists and said:

I hold that economic progress in the sense I have put it is antagonistic to real progress . . . That you cannot serve God and Mammon is an economic truth of the highest value. We have to make our choice. Western nations today are groaning under the heel of the monster-god of materialism. Their moral growth has become stunted. They measure their progress in £.s.d. American wealth has become standard. She is the envy of the other nations. I have heard many of our countrymen say that we will gain American wealth but avoid its methods. I venture to suggest that such an attempt if it were made is foredoomed to failure.

These words were spoken in 1916, but apart from decimalization they are just as valid today. During the question and answer session that followed the address, Gandhi responded to a question from Professor Jevons about whether it was necessary for economists to exist by saying that 'dirt was matter misplaced. So also when an economist was misplaced he was hurtful.'

Rosa Luxemburg (1871–1919)

Rosa Luxemburg is a good friend of the emancipatory economist. Like many Marxists, she focused especially on economic history, but she lived at a time when the experience of the expansion of capitalism on a global basis was still recent history, and when imperialist capitalism was in full swing. She takes up two issues of great importance to green economics: the destruction of the peasant economy and the struggle against the natural economy.

> The second condition of importance for acquiring means of production and realizing the surplus value is that commodity exchange and commodity economy should be introduced in societies based on natural economy as soon as their independence has been abrogated, or rather in the course of this disruptive process. Capital requires to buy the products of, and sell its commodities to, all non-capitalist strata and societies . . . For capital can indeed deprive alien social associations of their means of production by force, it can compel the workers to submit to capitalist exploitation.

Like so many critics of this economic system, Luxemburg saw the inevitable link between capitalism and war played out in real time, as she travelled across Europe trying to persuade elected socialist colleagues to vote against the war that would become the first global war. She failed, and the resulting history of horror and destruction was savagely attacked in her *Junius Pamphlet*, written in prison where she was serving a sentence for anti-war activity:

> Violated, dishonored, wading in blood, dripping filth – there stands bourgeois society. This is it, in reality. Not all spic and span and moral, with pretense to culture, philosophy, ethics, order, peace, and the rule of

law – but the ravening beast, the witches' sabbath of anarchy, a plague to culture and humanity. Thus it reveals itself in its true, its naked form.

She was also deeply sceptical of the economics discipline, which she viewed as deliberately obscurantist:

> It is but hollow phraseology and pompous prattle which we are being handed. And this in itself is an infallible sign. If you think soundly and if you have thoroughly mastered the subject under consideration, you will express yourself concisely and intelligibly. When you express . . . yourself in an obscure and rambling manner, you reveal that you are in the dark yourself – or that you have a motive for avoiding clarity.

Rosa Luxemburg was a role model for us all. As well as a thinker and a writer she was a political activist, and co-founder of the German Spartacist movement that later became the German Communist Party. She faced three serious disadvantages in the chauvinistic society she lived in, being a woman, Jewish and disabled. But it was not because of prejudice that she was murdered by those who had arrested her on behalf of the German state; rather it was because of her trenchant and rousing opposition to capitalism.

Joan Robinson (1903–83)

Joan Robinson was one of the most prominent economists of the twentieth century, a leading member of Keynes's circle at Cambridge, who was marginalized by the international profession because of her free-thinking attitudes. Her first major contribution was to challenge the theory of perfect competition and to substitute instead a theory of imperfect competition, offering ideas about how specific relationships to capital and the market could give some players an unfair advantage.

As a prominent economist of the 1930s, Robinson was particularly keen to make her subject relevant to the realities of the desperate slump: 'The Keynesian revolution brought us down from the neoclassical cloud-cuckoo-land, to here and now, facing the problems that we actually face.' She managed to draw useful insights from the work of Keynes but also from Marx, many of whose criticisms of capitalism she agreed with and whom she treated non-ideologically, as an economist rather than the bogeyman he had become to most economists. At the heart of her analysis was an interest in exploitation, which she shared with Marx. She provided a full-length discussion of the labour theory of value. Like Marx but unlike mainstream economists, her work did not ignore the importance of power in the allocation of value: 'The forces which govern the distribution of the product of industry between wages and profits are the central features of a capitalist economy.'

Her attitude to Marxian economics was much more positive than her attitude to neoclassical economics, which she considered almost entirely a waste of space: 'Robinson finds very little that is of use in terms of either her own research agenda or the pressing policy issues confronting contemporary economies. She advocates the abandonment, if not the utter destruction, of the entire neoclassical edifice.' She had much more time for Marx, not because she was a communist but because he was a better economist: 'Over the better part of four decades, Robinson drew heavily on Marx's ideas as she formulated and reformulated her own constructive contributions to economics.'

Robinson's idea of an economist involved a sense of duty to solve the problems of poverty, in her own society during the Great Depression, and also in developing countries.

> Effective demand in a capitalist world as a whole is interlinked through trade and finance . . . The United States is more than a major country, it is something like half of the whole. For our full employment we are largely beholden to holes in the ground that Americans dig. In the United States the declared military budget accounts for nearly 10 per cent of national income, and is equal to 60 per cent of gross investment . . . there is no physical, technical obstacle to prevent these resources from being deployed for peaceful purposes. But to do so would involve drastic political changes. Whatever might have been, in fact Keynesian prosperity has been a by-product of the Cold War.

The Iraq War has demonstrated the technologically advanced methods the USA has developed for creating holes, and the increasingly profitable way it has found to fund the refilling of those holes by manipulating the global financial system and the international oil market. Robinson's prescience touched many areas of economic life and her critique of capitalism is well worth reviving.

It is no coincidence that you have heard so much about Adam's Smith support for markets and so little about his concerns with morality. Nor that you have learned to associate William Morris with wallpaper rather than socialism. Radical critics of capitalism are marginalized. Their works are often neglected by publishers, while revisionist historians emphasize the anodyne aspects of their work and ignore its radical potential. Historians such as Francis Fukuyama and Niall Ferguson are lauded and promoted. It does not take much intelligence on the part of younger historians to spot the trend and abandon their more radical studies. But there is always a place for the critic, even if in the New Dark Ages it is sometimes difficult to keep the flame alight. This is a responsibility we must fulfil, if only because it is so much easier for us, with significant legal protections, than for others whose lives were destroyed by their beliefs.

As well as offering you a few new radical friends, I hope to have convinced my British readers of the radical potential of the country we live in and to rethink its history. We are not and never have been a nation of gardeners and beef-eaters. From the Peasants' Revolt and the Civil War, which were really two class revolutions, we have been a nation of dangerous radicals. The radical spirit that inspired Robert Owen and Tom Paine is now yours and it is our responsibility and our duty to take forward their confidence in the ability of mankind to live in justice and peace.

A conversion of economists?

In Chapter 2, I identified conventional economics as a key part of the problem with the global economy: as Joseph Stiglitz puts it, 'a triumph of ideology over science'. This triumph of pro-capitalist economics is a relatively recent development. Critical or 'anti-capitalist' economics was strong, especially in the UK, from the earliest days of that system's dominance. Its ideas led to the development of the cooperative movement, which may have provided nurturance of the early ideas of Marx. Towards the end of the nineteenth century, during a major international slump, vast popular movements were organized around the ideas of radical economists such as Henry George, whose *Progress and Poverty* was read by thousands across the globe. This activity was repeated in the economic crisis of the 1930s – then revolving around economists such as Major Douglas and Karl Marx – which was only ever satisfactorily resolved by the catastrophe of the Second World War. It is only since the end of that war and the deliberate hegemonic activity of US-trained economists, partly operating through apparently philanthropic activity such as the Marshall Plan, that European economics has become dominated by neoclassicists. The same process is now taking place to eradicate any alternative economic views from eastern Europe and the developing countries.

More recently, some economists who were trained in the conventional ideology have begun to ask some more interesting questions. An example was a session at the American Economics Association meeting in 2002 which debated the question 'Does money buy happiness?' The AEA has been the bulwark of conventional neoclassical economics, so although this question may seem banal to most of us, it is rather surprising to have it addressed there. We are probably less surprised to read the findings reported to the debate. Andrew Oswald, from Warwick University, has been researching this field for a number of years. His findings confirm the 'keeping up with the Joneses' view that what makes you happy is finding that you are at least as wealthy as most of the people around you. He concludes firmly that inequality, which I have argued throughout this book is an essential condition of capitalism, reduces happiness.

Within the discipline of economics there is now a major rebellion against the traditional narrow neoclassical line: the Movement for Post-Autistic Economics. This began in France in June 2000 when a group of students launched a web protest against the scientistic and dogmatic approach they were being forced to take towards this important subject. They called instead for a pluralism of approaches and an engagement with real economic problems. This is a political challenge to a system of thought that has long been about providing support for a single economic system rather than exploring alternative ways of arranging the distribution of resources. It has opened up the field to new thinking and real solutions.

A recent article in the *PAE Review* challenged directly the idea that growth brings happiness. It used the example of the tiny Himalayan kingdom of Bhutan, where King Jigme Singye Wangchuck committed the country to building an economy consistent with the country's Buddhist values after coming to the throne in 1972. The country was to focus on GNH (gross national happiness) rather than the conventional GDP (gross domestic product). In 2003 the government hosted a conference in the capital, Thimphu, with the aim of operationalizing the concept: that is, making it measurable. Bhutan has achieved significant advances in areas whose importance is unchallengeable, even if still, and perhaps forever, unmeasurable:

> Bhutan's insistence on the primacy of GNH over GNP inspires people far beyond its borders. Their commitment to GNH has meant that moral and ethical values are placed at the core of their economic strategies for ensuring better food, housing and health for their population of just over 710,000 people. It has allowed them to both expand their network of roads and increase their forest cover. In most other developing countries the arrival of roads is inevitably followed by deforestation. This is not to suggest that all is well in the Kingdom of Bhutan or that they are able to fully live up to their GNH commitment. Yet their achievements are notable.

Interestingly, work I carried out to explore the extent to which economies had moved into the new economic era of low carbon productivity also, and quite independently, identified Bhutan as one of the most advanced economies in the group (in Chapter 6, I discussed in more detail the research and the Contraction and Convergence model on which it is based). The measure I calculated is purely economic, relying on such considerations as the level of renewable energy that the economy uses and the sorts of goods it produces. It is amazing, and deeply reassuring, to find that an economy that has moved into the new era of sustainable production and consumption should already have demonstrated itself to be happier than the competitive, post-industrial economies most of us live in, and towards which other countries are encouraged to aspire.

We also have the support of a growing group of green economists and a burgeoning field of green political economy. The work of many of these economists has been drawn on throughout this book. I would mention especially Richard Douthwaite and James Robertson for their ground-breaking development of novel solutions. The additional feminist perspective of Hazel Henderson, Mary Mellor, Maria Mies and Vandana Shiva has deepened the commitment to care and subsistence that must underlie any sustainable economy. Frances Hutchinson has done important work reviving the work of economists whom capitalism would rather forget and, along with Mary Mellor and Wendy Olsen, has provided an excellent critique of the capitalist money system.

Conclusion: stop and smell the roses

As in so many areas of green economics, Richard Douthwaite is a great prophet of smelling the roses. At the end of a frenzied interview on the BBC's *p.m.* programme, about whichever latest economic crisis, he concluded by saying that he had just spent half an hour watching the bees feeding on a buddleia plant in his blissful garden on the west coast of Ireland. Interestingly, this is the only part of the interview that has stayed with me.

At the individual level, more and more people are giving up on as much of this competitive, dog-eat-dog economy as they can. Downshifting is becoming increasingly popular, with 12 million Europeans reducing their contribution to the economy by cutting their hours and accepting a reduction in earnings. Another 2 million, mostly better-educated people in their thirties and forties, have removed themselves from the labour market entirely. Their exit is more encouraging than the bare numbers suggest, since they are likely to be just the sort of creative and intelligent people that capitalism needs to make a successful adaptation to the new realities, and they are working on our side. At the individual level, we can make these decisions about our labour market involvement, and we need to follow them up with informed decisions about consumption and our involvement with the finance system. But this is not going to be enough. We cannot hide from the consequences of capitalism for ourselves or our planet. It will have to be tackled and replaced.

Smart and honest economists will admit that capitalism is a system which is far from efficient, and to an extraterrestrial it would appear irrational in the extreme. The humorous and avuncular posture they adopt towards this understanding is typified by the following famous quotation from J. M. Keynes:

> Ancient Egypt was doubly fortunate, and doubtless owed to this its fabled wealth, in that it possessed two activities, namely, pyramid-building as well as the search for the precious metals, the fruits of which, since they could not serve the needs of man by being consumed, did not stale

with abundance. The Middle Ages built cathedrals and sang dirges. Two pyramids, two masses for the dead, are twice as good as one; but not so two railways from London to York.

Ha ha! We can join in the joke, imagining ourselves in a large leather armchair at a London club, sipping brandy while the laughter of our peers loses its echo in the heavy wall-coverings. Except that this grossly inefficient and unfair system is now facing the sort of constraint that pulls this complacency up short. Even if economists might have argued that capitalism was the worst economic system apart from all the others, now that we have reached and surpassed the planetary frontier this languid response will no longer do. Our future depends on developing a system which is grown-up about resource constraints and responds to them intelligently and efficiently.

Sceptics will say that trying to replace globalized capitalism with a just and sustainable economic system is a misguided project. I am unconvinced by the claims of inevitability made on its behalf by its powerful apologists. Rather I take their increasingly strident tone to be evidence of the inherent weakness of their position. Most economic and political debates have a leisurely, almost enjoyable air, while history flows calmly on. But one issue has lent an irresistible urgency to this particular debate and that issue is climate change. This is a planetary limit, a real resource limit, which cannot be airbrushed away. First, the capitalists ignored the science and paid for their own lies to counter it. With the evidence of changing weather patterns all around, they have changed tack and are now working to adapt capitalism so that they may have their growth and their profits and their business as usual. But in reality climate change undercuts the unstable and unjust dynamic of capitalism as a system, and now is our chance to choose ways of arranging our economic affairs that would not only be better for the planet, but better for all of us too.

So, over to you. If you are worried about climate change or concerned about your own or other people's unhappiness, you know now that Bill Clinton was right: 'It's the economy stupid.' But the economy is not, as he has elsewhere suggested, determined by the irreversible and unchanging laws of capitalism. It is a system which is under political control, and since we live in a democracy it is, at least according to its own liturgy, under our control. You might think this is rather naïve, that if we challenged capitalism at the ballot box, democracy would rapidly be abolished. But we might at least call their bluff rather than willingly and passively cooperating in an economy and a polity that are not in our interests. The stakes are high, but the rewards are great. We have to think the unthinkable, and then we have to just do it.

Notes

Each source note below is introduced by a short phrase indicating the passage to which it refers on the page stated.

Chapter 1

p. 2   This is the sort of self-contradictory message . . .: *Consuming Passion: Do We Have to Shop until We Drop?* (London: Global Action Plan, 2004).

p. 3   The fact that ever-increasing consumption . . .: Hamilton, C., *Growth Fetish* (London: Pluto, 2004).

p. 3   The Worldwatch Institute . . .: *State of the World: The Consumer Society* (New York: Worldwatch Institute, 2004).

p. 3   Car use and the corresponding decline . . .: Roberts, I., 'The Second Gasoline War and How We Can Prevent the Third', *British Medical Journal*, 326, 18 Jan. 2003.

p. 3   A relationship has also been identified . . .: James, O., *They F*** You Up: How to Survive Family Life* (London: Bloomsbury, 2002); Lupien, S. J. et al., 'Can Poverty Get under Your Skin? Basal Cortisol Levels and Cognitive Function in Children from Low and High Socioeconomic Status', *Development and Psychopathology*, 13 (2001): 653–76; Matthews, K. A. et al., 'Does Socioeconomic Status Relate to Central Serotoninergic Responsivity in Healthy Adults?', *Psychosomatic Medicine*, 62 (2000): 231–7.

p. 3   between the West and the South . . .: I am using both these apparently geographical definitions as cultural or economic divisions, so that the West represents the capitalized, industrially developed richer nations, primarily the OECD, while the South represents the poorer nations whose economically vulnerable position leaves them open to exploitation by the nations of the West.

p. 5   Cocaine has a similar effect . . .: 'Low rank monkeys more prone to cocaine addiction', *New Scientist*, 20 Jan. 2002.

p. 6   The latest chapter . . .: 'Are Drugs the Answer?', *Telegraph* online, 27 Apr. 2004.

p. 6   This has been proven . . .: James, O., *Britain on the Couch: Why We're Unhappier Compared with 1950 Despite Being Richer: A Treatment for the Low-Serotonin Society* (London: Arrow, 1998), p. 230.

p. 6   532 million tranquillizers . . .: Foster, K., 'Prozac Link to Cancer Growth', *Scotsman*, 27 Mar. 2004.

p. 6   The most frightening aspect . . .: *Ecologist*, Mar. 2003.

p. 6   The idea that ADHD was invented . . .: 'Class action lawsuit against Ritalin maker asserts that ADHD was invented to sell drugs': www.pharmawatch.info/000081.html.

p. 7   people under 16 being given Prozac . . .: Townsend, M., 'Exam Fears Driving Teenagers to Prozac', *Observer*, 6 June 2004.

p. 7   A record 587 million drug prescriptions/offline survey . . .: Ahmed, K., 'Britons Swallow Cure-All Drugs: Commercially-Driven Hypochondria Means We Are Demanding Pills to Treat Everything', *Observer*, 26 Jan. 2003.

p. 8   26 million prescriptions . . .: 'Are Drugs the Answer?', *Telegraph* online, 27 Apr. 2004.

p. 8   mass medication . . .: Townsend, M., 'Stay Calm Everyone, There's Prozac in the Drinking Water', *Observer*, 8 Aug. 2004.

p. 8   top of the European league . . .: Data from Mind website: 'Is Psychiatry for Sale? National Conference Investigates the Controversial Relationships between Psychiatry and the Pharmaceutical Industry' (2003), www.mind.org.uk.

p. 8   as high as 1 in 50 . . .: Hickman, M., Higgins, V., Hope, V., Bellis, M. A., Tilling, K., Walker, A. and Henry, J., 'Injecting Drug Use in Brighton, Liverpool and London: Best Estimates of Prevalence and Coverage of Public Health Indicators', *Journal of Epidemiology and Community Health*, 58 (2004): 766–71.

p. 9   people prescribed opiates for pain relief . . .: Blakeslee, S., 'Drug Makers Hope to Kill the Kick in Pain Relief', *New York Times*, 20 Apr. 2004.

p. 9   To waylay suspicion . . .: Milburn, M. A., *The Politics of Denial* (London: MIT Press, 1996).

p. 9   It is also unsurprising . . .: Kierman, G. L., 'The Changing Rate of Depression', *Journal of the American Psychoanalytic Association*, 15 (1992): 641–85 reports a tenfold increase in rates of depression; Twenge, J. M., 'The Age of Anxiety? Birth Cohort Changes in Anxiety and Neuroticism, 1952–93', *Journal of Personality and Social Psychology*, 79 (2000): 1007–21 reports a huge increase in levels of anxiety; Amnesty International (United States of America: Rights for All, 1998) reports that slightly under 2 per cent of the whole US population is incarcerated.

p. 10   Suicide accounts for 20 per cent of all deaths . . .: Data from the Mind website.

p. 10   Between 1971 and 1998 . . .: *Safety First: National Confidential Inquiry into Suicide and Homicide by People with Mental Illness* (London: National Patient Safety Agency, 2001).

p. 11   supporting the capitalist system . . .: Fernández Durán, R., *Capitalismo (financero) global y Guerra permanente: el dòlar, Wall Street y la guerra contra Irak* (Barcelona: Virus editorial, 2003).

p. 13   We trade little pieces of paper . . .: 'Asia: The Military–Market Link', The US Naval Institute, January 2002, pp. 53–6. See http://www.nwc.navy.mil/newrulesets/AsiaTheMilitary-MarketLink.htm.

p. 13   The US plans to spend . . .: 'Defence and the Dollar', *Feasta Review*, 2004. All figures from World Military Spending, Center for Arms Control and Non-Proliferation: www.armscontrolcenter.org.

p. 13   This paranoid delusion . . .: Moore, M., *Dude, Where's My Country?* (London: Allen Lane, 2003).

p. 14   Records of 3km deep Antarctic ice core . . .: Brown, P., 'Melting Ice: The Threat to London's Future', *Guardian*, 14 July 2004.

p. 15   secret report from the Pentagon . . .: Townsend, M. and Harris, P., 'Now the Pentagon Tells Bush: Climate Change Will Destroy Us', *Observer*, 22 Feb. 2004.

p. 15   Work by the Geological Survey . . .: McDonnell, H., 'Scientists Alarmed at Increase in Melt Rate of Ice', *Scotsman*, 4 Aug. 2004.

p. 15   The loss of the Gulf Stream . . .: Edwards, R., 'Freezing Future: There's Now Alarming Evidence that Europe is Facing an Ice Age', *New Scientist*, 27 Nov. 1999.

p. 15   The implications may go wider . . .: McGuire, W., 'Will Global Warming Trigger a New Ice Age?', *Guardian*, 13 Nov. 2004.

p. 17   This is being seen in the North Sea . . .: McCarthy, M., 'Disaster at Sea: Global Warming Hits UK Birds', *Independent*, 30 July 2004.

p. 17   a whole book of evidence . . .: Such a project is also under way, called the Counting the Costs project and coordinated by the Centre for Holistic Studies. The Introductory Report was produced in September 2005. The plan of the project is to cost the negative consequences of the operation of global capitalism. The first report showed that the costs of escape strategies such as drug taking and alcoholism in the UK amount to around £50bn annually – about the same as the cost of the NHS.

p. 17   frog in the experimental vat . . .: Jamieson, B., 'UK Borrowers' New Boiling Point', *Scotland on Sunday*, 23 May 2004.

Chapter 2

p. 20   this solution fails . . .: Examples of privatization failures – including the withdrawal of several contracts to run benefits agencies from Capita, government bailing out of Connex South Eastern, and the fining of Cambridge Education Associates for their poor performance in running Islington schools

– are helpfully listed on Kensington and Chelsea Unison's website: www.kensingtonandchelseaunison.org.uk.

p. 20   These assumptions are very strict . . .: The text I have relied on most for this outline of neoclassical theory is Sloman, J., *Economics*, 5th edn (Englewood Cliffs, NJ: Prentice Hall, 2003).

p. 21   similar critiques . . .: See, for example, Ormerod, P., *The Death of Economics* (London: Faber, 1994).

p. 21   ideological rather than rational reasons . . .: See Gaffney, M. and Harrison, G., *The Corruption of Economics* (London: Shepheard-Walwyn, 1994).

p. 21   a standard economics text . . .: Sloman, J., *Economics*, 5th edn (Englewood Cliffs, NJ: Prentice Hall, 2003).

p. 22   The last time I taught this theory . . .: Mankiw, M. N., *Principles of Economics* (Fort Worth, Texas: Harcourt, 2001). I am now less surprised at how infuriating I found this book, having learned that Gregory Mankiw is chairman of the council of economic advisers to President Bush.

p. 24   James Dyson has described in detail . . .: See www.dyson.co.uk.

p. 24   564 pages . . .: Christie, A. and Gare, S., *Blackstone's Statutes on Intellectual Property*, 6th edn (Oxford: University Press, 2003).

p. 24   How surprising that an organization . . .: Hoekman, B. and Kostecki, M., *The Political Economy of the World Trading System: From GATT to WTO* (Oxford: Oxford University Press, 1995), p. 154.

p. 25   The price difference is staggering . . .: Boseley, S., 'USA: Bayer, Anthrax and the WTO', Guardian, 24 Oct. 2001; see also the information on the Oxfam website or on the Treatment Action Campaign (South Africa) website: www.tac.org.za.

p. 26   One textbook deals with consumers' lack of indifference . . .: Begg, D., Fischer, S. and Dornbusch, R., *Economics*, 8th edn (Maidenhead: McGraw-Hill, 2005).

p. 27   as shown by Naomi Klein . . .: Klein, N., *No Logo: No Space, No Choice, No Jobs: Taking Aim at the Brand Bullies* (London: Flamingo, 2000).

p. 29   chaos of the General Agreement on Trade in Services . . .: The latest WTO trade agreement designed to open 160 service sectors of the global economy up to international competition by 2005: see the box in Woodin, M. and Lucas, C., *Green Alternatives to Globalisation: A Manifesto* (London: Pluto, 2004), pp. 24–7.

p. 29   report from the World Bank's own research unit . . .: Dinar, A., Rosegrant, M. W. and Meinzen-Dick, R., *Water Allocation Mechanisms: Principles and Examples* (New York: World Bank, 1997).

p. 30   Association of Certified Chartered Accountants . . .: Edwards, P., Shaoul, J., Stafford, A. and Arblaster, L., *Evaluating the Operation of PFI in Roads and Hospitals* (London: ACCA paper no. RR84, 2004).

p. 30   was leaked to George Monbiot . . .: Monbiot, G., *Captive State: The Corporate Takeover of Britain* (London: Macmillan, 2000), p. 68.

p. 31   Unison has identified . . .: *Public Risk for Private Gain? The Public Audit Implications of Risk Transfer and Private Finance* (London: Unison, 2004).

p. 32   GATS . . .: Woodin, M. and Lucas, C., *Green Alternatives to Globalisation: A Manifesto* (London: Pluto, 2004), pp. 24–7.

p. 32   Lisbon Agenda . . .: 'EU insists it will not withdraw plans to free up services', *AFP*, 4 Feb. 2005.

p. 32   Wider Markets Initiative . . .: www.partnershipsuk.org.uk/widermarkets.

p. 33   The truth is . . .: Pollock, A., *NHS plc: The Privatisation of our Health Care* (London: Verso, 2004).

p. 33   some promising candidates . . .: Harvey, D., *Limits to Capital* (London: Verso, 1999).

p. 33   rational economic man . . .: Hewitson, G. J., *Feminist Economics: Interrogating the Masculinity of Rational Economic Man* (Cheltenham: Edward Elgar, 1998).

p. 33   personal relationships are reduced to bargaining games . . .: Becker, G. S., *A Treatise on the Family* (Cambridge, Mass.: Harvard University Press, 1991).

p. 33   Another prominent myth . . .: Douthwaite, R., *The Growth Illusion: How Economic Growth Has Enriched the Few, Impoverished the Many, and Endangered the Planet* (Bideford: Green Books, 1992).

p. 34   A more recent critique . . .: Hamilton, C., *Growth Fetish* (London: Pluto, 2004).

p. 34   The essence of the capitalist market system . . .: Mellor, M., *Breaking the Boundaries: Towards a Feminist Green Socialism* (London: Virago, 1992), p. 195.

p. 34   These quotations . . .: Cremer, A., 'Schroeder may lose German state elections amid welfare protests' (2004), http://quote.bloomberg.com/apps/news.

p. 35   Under the Lomé Convention . . .: See *Corporate Watch* 5 and 6, winter 1997.

p. 36   Markets are simply . . .: Barry, J., *Rethinking Green Politics: Nature, Virtue and Progress* (London: Sage, 1999), especially chapter 6, 'Green Political Economy', p. 159.

p. 36   the capitalist market cannot resolve . . .: Mellor, M., *Breaking the Boundaries: Towards a Feminist Green Socialism* (London: Virago, 1992), p. 190.

Chapter 3

p. 38   There is evidence that the New Labour government . . .: *The State of the Nation: An Audit of Injustice in the UK* (London: IPPR, 2004).

p. 40   Measures of absolute poverty . . .: Woodin, M. and Lucas, C., *Green Alternatives to Globalisation: A Manifesto* (London: Pluto, 2004), p. 48.

p. 40   Wade concludes his analysis . . .: Hunter Wade, R., 'Poverty and Income Distribution: What is the Evidence?' in A. Pettifor (ed.), *Real World Economic Outlook: The Legacy of Globalization: Debt and Deflation* (London: Macmillan, 2003).

p. 43   Under the new rules . . .: McCarthy, R., 'Foreign Firms to Bid in Huge Iraqi Sale', *Guardian* online, 22 Sept. 2003.

p. 43   Bremer Order #39 . . .: Juhasz, A., 'The Economic Colonization of Iraq: Illegal and Immoral', Testimony to the World Tribunal on Iraq, New York, 8 May 2004.

p. 44   Rather than models of speed and efficiency . . .: Klein, N., 'The Multibillion Robbery the US Calls Reconstruction: The Shameless Corporate Feeding Frenzy in Iraq is Fuelling the Resistance', *Guardian*, 26 June 2004.

p. 44   The big silver lining . . .: The article was actually written by Spencer Fitzgibbon: Cato, M. S. and Fitzgibbon, S., 'Oh, What a Lovely War!', *Morning Star*, 3 Apr. 2003.

p. 45   Data from the Office for National Statistics . . .: *Trends in Life Expectancy by Social Class 1972–1999* (London: SO), Tables 1–4.

p. 45   The paper suggests . . .: Kennedy, B. P., Ichiro, K. and Prothrow-Stith, D., 'Income Distribution and Mortality: Cross Sectional Ecological Study of the Robin Hood Index in the United States', *British Medical Journal*, 312 (1996): 1004–7.

p. 45   If at the earlier moment of industrialization . . .: Seabrook, J., *Landscapes of Poverty* (Oxford: Blackwell, 1985), p. 4.

p. 46   The advertising industry plays its own part . . .: See more on this in Cato, M. S., 'Sen and the Art of Market-Cycle Maintenance', *Sustainable Economics*, 12/5 (Oct. 2004): http://www.sustecweb.co.uk/past/sustec12-5/index.htm.

p. 46   Related findings on 'status anxiety' . . .: See de Botton, A., *Status Anxiety* (Harmondsworth: Penguin, 2004).

p. 46   control over our lives and opportunities . . .: Robert Sapolsky, author of *Why Zebras Don't Get Ulcers*, reviewing Marmot, M., *Status Syndrome: How Our Position on the Social Gradient Affects Longevity and Health* (London: Bloomsbury, 2004).

p. 46   James identifies the psychologically damaging effects . . .: James, O., *Britain on the Couch: Why We're Unhappier Compared with 1950 Despite*

Being Richer: A Treatment for the Low-Serotonin Society (London: Arrow, 1998), p. 232.

p. 46   a rare piece of psychological research into cooperation . . .: Rilling, J. K., Gutman, D. A., Zeh, T. R., Pagnoni, G., Berns, G. S., and Kilts, C. D., 'A Neural Basis for Social Cooperation', *Neuron*, 35 (2002): 395–405.

p. 47   Polly Toynbee finds that the rhetoric . . .: Toynbee, P., 'Family Man Gordon Should Make the Most of his Big Day', *Guardian*, 10 Dec. 2003.

p. 48   There is evidence that . . .: Garstka, T. A., Hummert, M. L. and Branscombe, N. R., 'Perceiving Age Discrimination in Response to Intergenerational Inequity', *Journal of Social Issues*, 61/2 (2005): 321–42.

p. 48   There are so many unspoken assumptions . . .: See *Arbeit Macht Frei and Other Lies About Work*, available online at: www.gaianeconomics.org/myths-about-work.

p. 48   stalling of class mobility . . .: Dustmann [sic!], C., 'Parental Background, Secondary School Track Choice, and Wages', *Oxford Economic Papers*, 56/2 (2004): 209–30; Li, Y., Savage, M. and Pickles, A., 'Social Capital and Social Exclusion in England and Wales (1972–1999)', *British Journal of Sociology*, 54/4 (2003): 497–526; Goldthorpe, J., 'The Myth of Education-Based Meritocracy', *New Economy*, 10/4 (2003): 234–9.

p. 50   Nursing neighbours . . .: Kropotkin, P., *Mutual Aid* (London: Pelican, 1902, 1939 edn), p. 225.

p. 51   The author of the pamphlet . . .: Anon., *The Source and Remedy of the National Difficulties*, letter to Lord John Russell (London, 1821).

p. 51   Owen wrote that the capitalist system . . .: Quotations from pp. 3 and 6 of Mellor, M., Hannah, J. and Stirling, J., *Worker Cooperatives in Theory and Practice* (Milton Keynes: Open University Press, 1988); see also Donnachie, I., *Robert Owen: Owen of New Lanark and New Harmony* (East Linton: Tuckwell Press, 2000).

p. 51   Syndicalism differed from socialism . . .: Hutchinson, F. and Burkitt, B., *The Political Economy of Social Credit and Guild Socialism* (London: Routledge, 1997), p. 16.

p. 51   swamped by political movements . . .: Hutchinson and Burkitt, pp. 94–5.

p. 52   Restricted to the dwarfish forms . . .: Speech in 1864 to the International Working Men's Association.

p. 52   The movement began . . .: For a brief history of Fagor, see: Mendizabal, A. and Errasti, A., 'Economic and Social Aspects of Productive Delocalisation (off-shoring?): The Case of Fagor Electrodomesticos', paper presented to the Mondragon Research Conference 2005, 28 June. For more about Mondragon as a whole, see: MacLeod, G., *From Mondragon to America: Experiments in Community Economic Development* (Sydney, NS: University of Cape Breton Press).

p. 53   Tower Colliery . . .: For a fuller account of the Tower story, see my earlier book *The Pit and the Pendulum* (University of Wales Press, 2004); a film script written by Colin Welland exists but is awaiting funding.

p. 53   International Cooperative Day 2004 . . .: *Co-operative News*, 3 July 2004, p. 5.

p. 53   We are by nature inclusive . . .: International Co-operative Alliance, *Cooperatives for Fair Globalisation: Creating Opportunities for All*, 82nd International Co-operative Day, 3 July 2004.

p. 54   Figures were massaged . . .: Thomas, M., 'Colliery Closure and the Miner's Experience of Redundancy', *Contemporary Wales*, 4 (1991): 45–65.

p. 55   The out-turn was over £15m less . . .: Pike, A. J., '"Shareholder Value" versus the Regions: the Closure of the Vaux Brewery in Sunderland', *Journal of Economic Geography*, 6/2 (2006): 201–22.

p. 55   Movimento dos Trabalhadores Rurais sem Terra . . .: http://www.mstbrazil.org.

p. 56   A film by Naomi Klein and Avi Lewis . . .: The film is called *The Take*, see: http://www.nfb.ca/webextension/thetake.

p. 57   [The social economy] . . .: Amin, A., Cameron, A. and Hudson, R., *Placing the Social Economy* (London: Routledge, 2002), pp. 19–20.

p. 58   This article is about . . .: Gordon, M., 'The Contribution of the Community Cooperatives of the Highlands and Islands of Scotland to the Development of the Social Economy', *Journal of Rural Cooperation*, 30/2 (2002): 95–117, p. 96; see also Scott Cato, M., Arthur, L. and Smith, R. 'The Social Economy: Failure of Definition or a Definition of Failure?', submitted to *Review of Radical Political Economy*.

p. 58   The key to unlocking interest . . .: Brown, J., *Co-operative Capital: A New Approach to Investment in Co-operatives* (Manchester: Co-operative Action, 2004), p. 4.

Chapter 4

p. 63   It has been established . . .: Milanovic, B., *The World Income Distribution, 1988 and 1993: First Calculation Based on Household Surveys Alone*, World Bank Policy Research Working Paper no. 2244 (1999).

p. 63   Direct evidence of the impact of trade . . .: *UNCTAD report on trade* (1997), Part Two, chap. IV, sect. B.1; World Bank report: Lundberg, M. and Squire, L., 'The simultaneous evolution of growth and inequality', Dec. 1999. Grateful thanks to Richard Douthwaite for both these references.

p. 64   Mies and Shiva argue . . .: Mies, M. and Shiva, V., *Ecofeminism* (London: Zed, 1993), pp. 235–6.

p. 64   The overall gains from trade . . .: Data from an unpublished report by Nick Robins called *Taming World Trade*, cited by Simms (2000). See below.

p. 64   According to Richard Douthwaite . . .: In an email to the author.

p. 65   To suggest, as Oxfam does . . .: Oxfam, 'Rigged Rules and Double Standards: Trade, Globalisation and the Fight Against Poverty', from Make Trade Fair website: www.maketradefair.com.

p. 65   G. D. H. Cole pointed out . . .: Cole, G. D. H., *Self-Government in Industry* (London: Bell, 1920), p. 65.

p. 66   Colin Hines's Jekyll-and-Hyde image . . .: Hines, C., 'Oxfam's Jekyll and Hyde Approach to Trade Will Worsen the Lot of the Poor' (unpublished, 2002).

p. 67   painted a disturbing picture . . .: Simms, A., *Collision Course: Free Trade's Free Ride on the Global Climate* (London: New Economics Foundation, 2000).

p. 69   One of the curious features . . .: Bush, J., 'America's Foes Prepare for Monetary Jihad', *New Statesman*, 4 Oct. 2004.

p. 69   it seems that the two largest economies . . .: E. Luce, 'India to Dip into Forex Reserves to Build Roads', *Financial Times*, 17 Oct. 2004; I. Stelzer, 'The Economic Consequences of the War', *Sunday Times*, 14 Sept. 2003.

p. 72   Evidence that this bandwagon is rolling . . .: Norberg-Hodge, H., Merrifield, T. and Gorelick, S., *Bringing the Food Economy Home: Local Alternatives to Global Agribusiness* (London: Zed, 2002), p. 21; see www.farmersmarkets.net.

p. 72   Specialization within the contemporary global market . . .: Barry, J., *Rethinking Green Politics: Nature, Virtue and Progress* (London: Sage, 1999), p. 4.

p. 72   Jules Pretty discusses . . .: Pretty, J., *Agri-Culture: Reconnecting People, Land and Nature* (London: Earthscan, 2002).

p. 74   Empowering local communities . . .: More information from: tymawr@lime.org.uk; or at the CAT website: www.cat.org.uk.

p. 74   the earliest trace is from Scotland . . .: Ryder, M. L., 'Probably Fibres from Hemp (*Cannabis sativa*) in Bronze Age Scotland', *Environmental Archaeology*, 1999.

p. 76   Hemp is now being seen as a solution . . .: More information from www.flaxandhemp.bangor.ac.uk.

p. 77   Retail sales of fairly traded products . . .: Brown, J., *Co-operative Capital: A New Approach to Investment in Co-operatives* (Manchester: Co-operative Action, 2004).

p. 78   It goes without saying . . .: This issue is discussed at some length in Woodin, M. and Lucas, C., *Green Alternatives to Globalisation: A Manifesto* (London: Pluto, 2004), pp. 77–82.

p. 78   re-creation of bioregions . . .: www.bioregional.com.

p. 78   We harvested our first crop . . .: Desai, P. and Riddlestone, S., *Bioregional Solutions for Living on One Planet*, Schumacher Briefing no. 8 (Totnes: Green Books, 2002), p. 80.

p. 80   moral standard developed by General Motors . . .: In connection with what is a need and what an unnecessary desire, see my paper 'Sen and the Art of Market Cycle Maintenance', published as 'The Freedom to be Frugal', in *Growth: The Celtic Cancer* (Dublin: FEASTA, 2004), pp. 48–53.

p. 80   Contraction and Convergence framework . . .: Meyer, A., *Contraction and Convergence: The Global Solution to Climate Change*, Schumacher Briefing no. 5 (Totnes: Green Books, 2000).

p. 83   Glastonbury Festival is some sort of prototype . . .: As an ideas merchant, I especially value the free thinking that Glastonbury and the Green Gathering encourage and I would like to thank participants in discussions I have had there for their contribution to the development of these ideas.

p. 85   system of global distribution creates conflict and instability . . .: Schumacher, E. F., *Small is Beautiful: A Study of Economics as if People Mattered* (London: Abacus, 1973), pp. 56–7.

Chapter 5

p. 88   The response by the more pioneering fans . . .: For more information, see the Football Governance Research Centre at Birkbeck, University of London and their report *Back Home: Returning Football Clubs to their Communities* by Oughton, C., McClean, M., Mills, C. and Hunt, P.

p. 89   The origins of globalisation . . .: Arthur, L., Keenoy, T. and Smith, R., 'Capital Anchoring and Co-operative Ownership: The Reality of the Operation of a Co-operative Enterprise in a Globalising Economy', 16th Annual Employment Research Unit Conference: Politics, Public Policy and the Employment Relationship, held at Cardiff Business School, 10–11 Sept. 2001; available for download at: http://www.uwic.ac.uk/ubs/research/wirc/publications.asp.

p. 89   [Globalization's] common feature . . .: Cox, R. W., 'Global Restructuring: Making Sense of the Changing International Political Economy', in Stubbs, R. and Underhill, G. R. D. (eds), *Political Economy and the Changing Global Order* (Basingstoke: Macmillan, 1994): 45–59, p. 49.

p. 89   report published in 1999 . . .: Ford Foundation, *Summary of Broadening Capital Ownership in the Global Economy: Creating an International Network to Develop Policy Options*; summarized by Arthur et al., 'Capital Anchoring' (1999).

p. 90   massive increase in trade-related pollution . . .: Simms, A., Kumar, R. and Robbins, N., *Collision Course: Free Trade's Free Ride on the Global Climate* (London: New Economics Foundation, 2000).

p. 92   shareholder becomes the only stakeholder . . .: Minford, P., *Markets not Stakes* (London: Texere, 1998); for more on the relationship between shareholder value and Corporate Social Responsibility, see Arthur, L., Scott Cato, M., Keenoy, T. and Smith, R., 'Corporate Social Responsibility in Your Own Backyard', paper presented at the conference Corporate Social Responsibility: Thought and Practice, University of Glamorgan Business School, 23–4 Sept. 2004.

p. 92   creative accountants' training manual . . .: Libert, B. D., Samek, S. S. and Boulton, R. E. S., *Cracking the Value Code: How Successful Businesses are Creating Wealth in the New Economy* (New York: HarperBusiness, 2000).

p. 93   reworks the hierarchy of management . . . : Williams, K., 'From Shareholder Value to Present-Day Capitalism', *Economy and Society*, 29/1 (2000): 1–12, p. 6.

p. 94   narrative of the decline and death . . .: Pike, A. J., '"Shareholder Value" versus the Regions: the Closure of the Vaux Brewery in Sunderland', *Journal of Economic Geography*, 6/2 (2006): 201–22.

p. 95   From the perspective of capital, the locality no longer matters . . .: Martin, R., 'The New Economic Geography of Money', in R. Martin (ed.), *Money and the Space Economy* (Chichester: Wiley, 1999), pp. 3–27; Pollard, J., 'Small Firm Finance and Economic Geography', *Journal of Economic Geography*, 3/4 (2003), 429–52; O'Brien, R., *Global Financial Integration: The End of Geography* (London: Pinter, 2001).

p. 95   corporate drive towards the enlargement . . . : Note the glee evident in the 'achievements' listed on the website of the largest corporate pressure group in the EU, the European Roundtable of Industrialists: http://www.ert.be/pg/eng_frame.htm.

p. 95   The reality, however . . . : Bahumik, T. K., 'Outsourcing outcry: West should compete, not whine', *Times of India*, 17 Feb. 2004.

p. 96   Comparison of hourly pay rates . . .: A. Mendizabal and A. Errasti, 'Economic and Social Aspects of Productive Delocalisation: The Case of Fagor Electrodomesticos', paper presented to the Mondragon Research Conference, 28 June 2005.

p. 96   At any given time . . .: Wood, A., *North–South Trade, Employment, and Inequality: Changing Fortunes in a Skill-Driven World* (Oxford: Clarendon Press, 1994), pp. 29–30.

p. 98   attempts by unions to defend . . .: Ahmed, R. Z., 'UK unions twisted report to rubbish Indian BPO: analyst', *Times of India*, 15 Jan. 2004.

p. 98   India has been . . . : Figures from O'Connell, D. and Armitstead, L., 'The Great Indian Takeaway', *Sunday Times*, 8 June 2003, p. 5.

p. 98   A whole range of pathology tests . . . : 'British Hospital Tries Out Scheme to Outsource Lab Testing to India', *Sunday Times*, 2 July 2004.

p. 98   On current trends . . . : *Manufacturing Now: Delivering the Manufacturing Strategy* (London: Trades Union Congress, 2004).

p. 98   The British government itself . . .: Griffin, Z., 'Protest as Army Buys Uniforms from China', *Daily Telegraph*, 3 Aug. 2004.

p. 98   Wingfield Hayes quotes the conclusion . . .: Wingfield Hayes, R., 'On China's Fast-Track to Luxury', *From Our Own Correspondent*, BBC website, 2004.

p. 101   reported by Burt . . .: Burt, T., 'Multinational Retailers Expand by a Third in Emerging Markets', *Financial Times*, 22 June 2004.

p. 101   The global food economy . . .: As we might perhaps expect, it is the UK farmers who follow the activities of UK supermarkets with most interest, having been their first victims: these data on Tesco come from the *Farmers' Guardian*, 18 and 25 June 2004.

p. 102   Bioregionalism has at its heart . . .: The concept of bioregionalism has not been adequately theorized yet, but practical ideas about achieving balance are available from the Bioregional Group: www.bioregional.com or published in Desai, P. and Riddlestone, S., *Bioregional Solutions for Living on One Planet*, Schumacher Briefing no. 8 (Totnes: Green Books, 2002).

p. 102   development of the local food economy . . .: See more about the work of her International Society for Ecology and Culture at www.isec.org.uk.

p. 103   Foundation for Local Food Initiatives . . .: www.localfood.org.uk.

p. 103   Foremost among these is Colin Hines . . .: Hines, C., *Localization: A Global Manifesto* (London, Earthscan, 2000).

p. 104   Expenditure by local authorities in England . . .: DTI (Department of Trade and Industry), *Public Procurement: A Toolkit for Social Enterprises* (London: SO, 2003); ref. as DTI Toolkit.

p. 104   they only apply to contracts . . .: For 2004 and 2005 the sterling threshold for supplies and most services (e.g. stationery or building maintenance) is £153,376; for construction and engineering works it is £3,834,411: IDeA Procurement, *Sustainability and Local Government Procurement* (London: IDeA, 2003), www.idea.gov.uk.

p. 106   There has been much concern . . .: In the US context the most prominent is Putnam, R. D., *Democracies in Flux: The Evolution of Social Capital in Contemporary Society* (Oxford: University Press, 2002); in the UK the political argument is made by Hirst, P. Q., *Associative Democracy : New Forms of Economic and Social Governance* (Cambridge: Polity, 1994) and the sociological argument by Giddens, A., *The Third Way: The Renewal of Social Democracy* (Cambridge: Polity, 1998).

p. 106   I would ask you to imagine . . .: One of the hidden perks of writing is that people actually tell you how this feels. After publishing a longer discussion of the contrast between MFI and Adam Bede ('Butcher, Baker, Candlestick-maker' etc.) I was approached by a campaigner from Manufacturers Fighting Injustice (MFI), a pressure group specifically established to blow the whistle on the dreadful working conditions at MFI's Runcorn factory. In a similar way I received a detailed account of working life at LG following my discussion of that fiasco in *The Pit and the Pendulum.*

p. 107   the utilitarian design of Safeway . . .: Interestingly, in contrast to the workers, the managers of corporations are remarkably cagey. I was told to leave my local Safeway when taking these photographs. I have no idea what the manager was hoping to hide.

p. 107   Helen Petrie . . .: Professor of human–computer interaction at London City University.

Chapter 6

p. 111   The finance industry lies at the heart of globalisation . . .: Hutchinson, F. Mellor, M. and Olsen, W., *The Politics of Money* (London: Pluto, 2002), p. 5.

p. 111   The financial system now completely dominates . . .: Martin, R. and Minns, R., 'Undermining the Financial Basis of Regions: The Spatial Structure and Implications of the UK Pension Fund Industry', *Regional Studies*, 29 (1995): 127–44, p. 128.

p. 112   In reality, people who save and invest money . . .: Hutchinson, F. and Burkitt, B., *The Political Economy of Social Credit and Guild Socialism* (London: Routledge, 1997), p. 39.

p. 117   At that time US bankers . . .: Roberts, P., 'Benjamin Strong, the Federal Reserve and the Limits to Interwar American Nationalism', *Economic Quarterly*, spring 2004.

p. 117   when Chancellor Gordon Brown sold 415 tonnes . . .: 'Treasury to Sell 415 Tonnes of Gold Reserves': http://www.24carat.co.uk/goldsales.html.

p. 117   The process by which banks create money . . .: As banking developed . . .: Galbraith, J. K., Money: *Whence it Came; Where it Went* (London: Deutsch, 1975), p. 21.

p. 119   By November 1923 . . .: Schacht, H., *The Magic of Money* (London: Oldbourg, 1967), p. 62.

p. 119   to create confidence it was backed by land . . .: Currency nerds may be interested in the parallel with the proposal for a land bank rather than a joint-stock bank (on the Bank of England model) to restore credibility in the Irish currency following the South Sea Bubble fiasco in 1720: P. Kelly, 'Swift on Money and Economics', in C. Fox (ed.), *The Cambridge Companion to Jonathan Swift* (Cambridge: University Press, 2003), pp. 128–45.

p. 120   The government froze bank accounts . . .: Elliott, L., 'Do Cry for Us', *Guardian*, 7 June 2002.

p. 120   So, the Argentinian economy has collapsed . . .: Salinas Price, H., 'What Really Killed Argentina?', *Asia Times*, 10 Apr. 2002.

p. 121   The 1997–99 contagion . . .: Desai, P., *Financial Crisis, Contagion and Containment: From Asia to Argentina* (Princeton, NJ: Princeton University Press, 2003), p. 9.

p. 122   Speculating against these economies . . .: Barlow, M., *Blue Gold: The Global Water Crisis and the Commodification of the World's Water Supply* (San Francisco: International Forum on Globalization, 1999).

p. 122   Castro introduced a 10 per cent commission . . .: 'Fidel Castro has Banned the Dollar – Helped by America's Embargo', *Economist*, 28 Oct. 2004.

p. 122   Multi-millionaire and Falangist . . .: Beevor, A., *The Spanish Civil War* (London, Cassell, 1982).

p. 124   Hence the national debt of the UK . . .: *Government Debt and Credit Creation: A Study of the Creation of Credit and Its Effect on the British Economy* (London: Economic Research Council, 1981).

p. 124   two Early Day Motions . . .: Sterling work to take democratize the process of money creation is being undertaken by the Forum for Stable Currencies. See its *Publicly Created Money and Monetary Reform: A New Finance Initiative* (London: Forum for Stable Currencies, 2003).

p. 124   Dr William Temple . . .: Temple, W., *The Hope of a New World* (London: Student Christian Movement Press, 1941).

p. 124   The evidence collected . . .: Holloway, E., *Money Matters: A Modern Pilgrim's Economic Progress* (Sherwood, 1986).

p. 125   Total lending rose by £9.4bn . . .: 'The Life and Debt of Capitalist Economics: Time for a Genuine Sustainable Alternative', Green Party Budget Statement, 2003.

p. 125   the credit structure . . .: Hutchinson, F. and Burkitt, B., *The Political Economy of Social Credit and Guild Socialism* (London: Routledge, 1997), pp. 40–1.

p. 126   The effect of this method of creating money . . .: Madron, R. and Jopling, J., *Gaian Democracies: Redefining Globalisation and People-Power* (Foxhole: Green Books, 2003), pp. 70–1.

p. 127   LETS received huge interest . . .: For more information on LETS and to find a scheme in your area, visit the LETSlink UK website at: http://www.letslinkuk.org.

p. 127   'barter clubs' . . .: Pearson, R., 'Argentina's Barter Network: New Currency for New Times?', *Bulletin of Latin American Research*, 22/2(2003): 214–30, p. 216.

p. 129   Outstanding bank loans have fallen . . .: Dvorak, P., 'Puzzle in Japan: Despite Lowering Rates To Rock-Bottom, Banks Lack Borrowers', *Wall Street Journal*, 25 Oct. 2001.

p. 129   Japan is now the world leader . . .: Malcolm Currie offered feedback on the Conference on Community Currencies in Kuriyama, August 2002, at the Sixth Annual Conference of the Bromsgrove Group in 2002.

p. 130   It is based in Japan's strong culture . . .: Readers of Japanese, and those able to fight their way through the peculiarities of online translations, can find out more on the Yamato website: http://www.city.yamato. kanagawa.jp.

p. 130   The Chiemgauer was launched . . .: Information on the Chiemgauer from the website: http://www.chiemgau-regional.de.

p. 135   The big idea is the creation of the EBCU . . .: Much of the content of this section is taken from a paper I wrote jointly with Tony Cooper of the Global Commons Institute and I would like to pay tribute to his substantial work towards finding a solution to climate change.

p. 135   'bancor' proposed by Keynes at Bretton Woods . . .: For more detail, see: Rowbotham, M., *Goodbye America! Globalisation, Debt and the Dollar Empire* (Charlbury: Jon Carpenter, 2000).

p. 135   Contraction and Convergence . . .: Meyer, A., *Contraction and Convergence: The Global Solution to Climate Change*, Schumacher Briefing no. 5 (Totnes: Green Books, 2000).

Chapter 7

p. 140   I have written about this at great length elsewhere . . .: In 1996 I published *Seven Myths About Work*, which was produced in a second electronic edition in 2002 and is available as *Arbeit Macht Frei and other Lies About Work* from: http://www.gaianeconomics.org/myths-about-work.htm.

p. 140   We are laughed at when we say . . .: Kropotkin, P., *Mutual Aid* (Harmondsworth: Pelican, 1902, 1939 edn), p. 160.

p. 140   Soul-destroying, meaningless . . . work . . .: Schumacher, E. F., *Small is Beautiful: A Study of Economics as if People Mattered* (London: Abacus, 1973), p. 35.

p. 141   Under market conditions . . .: Eagleton, T., *Marx and Freedom* (London: Phoenix, 1997), p. 28. Other quotations also from Eagleton.

p. 143   a conference on identity in 1996 . . .: This has now been published as Chapter 4 in *The Pit and the Pendulum: A Cooperative Future for Work in the Welsh Valleys* (Cardiff: University of Wales Press, 2004).

p. 144   consumer identities as discussed by Baudrillard . . .: Baudrillard, J., *Selected Writings*, ed. M. Poster (Stanford, Calif.: Stanford University Press, 1988).

p. 144   According to Oliver James . . .: James, O., *Britain on the Couch: Why We're Unhappier Compared with 1950, Despite Being Richer: A Treatment for the Low-Serotonin Society* (London: Century, 1997).

p. 144   Shackled free commercial intercourse . . .: Gross, C., *The Gild Merchant* (Oxford: Clarendon Press, 1890).

p. 144 seldom regulated wholesale trade . . .: Richardson, G., 'A Tale of Two Theories: Monopolies and Craft Guilds in Medieval England and Modern Imagination', *Journal of the History of Economic Thought*, 23/2 (2001): 217–42, p. 218.

p. 146 is not a realizable project . . .: Williams, K., 'From Shareholder Value to Present-Day Capitalism', *Economy and Society*, 29/1 (2000): 1–12, p. 6.

p. 146 The masters did not provide much testimony . . .: Epstein, S. A., *Wage Labor and Guilds in Medieval Europe* (Chapel Hill, NC: University of North Carolina Press, 1991), p. 100.

p. 147 sharing power in a democratic setting . . .: Brown, J., *Co-operative Capital: A New Approach to Investment in Co-operatives* (Manchester: Co-operative Action, 2004), p. 30.

p. 147 Their development was a natural consequence . . .: Kropotkin, P., *Mutual Aid* (Harmondsworth: Pelican, 1902, 1939 edn).

p. 147 discovery of the Census of 1388 . . .: Smith, T. and Smith, L., *English Gilds: The Original Ordinances of More Than One Hundred Early English Gilds* (London: Oxford University Press, 1869).

p. 148 acting directly against monopolistic practices . . .: Richardson, G., 'A Tale of Two Theories: Monopolies and Craft Guilds in Medieval England and Modern Imagination', *Journal of the History of Economic Thought*, 23/2 (2001): 217–42.

p. 148 The craft guild was then a common seller . . .: Kropotkin, P., *Mutual Aid* (Harmondsworth: Pelican, 1902, 1939 edn), p. 158.

p. 150 When the German Emperor Barbarossa . . .: Nelson, L. H., 'The Rise of Capitalism', from lecture series, Introduction to Medieval History, University of Kansas website: www.ukans.edu/kansas/medieval.

p. 150 It may be no coincidence . . .: Thompson, E. P., *The Making of the English Working Class* (London: Gollancz, 1963).

p. 151 guild socialists opposed wage slavery . . .: The argument throughout this section leans heavily on the work of Frances Hutchinson, who, with her co-author Brian Burkitt, is virtually alone in recording let alone propagating the ideas of the guild socialists. The major reference source, as here, is: Hutchinson, F. and Burkitt, B., *The Political Economy of Social Credit and Guild Socialism* (London: Routledge, 1997), p. 14.

p. 151 denial of the opportunity for creative labour . . .: Noel Thompson discussing *The Restoration of the Gild System* by A. J. Penty (1906) in *Political Economy and the Labour Party: The Economics of Democratic Socialism* (London: UCL Press, 1996).

p. 151 a transition period . . .: Morris, W., *Political Writings of William Morris* (London: Lawrence and Wishart, 1973).

p. 152 Although the Marxian analysis . . .: Hutchinson, F. and Burkitt, B.,

The Political Economy of Social Credit and Guild Socialism (London: Routledge, 1997), p. 18.

p. 152   the political emphasis . . .: Hutchinson, F. and Burkitt, B., *The Political Economy of Social Credit and Guild Socialism* (London: Routledge, 1997), p. 27; quoting P. Kropotkin, *The Conquest of Bread* (London: Chapman and Hall, 1906).

p. 152   the demoralizing tyranny . . .: Penty, A. J., *Old Worlds for New: A Study of the Post-Industrial State* (London: G. Allen & Unwin, 1917).

p. 153   Already by the end of the Middle Ages . . .: Ferguson, J., *Foundations of the Modern World* (Cambridge: Cambridge University Press, 1963).

p. 153   several important aspects of London life . . .: M. Rubin, *The Hollow Crown: A History of Britain in the Late Middle Ages* (London: Penguin, 2005), p. 137.

p. 153   In a striking parallel . . .: Nelson, L. H., 'The Rise of Capitalism', from lecture series, Introduction to Medieval History, University of Kansas website: www.ukans.edu/kansas/medieval.

p. 154   In London a political struggle was at play . . .: M. Rubin, *The Hollow Crown: A History of Britain in the Late Middle Ages* (London: Penguin, 2005), p. 249.

p. 155   Schumacher expressed the tragedy . . .: Schumacher, E. F., *Small is Beautiful: A Study of Economics as if People Mattered* (London: Abacus, 1973), p. 187.

p. 155   There are two possible courses to affluence . . .: Sahlins, M., *Stone Age Economics* (Chicago: Aldine Altherton, 1972), p. 2.

p. 156   Thompson describes the difficulty . . .: Thompson, E. P., *The Making of the English Working Class* (London: Gollancz, 1963).

p. 156   Capitalism is the first economic system . . .: Mellor, M., *Breaking the Boundaries: Towards a Feminist Green Socialism* (London: Virago, 1992), p. 205.

p. 156   the culture of subsistence was carried forward . . .: Burchardt, J., *The Allotment Movement in England, 1793–1873* (London: Royal Historical Society, 2002).

p. 157   Where wage labor expands . . .: Illich, I., *Shadow Work* (London: Marion Boyars, 1981), p. 21.

p. 157   The same thing is happening now . . .: Robertson, J., *Future Wealth: A New Economics for the 21st Century* (London: Cassell, 1989), p. 114.

p. 158   You may have heard of . . .: Find out more about guerrilla knitting at www.castoff.info. Information on eco-building is available from the Association for Environment Conscious Building: http://www.aecb.net or the Centre for Alternative Technology: www.cat.org.uk.

p. 158   The proposal for a basic weekly income . . .: Mellor, M., *Breaking the Boundaries: Towards a Feminist Green Socialism* (London: Virago, 1992), p. 206.

p. 158   Robertson has gone further . .   .: Robertson, J., 'A Green Benefits and Taxation System', in Scott Cato, M. and Kennett, M. (eds), *Green Economics: Beyond Supply and Demand to Meeting People's Needs* (Aberystwyth: Green Audit, 1999).

p. 158   an income pooling scheme . . .: Smith, A., 'Fair Shares for Everyone', *Guardian*, 22 Sept. 1999.

p. 158   disgust for those who would rather couch out . . .: 'The Atheist Sloth Ethic, or Why Europeans Don't Believe in Work', *Telegraph*, 14 Aug. 2004.

p. 159   More interesting is the fact . . .: International Institute for Management Development, *World Competitiveness Yearbook* (Lausanne: IIMD, 2002).

Chapter 8

p. 160   According to Renato Ruggiero . . .: Quoted by Lucas, C., 'Can We Create a Local World?', Schumacher Lecture, Bristol, 2 Nov. 2002.

p. 160   Michael Portillo described . . .: 'Big Business Needs Taming, and Guess who Should Do It?', *Sunday Times*, 9 May 2004.

p. 161   The assumption of the naturalness . . .: Hutchinson, F., Mellor, M. and Olsen, W., *The Politics of Money: Towards Sustainability and Economic Democracy* (London: Pluto, 2002), p. 24.

p. 161   Such awareness of the ethics . . .: M. Rubin, *The Hollow Crown: A History of Britain in the Late Middle Ages* (London: Penguin, 2005), p. 249.

p. 161   The description of the moral strictures . . .: Ferguson, J., *Foundations of the Modern World: John Ferguson* (Cambridge: Cambridge University Press, 1963), p. 154.

p. 164   The growth in individualist pensions . . .: Clark, G., *Pension Fund Capitalism* (Oxford: Oxford University Press, 2000).

p. 165   the Bishop of Durham said . . .: Pike, A. J., '"Shareholder Value" versus the Regions: the Closure of the Vaux Brewery in Sunderland', *Journal of Economic Geography*, 6/2 (2006): 201–22.

p. 167   Elsewhere I have explored . . .: Cato, M. S., 'The Freedom to be Frugal', in *Growth: The Celtic Cancer* (Dublin: FEASTA, 2004), pp. 48–53.

p. 167   Modern capitalist societies . . .: Sahlins, M., *Stone Age Economics* (Chicago: Aldine Altherton, 1972), pp. 3–4.

p. 169   Thanks mainly to Matthew Arnold . . .: Muriel Spark discusses the creation of the Shelley myth by both Mary Shelley and Matthew Arnold in *Mary Shelley* (London: Penguin, 2002).

p. 169   Although Shelley has been championed . . .: *Shelley's Revolutionary Year: Shelley's Political Poems and the Essay, A Philosophical View of Reform*, ed. P. Foot (London: Red Words, 1990).

p. 169   In historical moments . . .: Duff, D., *Romance and Revolution: Shelley and the Politics of a Genre* (Cambridge: University Press, 1994).

p. 169   As well as prefiguring anti-capitalism . . .: See his impressively titled *Proposal for an Association of Philanthropists Who Convinced of the Inadequacy of the Moral and Political State of Ireland to Produce Benefits Which Are Nevertheless Attainable Are Willing to Unite to Accomplish its Regeneration* (1812), which led to the establishment of the Hunt Circle of political reformers.

p. 171   The cultivation of those sciences . . .: From *Defence of Poetry*, quoted in Duff, D., *Romance and Revolution: Shelley and the Politics of a Genre* (Cambridge: University Press, 1994), p. 199.

p. 171   he met no sticky end . . .: D. Oakleaf, 'Politics and History', in C. Fox (ed.), *The Cambridge Companion to Jonathan Swift* (Cambridge: University Press, 2003), pp. 31–47.

p. 171   If your little Finger be sore . . .: C. Fabricant, 'Swift the Irishman', in C. Fox (ed.), *The Cambridge Companion to Jonathan Swift* (Cambridge: University Press, 2003), pp. 48–72.

p. 172   His suggestion that Irish women . . .: Swift attacked the Woollen Act of 1699 which restricted Ireland's trade in *A Proposal for the Universal Use of Irish Manufacture* (1720); the political manipulation of the apparently 'free' trade system was discussed in Chapter 4, above. See also Swift's *A Proposal that All the Ladies and Women of Ireland Should Appear Constantly in Irish Manufactures* (1729).

p. 172   His most famous polemical attack . . .: *A Modest Proposal for Preventing the Children of Poor People in Ireland from Being a Burthen to Their Parents or Country, and for Making them Beneficial to the Public* (1729).

p. 172   With the domestic needs for meat met . . .: Gravil, R., *Gulliver's Travels, and, A Modest Proposal* (Harlow: Longman, 2001).

p. 172   He was fortunate enough to view . . .: P. Kelly, 'Swift on Money and Economics', in C. Fox (ed.), *The Cambridge Companion to Jonathan Swift* (Cambridge: University Press, 2003), pp. 128–45.

p. 173   Most of those who are well-to-do . . .: Morris, W., 'Useful Work vs. Useless Toil', in A. L. Morton (ed.), *Political Writings of William Morris* (London: Lawrence and Wishart, 1973), p. 86.

p. 173   Whatever England . . .: 'Under an Elm Tree, or Thoughts in the Country-side', *Commonweal*, 6 July 1889.

p. 174   *Swadeshi* carries a great and profound meaning . . . .: 'New Year', *Indian Opinion*, 2 Jan. 1909; reprinted in Raghavan, I. (ed.), *The Essential Writings of Mahatma Gandhi* (Delhi: Oxford University Press, 1991).

p. 175   I hold that economic progress . . .: Gandhi, M. K., 'Speech at Muir College Economic Society, Allahabad', *The Leader*, 25 Dec. 1916; reprinted in Raghavan, I. (ed.) (1991), *The Essential Writings of Mahatma Gandhi* (Delhi: Oxford University Press, 1991).

p. 175   The second condition of importance . . .: Luxemburg, R. *The Accumulation of Capital* (London: Routledge, 2003), p. 366; first published as *Die Akkumulation des Kapitals*, 1913. A collection of her writings is available online at http://www.marxists.org/archive/luxemburg.

p. 175   Violated, dishonoured, wading in blood . . .: Luxemburg, R., *The War and the Workers*, 'The Junius Pamphlet' (1916).

p. 176   It is but hollow phraseology . . .: 'What is Economics?', university lecture by R. Luxemburg reprinted in M.-A. Waters (ed.), *Rosa Luxemburg Speaks* (New York: Pathfinder, 1970).

p. 176   The Keynesian revolution . . .: Robinson, J., foreword to K. Kuhne, *Economics and Marxism*, vol. I (New York: St Martin's Press, 1979).

p. 176   The forces which govern . . .: Robinson, J., 'The Theory of Value Reconsidered', lecture delivered at University College London in 1963; republished in *Contributions to Modern Economics* (Oxford: Blackwell, 1978), p. 186.

p. 177   Over the better part of four decades . . .: Baragar, F., 'Joan Robinson on Marx', *Review of Political Economy*, 15/4 (2003): 467–82.

p. 177   Effective demand in a capitalist world . . .: Robinson, J., 'Latter-Day Capitalism', published in *New Left Review*, 1962; reprinted in *Contributions to Modern Economics* (Oxford: Blackwell, 1978), p. 231.

p. 178   Critical or anti-capitalist economics . . .: For details of the work of anti-capitalist economists Thomas Hodgkin, William Thompson and others see 'Labour Economics and Co-operation in the 1820s', in G. C. H. Cole and A. W. Filson (eds), *British Working Class Movements: Select Documents 1789–1875* (London: Macmillan, 1967).

p. 178   Does money buy happiness? . . .: Hilsenrather, J. E., 'Does Wealth Produce Happiness? Economists' Answer Isn't So Simple', *Wall Street Journal*, 4 Jan. 2003.

p. 179   The Movement for Post-Autistic Economics . . .: For more information on the movement see www.paecon.net.

p. 179   Bhutan's insistence on the primary of GNH . . .: Bakshi, R., 'Gross National Happiness', *Post-Autistic Economics Review*, 26/2 (2004): article 6.

p. 180   Another 2 million . . .: Data from Datamonitor.

p. 180   Ancient Egypt was doubly fortunate . . .: Keynes, J. M., *General Theory of Employment, Interest and Money, Collected Writings of John Maynard Keynes*, vii (London: Macmillan, 1974), p. 131.

p. 181   working to adapt capitalism . . .: See especially Jonathon Porritt's latest book, *Capitalism as if the World Matters* (London: Earthscan, 2005).

Index

History and politics from New Clarion Press

CONSENSUS OR COERCION?

THE STATE, THE PEOPLE AND SOCIAL COHESION IN POST-WAR BRITAIN

Lawrence Black et al.

'Collectively, these essays serve as an antidote to the somewhat unchallenging notions of post-war stability and cohesion in British society . . . The authors are to be complimented for their initiative in putting this volume together, and it is worth reading in order to recognise the continuing strength of modern British social history in its broadest sense.' *Labour History Review*

'This book is a welcome addition to the growing number of recent studies which have sought to reassess British society through the post-war period . . . *Consensus or Coercion* will undoubtedly be an important read for undergraduates in history and a range of the social sciences.' *Contemporary British History*

ISBN   1873797311   paperback   £12.95
           187379732X   hardback   £25.00   Published 2001

NEW APPROACHES TO SOCIALIST HISTORY

edited by Keith Flett and David Renton

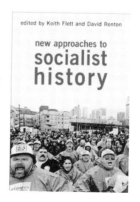

'When we were at school, most of us were taught history in terms of battles and treaties secured by great soldiers and statesmen. So it is a refreshing change to read *New Approaches to Socialist History*, a set of essays that looks at history through the prism of working-class movements, their struggles and strikes, and their trade union and political leaders . . . a thoughtful and stimulating contribution to a frequently neglected labour history.' Connect *Review*

'In an age of global capitalism it is vital and refreshing to see a collection of lived histories relating local struggles to worldwide resistance . . . [This collection] captures the cultural changes in socialism, and questions what constitutes socialist struggle at the end of the 20th century.' *Bookmarks Review of Books*

ISBN   1873797419   paperback   £12.95
           1873797427   hardback   £25.00   Published 2003

'A PLEASANT CHANGE FROM POLITICS'

MUSIC AND THE BRITISH LABOUR MOVEMENT BETWEEN THE WARS

Duncan Hall

'This is an excellent book from a relatively new publisher, which is itself a workers' co-operative. Many such co-operatives have failed in the past. If New Clarion Press continues to produce books of this quality, then it will deserve not to follow them.' *Contemporary British History*

'an evidently well-researched book . . . most likely to be fascinating to those who are drawn to the linkages between music and politics' *British Music Society Newsletter*

'a thoughtful and well-researched history of a fascinating byway in British musical history' *BBC Music Magazine*

ISBN	187379729X	paperback	£12.95	
	1873797303	hardback	£25.00	Published 2001

GENETIC POLITICS

FROM EUGENICS TO GENOME

Anne Kerr and Tom Shakespeare

'a thought-provoking book, laden with information and detailed historical records' *Times Higher Education Supplement*

'a very welcome and timely analysis of "the new genetics" from a disability rights perspective . . . an important text, offering a well-argued and reasoned analysis of current genetic policy' *Disability and Society*

'a superb, historically rooted narrative . . . highly readable' *Health, Risk and Society*

ISBN	1873797257	paperback	£12.95	Published 2002

WHEN ADAM DELVED AND EVE SPAN

A HISTORY OF THE PEASANTS' REVOLT OF 1381

Mark O'Brien

'There cannot be a better sight than oppressed, exploited people standing up for themselves and demanding rights. These are people to remember and honour . . . Huzzah.' *Bookmarks Review of Books*

ISBN   1873797451   paperback   £8.95   Published 2004

WHEN WE TOUCHED THE SKY

THE ANTI-NAZI LEAGUE 1977–1981

Dave Renton

'This carefully researched and eloquently written book provides the first full-length history of the Anti-Nazi League. It shows how ordinary people can affect the course of history, providing stirring memories and valuable lessons.' Peter Alexander, Professor of Sociology, University of Johannesburg

'a very readable new history of the ant-Nazi campaign of the 1970s . . . This book should inspire a new generation of activists.' Paul Mackney, General Secretary, NATFHE, *The Lecturer*

ISBN   1873797486   paperback   £13.95
        1873797494   hardback   £27.50   Published 2006

CLASSICAL MARXISM

SOCIALIST THEORY AND THE SECOND INTERNATIONAL

David Renton

'Given the current fashion for "pop history" it is a somewhat ironic fact that never has the dearth of well-written, intellectually accessible socialist historiography been more acute. Classical Marxism takes up the challenge and steps into the breech, providing a valuable addition to the canon of labour and progressive history.' *North West Labour History Bulletin*

ISBN   1873797354   paperback   £12.95
           1873797362   hardback   £25.00   Published 2002

THE FIRST DARWINIAN LEFT

SOCIALISM AND DARWINISM 1859–1914

David Stack

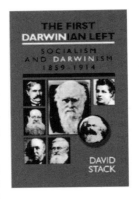

'brisk, readable and theoretically savvy . . . Stack has made a useful contribution to the history of the left. He sparks interest, raises questions and occasionally provokes irritation, and that is reason enough to read his book.' *Human Nature*

'In this well-written and sophisticated book David Stack argues that the importance of Darwinism to socialist thought has been underestimated. He argues convincingly that after the publication of Darwin's *On the Origin of Species* evolution became integral to socialist theorising . . . A book that offers real insights.' *Bookmarks Review of Books*

ISBN   1873797370   paperback   £12.95
           1873797389   hardback   £25.00   Published 2003